The Leaving Care Handbook

Helping and Supporting Care Leavers

Edited by
Ann Wheal

Russell House Publishing

First published in 2005 by:
Russell House Publishing Ltd.
4 St. George's House
Uplyme Road
Lyme Regis
Dorset DT7 3LS
Tel: 01297-443948
Fax: 01297-442722
e-mail: help@russellhouse.co.uk
www.russellhouse.co.uk

© Ann Wheal and the various contributors

The moral right of Ann Wheal and the various contributors to be identified as the authors of this work has been asserted by them in accordance with The Copyright Designs and Patents Act 1988.

All rights reserved. No part of this publication may be reproduced, apart from the exception, stored in a retrieval system or transmitted in any form, or by any means, electronic, mechanical, photocopying, recording or otherwise, without the prior permission of the copyright holder and the publisher.

The copyright holder and the publisher grant permission for forms, handouts and OHTs from this book to be photocopied solely for 'not for profit' use locally within the institution purchasing the material.

British Library Cataloguing-in-publication Data:

A catalogue record for this book is available from the British Library.

ISBN: 1-903855-67-5; 978-1-903855-67-6

Typeset by TW Typesetting, Plymouth, Devon
Printed by Antony Rowe, Chippenham

About Russell House Publishing

RHP is a group of social work, probation, education and youth and community work practitioners and academics working in collaboration with a professional publishing team.

Our aim is to work closely with the field to produce innovative and valuable materials to help managers, trainers, practitioners and students.

We are keen to receive feedback on publications and new ideas for future projects.

For details of our other publications please visit our website or ask us for a catalogue. Contact details are on this page.

Contents

Acknowledgements	viii
About the Authors	ix

Section One: Introduction — 1

1 Introduction — 1
Ann Wheal

2 Resilience — 4
David Woods
- Difficulties — 4
- Life-skills and resilience — 5
- Conclusion — 11

Section Two: Nature and Level of Personal Support — 13

3 Personal Support — 13
Ann Wheal
- Pathway planning — 13
- Personal advisors — 14
- Mentoring — 15
- Advocacy — 16
- Complaints, and redress, when things go wrong — 17
- Using the Web for support — 17
- Conclusion — 19

4 Young Disabled People Leaving Care: Pathway Planning — 20
Julie Harris
- What do we mean by 'leaving care'? — 21
- Transitions for young disabled people — 22
- Personal advisors — 23
- Involving young disabled people — 24
- Person-centred approaches to needs assessment and pathway planning — 24
- Keeping in touch: communication and information — 25
- Young people living out of authority — 26
- Self-advocacy and empowerment — 27
- Independent living — 28
- Resources — 34

5	**Working Together – Connexions and Leaving Care Services** *Amanda Allard and Roger Clayphan*	**37**
	Leaving care services	37
	Connexions service	37
	Working with care leavers – a co-operative approach	38
	Partnership working	40
	Resources	45

Section Three: Accommodation — 46

6	**Accommodation** *Jane Murphy and Rachel Strahan*	
	The local authority's duties and powers to help young care leavers	46
	The different types of accommodation	49
	The eviction process from private and local authority housing	49
	Resources	57

Section Four: Education, Training and Employment — 60

7	**Education in School, in Further and Higher Education** *Ann Wheal and Peter James*	**60**
	Introduction: care leavers and research	60
	Changing behaviour and attitudes: care leavers and education	65
	Personal Education Plan (PEP)	67
	How the education system works: a guide for young people	68
	Getting qualified	70
	Thinking of going into higher education?	77
	Grants, loans and other financial help	78
	University jargon-buster	80
	Conclusion	82
	Resources	82
8	**Training, Employability and Work Experience** *Linda Daniel and Ena Fry*	**83**
	Introduction	83
	Training, employability and work experience	83
	The world of work today	84
	Where are we now?	85
	Work experience	86
	How to get help when things go wrong	89
	Conclusion	90
9	**Employment – Getting a Job; and Keeping It** *Linda Daniel and Ena Fry*	**99**
	Tips on applying for a job	99
	Job application forms	100

	Writing a Curriculum Vitae	102
	Conclusion	103
	Resources	103

Section Five: Support to Sustain Family and Social Relationships — 105

10 Family and Friends: Getting in Touch and Staying in Touch — 105
Shelagh Beckett

Introduction	105
Self-esteem, relationships and contact	106
Trust, and keeping confidences: who can I talk to?	107
Taking care of my own needs	107
All on my own: alone or lonely?	108
Thinking about re-starting contact: pointers to consider	108
Building new relationships	109
Valuing important people in our lives, and feeling valued	110
Conclusion	112
Resources	112

Section Six: Practical and Other Skills — 114

11 Practical Help — 114
Ann Wheal

Helping young adults to cope with practical skills	114
Managing money	116
Housing	117
Hygiene	117
Cooking, menus, diets	118
Conclusion	119
Resources	119
Budgeting exercise	121
Accommodation checklist	122
Other practical skills checklist	124
Money checklist	124
Food checklist	124

12 Social and Emotional Skills — 126
Ann Wheal

Helping young adults to cope with personal skills	126
Some social skills	126
Self-confidence and self-esteem	128
Coping strategies	130
Making friends and forming relationships	132
Decision-making	134
Negotiating skills	136
Problem solving	137
Culture, values, beliefs and religion	138
Sex, getting pregnant and being a young parent	139

	Health and sexuality	142
	Conclusion	144
	Resources	144
	Life plan	145

13 Involving Young People in Decisions that Affect Their Lives — 148
Martin Hazlehurst

Introduction	148
User involvement and participation	148
Involvement or consultation	151
Different methods of involvement	153
Involving young people in selection and recruitment	155
Conclusion	156
Resources	157

Section Seven: Financial Support — 158

14 Financial Matters — 158
Ena Fry and Ann Wheal

Good practice	158
Statutory entitlements	158
Money	160
Special payments	163
Conclusion	163
Resources	166

Section Eight: Health Needs: How Are They Best Met — 167

15 Health and Healthy Lifestyles — 167
Jane Scott

Introduction	167
Some roles and responsibilities in health	167
How to access doctors, dentists and opticians	168
Healthy eating strategies: prevention is better than cure	171
Food	172
Physical exercise	174
Sexual health	174
Sexual orientation	178
Conclusion	178
Resources	179

16 Mental Health of Care Leavers — 181
Cynthia Fletcher

Introduction	181
A definition of mental health	181
The national service framework	183
The role of the Child and Adolescent Mental Health Service (CAMHS)	184

Anticipating and managing difficult behaviours	186
How care leaver workers can help	196
Conclusion	198
Resources	198

Section Nine: Legal Matters — 200

17 The Law and Your Rights — 200
Amanda Allard and Jane Sufian

Introduction	200
The Children (Leaving Care) Act 2000 and its associated guidance and regulations	201
Criminal injuries compensation awards and other money	203
Sleepovers for looked after children	204
Access to files	204
Being a parent, parental responsibility and entitlements	205
The police	207
Drugs	209
Debt	211
Health care	214
Resources	218

Useful Organisations	220
Appendices	224

Acknowledgements

A book such as this could not have been produced without the help, advice and assistance of a wide variety of people.

First of all I would like to thank all the young people who helped by making suggestions, sometimes revealing very personal feelings about themselves.

Sometimes, people make promises to help with such a book and then for a variety of reasons fail to do so. In this case other people have stepped in and provided material that has been invaluable and I would like to especially thank those people.

I would like to thank Davina Pandya and Vanessa Frylinck from Hounslow leaving care team; John Short, an independent consultant; Norfolk Social Services; Fostering Network's Young People's Project and VCC who provided additional material to enable certain chapters to be completed.

I would like to thank Linda Morgan who unravelled many of my scribbles to make them into coherent sections.

I would particularly like to thank Ena Fry not just for being a super critical reader but also for the material she provided.

Finally, I would like to thank my husband for his patience, tolerance and love.

About the Authors

Amanda Allard is a Senior Public Policy Officer for NCH, one of the UK's leading children's charities. NCH works with some of the most vulnerable and excluded children and young people in the UK. As policy officer Amanda's role is to influence public policy in favour of NCH's client group. Her fields of expertise include leaving care, youth homelessness and young people's education, employment and training issues. Amanda has written and contributed to various publications on homelessness, leaving care employment, and benefit issues. Both in her work at NCH and in previous jobs Amanda has promoted the importance of enabling children and young people to lobby policy makers on their own account.

Shelagh Beckett has extensive experience as a practitioner and manager. She now provides consultancy to local authorities, voluntary adoption agencies and the BBC. Shelagh is frequently used as an expert witness in complex cases. She maintains a commitment to direct work with individual children as well as policy review and development work with senior managers.

Roger Clayphan is Assistant Director of Children's Services, NCH, and has over 20 years experience in social care, working in a range of services including Probation, Education, Youth Justice, Social Services and the Voluntary Sector. Roger has been committed to working with young people leaving care for the past 15 years as practitioner and service manager, and for the past five years in NCH as the regional senior manager for youth services in the North East.

Linda Daniel works for Hounslow's Leaving Care Team in the Education and Employment Office. Linda has held posts in the commercial, national health and education sectors. Her passions are the value of education for young people and levelling the playing field for the disadvantaged.

Cynthia Fletcher has worked for all three main agencies; in Child and Adolescent Mental Health, as a project manager of a multi-agency project to support the Psychological needs of Looked After Children, in Education, as a Senior Educational Psychologist for Looked After Children; and as a Child Psychologist working for Social Services, but jointly funded by the Health Services supporting children in residential and foster care. Cynthia believes that all children should be given the opportunity to have a voice and should be listened to by those providing services.

Ena Fry has been development worker for the Fostering Network's Young People's Project since 1990. The project provides information, advice and training on teenage fostering as well as working with local authorities to develop better services for young people leaving foster care. Prior to joining the Fostering Network, Ena worked directly with young people in a range of local authority settings including ten years developing 'leaving care' resources in an inner London authority.

The Leaving Care Handbook

Julie Harris is an independent specialist in social care, providing qualitative and collaborative research, consultancy and training particularly in the areas of improving services for looked after young people and those leaving care, especially services for young disabled care leavers. She also has an interest in quality assurance in the voluntary sector, the subject of her Masters degree from Leeds University.

Martin Hazlehurst is the manager of the National Leaving Care Advisory Service, part of the Rainer Standards and Development Unit. Prior to this he was the Assistant Director of First Key. He has had ten years experience of facilitating and managing projects to involve care leavers in service development and review, working at a local authority level and establishing 'A National Voice', as an organisation, led by young people, for looked after young people and care leavers. He has also devised and delivered training courses for leaving care and others on involving young people.

Jane Murphy spent eight years working for social landlords before joining Shelter's Young Persons Team as Information Officer. Her current role involves promoting good practice and assisting local authorities in developing common monitoring systems for single homeless people.

Jane Scott is employed as a Senior Nurse for Looked after Children and Young People. She works within a team dealing with vulnerable children in the North of Durham. Jane looks after the two PCTs in the North of the County and is responsible for the planning, development and implementation of services for looked after children and young people. Jane has a particular interest in the young people who are preparing to leave care, and works closely with the leaving care team, to deliver a first class service to the young people leaving care.

Rachel Strahan is the Education Officer for Shelter's Young Persons Team. Her role involves developing housing education resources for professionals working with young people. Her background is in youth and community work.

Jane Sufian is a Senior Policy Officer (Leaving Care) at Rainer's National Leaving Care Advisory Service, Chair of Action on Aftercare Consortium and co-author of Supporting Care Leavers: A Training and Resource Pack for People Working with Young People Leaving Care. She is a qualified (non-practicing) solicitor.

Ann Wheal is a Senior Visiting Research Fellow in the Division of Social Work at the University of Southampton. Ann was a teacher in multi-racial inner city schools and colleges before joining the University in 1990. She has published widely in the child care field.

David Woods is employed by Centrepoint as Policy and Practice Development Manager (Leaving Care) and works with local authorities and individual agencies across the country to develop services for care leavers. At Centrepoint he worked with the Department of Health and the Office of the Deputy Prime Minister (ODPM) to write Care Leaving Strategies: A Good Practice Handbook. He is also Chair of the Care Leavers Association.

Section One: Introduction

Introduction

Ann Wheal

The Children Leaving Care Act 2000 imposed on local authorities a wide variety of duties and responsibilities. However, preparation and support for leaving care should not just be about entitlements; preparation for leaving care should begin from the first day a young person is 'looked after' and continue for as long as is necessary to ensure young people who have been in the care system have the skills and resources necessary to enable them to fulfil their potential and take their rightful place in society.

About this book

This book is for anyone working or studying in the area of leaving care. It is for leaving care workers, Connexions or other similar staff, personal advisors, educationalists, foster and residential carers. It is also for trainers and for management so that they know and can plan to ensure their staff are conversant with what is required, and that resources are available to meet the full cost of the implementation of the Act. This book is also an important information resource for young people; a copy should be available in every leaving care office so care leavers can read, copy relevant information and use it when they wish, though ideally they should be given their own copy.

Many of the chapters have been written by individual authors and these have retained their own distinct style. The remaining chapters have been written using material from a variety of sources. However, the topics have all been highlighted by young people as important. The chapters reflect the views of the authors which may not necessarily be the views of the editor or the publisher.

The book is written in a format which is easy to use and understand. The sections have been put in the order of a Pathway Plan.

The appendices at the end of the book contain checklists that a young person can use to highlight areas where they need further information on any of the topics in the Pathway Plan. The book also provides key information, tips, guidance sheets, notes, charts and diagrams. Most of the time, the material is aimed at the worker, but sometimes it is specifically aimed at the young person, so it can be copied and handed to the care leaver. (See page ii for photocopying guidance.)

The book has been designed so that it can be dipped into at any time, used in any order and developed for use to help staff who have differing levels of ability, knowledge and experience. Information from the book may be given to young people. Much of the material is produced so that it may be copied or used as OHP foils that can be adapted to meet specific needs or for use as handouts to staff or young people.

Young people leaving care

If you ask any young person who is in the care system about the future, they will almost always tell you that they dread leaving care, and that they worry about what will happen to them. Unfortunately, they will have read a variety of quite depressing statistics about outcomes for care leavers and don't want to land up being one of the statistics.

There are many practical aspects of leaving care such as providing appropriate information – legal aspects and entitlements, cooking, budgeting, keeping healthy and knowing about accommodation options – and these are covered in this book. However, there are other aspects that need to be considered:
- Raising aspirations and self-esteem.
- Creating opportunities so care leavers can be equal to other young people who have not been in the care system, helping them achieve educational potential.
- Reducing social isolation.
- Reducing the stigma of care.
- Having high but realistic expectations.
- Involving young people in decisions that affect their lives.

A variety of young people were asked what help, advice, or support they would like, or would like to have received. Some of the answers were surprising. Some were just common sense, and we have covered many of them in this book such as:
- Sharing.
- Talking and listening.
- Knowing when to keep quiet.
- Being reliable.
- Social skills.
- Identity and race issues.
- Blaming.
- Giving the wrong impression.
- Relationships.
- Making contact.
- Friendships.
- Getting rid of the 'care baggage'.
- Saying 'thank you'.
- Having fun.
- Overcoming social barriers.
- Coping with reality.

This book also looks at ways to enable young people to have a real sense of involvement in improving the care service by preparing them to be involved in:
- Recruitment of foster carers and social workers.
- Preparation and training of foster carers.
- Being a member of a fostering panel.
- Recruitment of social work students and involvement in all aspects of their training.
- Co-leading courses on preparation for adult life, for other young people.
- Involvement in commissioning services.
- Enlightening government officers.

Sometimes a topic is covered in two places. For example, in Health, there is mention of dentists, and in the legal section what the entitlement for seeing a dentist is. In this way the information can be found in the place that seems most appropriate at the time.

The role of leaving care workers

Many people use the term 'preparation for independence' but in this book we have used the term 'preparation for adult life'. Very few of us are ever totally independent, more interdependent. Also, the term may give the impression that once *prepared*, a young person will be 'on their own' which certainly should not be the case.

Leaving care workers and personal advisors have a very important role when working with young people who have experienced care by providing support. Support is:

- Preparation.
- Information.
- Being there.
- Taking the initiative.

'If only everyone had a Mark' was said at a national conference following comments by a series of young people. This statement referred to a particular leaving care worker who seemed to be willing to 'go that extra mile' for the young people; who was there to support and to listen to them and to fight to ensure they received the service to which they were entitled. All young people should receive such help and support. It is hoped that this book will help all those working with them to provide a service of which workers can be proud, from which young people can benefit, and which they will appreciate.

The Children Leaving Care Act (CLCA) provides a very simple framework on how to prepare young people to leave care. This book is like a coat hanger where the CLCA is the broad shoulders of the hanger. The book puts the act into practice. It is based on questions young people have asked, and aims to provide practical solutions to help each and every care leaver. Every care leaver is unique, so will need different help and advice, at different times, in different quantities and in different ways.

NOTE: In some parts of the country the Connexions service may be known by another name. However, the service provided will largely remain the same.

Resilience

David Woods

Preparing young people for leaving care has been an area of work with which many agencies and local authorities have struggled over the years. It is also an area that has generated a substantial body of research, some of which highlights the ongoing failings of much of this preparation.

Centrepoint has been working with care leavers across the country to identify the key issues which these young people feel are important when preparing young people to leave care.

This chapter is extracted from Centrepoint's larger research report (2002) and highlights some of the difficulties and structural issues that arose from the research. It also identifies some of the key issues that carers and agencies need to address when working with looked after children. All quotes are from interviews with care leavers.

Difficulties

There are many difficulties linked to preparing young people for leaving care. Some of these are related to the young person's care experience, some to a lack of knowledge amongst staff and carers, and some due to the age that young people leave care.

Many foster carers and residential staff do not have an understanding of the impact on a young person of leaving care or the support that may (or may not) be available to that young person. There is often a view that the young person is looking forward to, and ready for, more independence and leaving care. Indeed this may be how the young person *presents*, but this is often at odds with how they *feel*. Without a greater understanding of the reality of leaving care, foster carers and residential staff will continue to struggle to help young people equip themselves for leaving care.

For many young people in the care system there is often a 'crisis-intervention' model of work, with staff focusing on day-to-day issues to the detriment of long-term ones, such as identity and education. Equally, many carers find it difficult to balance preparing a young person for leaving care with their everyday caring role, choosing to 'protect' the young person from the future reality.

The average age of young people leaving home is rising, with many young people feeling unable to face the personal, emotional and financial challenges of living independently until well into their mid-twenties. For most, their transition to independent living is a gentle one with ongoing support from their families, as and when they feel they need it.

It is in stark contrast to this that we still expect young people in care to have left that care by eighteen. It does not need much time spent with these care leavers to realise that this is far too early an age for most of them to face the challenges of life, with often minimal support networks. Many young people report that their 'preparation for leaving care' is too constricted and too compressed. In the words of one seventeen-year-old:

My social worker told me on the Monday that I would need to think about moving from my foster placement, by the Thursday I was moving into my council flat.

A problem that many of the care leavers reported was the sharp transition, and the huge difference between their experience in care, and after leaving care:

My care experience was totally dis-empowering, I had no say in any of the major decisions made about me, then bang! There's no-one to turn to or ask for help, suddenly you're supposed to be an adult-I had to really struggle to learn how to survive.

Many of the young people reported that leaving care seemed to be looked at far too simplistically and 'sold' to young people on an unrealistic basis. Quite often, independent living is portrayed as getting away from the restrictions imposed by the current placement, without an understanding of the realities.

They think if they give you a flat, a bit of money and a mentor for an hour every now and then you'll do fine. What you really need is to know beforehand what's coming, then you'd do all you could to stay in care.

Couldn't take it man, all the loneliness, isolation, but didn't want to admit it. I looked forward to it but when it happened I was just scared, I'd thought I'd die and no-one will come for me.

Life-skills and resilience

We need to recognise that many of the issues and difficulties facing care leavers may never be completely removed and that the transition to adulthood may always be difficult for some young people. Indeed, the majority of young people will leave care before they are prepared and ready to leave. Developing resilience in young people is therefore about equipping them with the skills and qualities to help ease that transition.

Most children and young people will develop these skills and qualities through their everyday experiences and observations of life around them, at home, at school and at leisure. For many young people in the care system, this process is often disrupted and fragmentary. As a result, many care leavers report difficulties with issues of self-esteem, confidence, aspirations and relationships.

These areas that care leavers highlighted were, unsurprisingly, very close to those that much research identifies. The marked difference was that many of these issues are not those addressed in many 'preparation for independence schemes' run by local authorities.

In these, there is often either an expectation that these 'soft' skills will be 'picked up' by looked after children without any direct intervention, or no real understanding of these issues and how to address them.

As stated, the aim of this project was to work with care leavers to identify areas that they thought were the most important when preparing young people for leaving care.

Although finance and accommodation were mentioned, as care leavers regularly struggle with these issues, there was a clear focus on areas that can be identified as 'soft skills' or resilience factors.

There were two key interlinked issues that young people raised over and over again. Preparation for leaving care should be seen as an integral part of the care process with all staff and carers working in a way that develops resilience as soon as a young person comes into care. It should not be something that one individual worker has responsibility for but something that is fundamental to all interactions with the child:

> *What's the point in one person trying to help you move yourself forward when everyone else seems to want to hold you still?*

It is also something that cannot be a 'tagged on' addition to a child's care history:

> *You've got to start doing this straight away, there's no point suddenly trying to be different with young people because they're about to leave care, it's too late.*

The factors that the young people identified are interlinked and working to develop one area undoubtedly has a positive effect on other areas. The areas that they identified as being of importance are:

- Self-esteem and identity.
- Communication skills.
- Negotiation skills and problem-solving.
- Interpersonal skills.
- Understanding and identifying with others.
- Exploring and managing feelings.
- Action planning and reviewing.

Self-esteem and identity

Low self-esteem may mean that the young people have a lack of motivation or confidence and this will affect how they interact with others, how well they achieve and whether they have aspirations and goals for themselves. Self-esteem, and the related issue of identity, were the areas that care leavers spent the most time discussing and thought were the most important. Indeed, each of the other areas were discussed in terms of how they can help to develop greater self-esteem.

It is useful to identify the two components of self-esteem as competence and worthiness. Competence may include the successes that young people have, the skills they have learnt and the impact that they have. Worthiness may be composed of how the young person views themselves, how they accept themselves and whether they see themselves as having value.

It is obvious that young people's thoughts and behaviour will be affected by how they view themselves. For many young people in the care system there is often a lack of knowledge about their background and their birth families, and this can lead to these young people feeling unsure about who they are:

> *There was a time when I thought who am I? I've not had a proper identity whilst in care, my family history, who I am, who I'll be – how can I just invent myself?*

> *You end up with an institutionalised identity and you want to be normal.*

It was clear that this difficult area was one that the young people wished carers had spent more time exploring with them whilst they were looked after. Indeed, this is an issue that continues to affect many care leavers of a much older age:

> *Foster carers need to talk to young people at an understandable level about their background, you need a knowledge of yourself and your history.*

Many of the young people reported feeling different due to their background and care history, with some of this coming from the uncertainty surrounding their past:

> *Talk to them gently and build a relationship, talk about their family and history, where they've come from, so they don't think they're the only one with this experience.*

All young people explore who they are and many report 'trying on' a number of different identities as they developed an understanding of themselves. Positive role models may be of some use here and these role models may come from a number of areas. Real life role models, who the young people can meet and talk to, may include other care leavers or older siblings. There are also 'distance' role models who the young people may possibly not meet but access through the media. These models may show similar backgrounds or have experienced similar issues to the young people.

The young people were clear that this area was one where positive ongoing input from staff and carers was necessary:

Confidence and self-esteem – you need good feedback from adults.

Building my confidence was the most important and hardest part, but they were kind and always helping, showed they were trustworthy.

Many of the young people reported that support with activities and sports had been instrumental in developing self-esteem, even though some of the young people had tried many activities before they found one that they liked and felt good at.

Positive, genuine feedback from carers is needed to help address young people's often negative self-image:

It's when someone says you're good at something and you think . . . yeah, I'm good at something.

Help young people to identify individual strengths and build on them, it's brilliant when someone helps you see you can actually do something.

If they're good at football, English, maths, whatever, they should be given assistance and recognition – let them know they're good at something.

Many of the young people recognised the vulnerability of an individual's self-esteem and identity; they were clear that it was important to surround yourself with people who would promote rather than damage this:

I think the key things are to avoid having your identity spoilt by peer pressure or bad examples and to have positive role models, a strong sense of identity is the most important.

You've got to make good friends, you'll always be in trouble if that's the scene, get a good strong group of mates for support.

It is often the case that 'noisy' young people, those that draw attention to themselves, are the ones that services are seen to concentrate on. If young people are getting on with their lives they often feel that they are ignored or not offered as much input as they would like:

You've got to act up to get any attention.

It was with this issue that young people were insistent that good working relationships with staff and carers was important. If staff and carers spent time with the young people, discussing issues of importance to them, doing activities that they wanted then this could promote a sense of being valued.

Spending time with the young person, on their terms, is necessary to develop a sense of valuing.

Help young people to identify their strengths and weaknesses, their likes and dislikes.

Positive displays of, and reference to, appropriate role models is important.

Communication skills

Communication skills are very important as is self-awareness.

All human interactions involve communication, and it is important for this communication to be clear and effective. Young people often feel that the power imbalance in a relationship can work against good communication, with staff and carers often not giving enough time and weight to the young person's views. Often the language and structure of meetings can intimidate young people. Young people may need assistance in these situations:

I've had help to put my views across, to explain what I need and to justify it.

Adults not communicating effectively with young people can hinder even everyday communication. If young people are not supported in developing these skills it may continue to affect them in other aspects of their lives:

Learning how to deal with management at work was a challenge.

The young people were adamant that support and assistance would not be forthcoming if they did not chase it and that they needed to argue for appropriate support:

I felt dumped when I left care but my outdoor education had given me a sense of my abilities. I felt internally strong and am a good communicator so I pushed for ongoing advice and support.

The dangers inherent in not having these skills are that young people are left unsupported:

Too many young people are shy and just do what they are told.

Staff and carers need to develop effective communication skills to use with young people. Avoidance of blaming or condescending language is very important if young people are to stay involved.

It is also important that communication is two way, with the young person given time and encouraged to present their thoughts and feelings. 'Communication' needs to avoid becoming a monologue that allows the staff or carer to vent their frustration.

Negotiation skills and problem-solving

For many looked after children their time in care often feels very dis-empowering, with major decisions, such as where the young person will live, who they'll live with, where they'll go to school and how often they will see their birth family, seemingly made without taking into consideration the young person's wishes. This can often leave the young person feeling disengaged from the decision-making process. Yet when they leave care they are expected to have well-developed decision-making skills:

To develop responsibility you need better involvement in life decisions.

The young people were clear that these skills, linked to communication, were ones that many carers would find difficult or may not want to promote in young people:

Negotiation skills are important, communication full stop. I look back to when I was 13 or 14 and I'd argue, argue, argue and get nowhere, but it takes two to argue, so staff need to negotiate as well.

Problem-solving skills are important. I did outdoor education which started me with team skills, interpersonal skills, negotiation and planning.

The older care leavers interviewed were clear that good problem-solving skills were necessary skills for young people leaving care and that they needed to have rehearsed these skills in the safety of their placements before they live independently.

It is important for these young people to identify where there are problems and where the 'ownership' of the problem lies. Many care leavers are left with a legacy of taking the blame for issues that they are not responsible for:

If there is a problem at work, I automatically feel guilty, that somehow it's my fault, even though I know it can't be.

It is clear that these young people need to be able to make sense of what the problem is and to have the skills to identify different possible solutions or responses to the problem. For many care leavers the lack of scope for mistake-making works against developing an ability to solve problems; the repercussions for making the wrong decision, or past experience, often lead them to avoid making decisions at all:

When you just know you're going to be wrong, you stick your head in the sand and hope you don't have to make a decision; after all, you were never allowed to make decisions before.

In care I didn't have to take responsibility, I'd be baled out. But that's not real. How can I practice and learn from my mistakes? Responsibility? – Nothing to do with me!

It is important that permission to make mistakes is given; it is learning from those mistakes which is important.

Make a plan, and then implement, and then evaluate.

Negotiation can be practised on a small scale, for example earning a treat for doing an extra job.

Interpersonal skills

Care-experienced young people may have to interact with a much wider range of people and at a much earlier age than their non-care peers: family, peer group, foster carers, residential staff, personal advisors, social workers. Good interpersonal skills are needed in all of these interactions but may be more important in those situations where the other person's positive response is crucial, such as Pathway Planning meetings, see Chapter 3.

These interpersonal skills may include:
- Being aware of one's own starting position, including feelings and intention.
- Being able to read other people correctly.
- Measuring and making an appropriate response.
- Ensuring the response has been correctly understood.

This was an area that many of the young people reported was strongly linked to the quality of relationships they had developed with staff and carers. If these relationships are not seen as positive:

I don't think we get enough respect. I give them as much respect as they give me – sometimes none.

Then, the development of these interpersonal skills may be severely inhibited. Equally, when the relationships are seen in a positive light, then these skills are reported as more developed:

Having a real relationship, choosing what and when to share, just talking about day-to-day life is a more real, a more two-way relationship.

Many of the young people took a slightly different approach to engendering respect within these relationships:

Outer confidence – how I present myself affects how I think about myself and people are more respectful of me.

Demonstrate these skills yourself, let young people see them in action!

Think about how you respond to young people, when you're tired, busy, or ill.

Understanding and identifying with others

An area of interpersonal skills that the young people thought was important was the area of understanding and identifying with others. Many of the care leavers explained that having had little choice in their care history of who they live with, whether adults or other young people, can leave them unsure of themselves when meeting new people. Having had to accept, at least superficially, many different people, and to adjust their behaviour to live with them, also has an impact.

Some of the care leavers reported that they had entered into unsuitable friendships on leaving care. This may have been for a number of reasons, but an inability to assess other people and your own impact on others can be dangerous:

> *Knowing how to make friends is important, but you have to know how to understand people to avoid bad situations.*

> *You need self-awareness, it's how you affect those around you that you need to understand.*

An understanding that people bring many different values, both positive and negative, to relationships is important, in making good friendships and relationships, and in looking after oneself.

Use youth culture, popular television or news items to explore these issues with young people.

Encourage young people to explore a different point of view.

Exploring and managing feelings

> *You need to be honest about your feelings. Sooner or later it'll come out and maybe in a bad way.*

Many care leavers make the transition to adulthood and become successful, confident adults who can view their childhood in care in context and recognise both the positive and negative elements of their experiences. These young people can move forward without their past unduly holding them back. Other care leavers struggle to make sense of their history and may feel angry, confused or ashamed of their childhood. These feelings may affect them on a day-to-day basis or lie just under the surface and emerge, sometimes violently, when difficult situations leave them feeling that they cannot cope.

The young people interviewed suggested that a good understanding of their own feelings and what triggered them was essential if they wanted to interact effectively with others and be successful:

> *You've got to work out your feelings, it helps you in relationships, with jobs, school, college, benefits – being angry keeps you on your own.*

> *You need to understand your feelings and actions, they call it emotional intelligence.*

Working with staff and carers, in a positive way, to explore reactions to situations and how the young person felt, was beneficial in developing this understanding. For these young people, focusing on the emotions and not the presenting behaviour allowed them to avoid blaming language and move towards understanding what had happened and why. This also enabled planning for future incidents to allow a better emotional response:

> *It helps me to explain the 'why's' of my thinking and actions, and helps me to understand my thought processes.*

It is also important to explore feelings and emotions in relation to positive events, so the young person can explore what makes them feel happy, strong or positive. Many young people report that behaviour and emotions had only ever been discussed in a negative context:

> *Before that we only talked about my behaviour if I was naughty.*

Focusing on behaviour and emotions had proved to be beneficial for those young people who had experienced it:

> *Using the day sheet, and reviewing it daily, helps you learn your behaviour.*

The young people recognised that this was not just an exploration of events past, but a learning tool that will help them in the future:

> *Discussing the issue has got to be good, there's always another bump in the road.*

Be aware of your own feelings before discussing issues with young people; anger and frustration will not ease dialogue.

Avoid blaming language with young people, use 'the situation made me feel', rather than 'you made me feel'.

Action planning and reviewing

Action planning and reviewing skills are important for young people if they are to develop a greater understanding of themselves and their impact on the world. Learning from their own experience may be the obvious choice, but unless effective reviewing skills are developed many young people will be unable to do this, and may be set to repeat and re-repeat damaging behaviours.

Unfortunately for many young people, those at home as well as those in care, this 'reviewing' can often amount to nothing more than a telling off, followed by 'I hope you learn something from this'.

For many looked after children their files may seem to be a record of all of the negatives that have happened in the young person's life, with little of the positives being recorded:

> *I read my file and felt they'd only recorded my evil twin. Where was the other side of me that I remember?*

Recording positive behaviour allows the young person to develop a more balanced sense of themselves:

> *Having praise regularly recorded in your file helps to give a balanced history.*

Even 'minor' successes are important for many young people:

> *Celebrating minor successes felt odd at first, but that's because I'd never celebrated anything at all.*

An example that a number of young people mentioned was the 'bonus points system'. These were a record of the young person's behaviour over the day, including sections on interactions, activities, household tasks and any specific behaviours relevant to the individual young person. The young person was encouraged to self-review and score their own behaviour, rather than having staff score it for them:

> *A sense of achievement – my achievement, not the staffs.*

These points were then accumulated and could be exchanged for items in a 'catalogue'.

Help the young person to record positive experiences and behaviour, however small or insignificant it may seem.

Identify 'progress' and encourage the young person to recognise this.

Conclusion

Carers and staff need to be clear about the intended impact of any intervention, and have an idea about the type of outcomes they wish to promote: they should be aiming to elicit active responses from young people such as 'I can do . . .' or 'I know . . .'. There is also a clear need to evaluate the effectiveness of any interventions.

The promotion of 'resilience' and life skills should not be seen as the responsibility of any one individual carer or agency. There needs to be a 'whole of service' approach.

We should recognise that many young people feel that much of their care experience works against them developing and practising these skills. Many care leavers report that their care experience was dis-empowering and constrained, and that they felt they had little choice in any major decisions.

Young people need to be supported in making decisions about their lives and may need to be encouraged and supported in challenging decisions that they are unhappy about.

We are living in a society that is increasingly worried about, and aiming to reduce, risk. Yet taking risk is an important and necessary learning process that all young people need to take part in. It is even more important for looked after children as their transition into independent living is, generally, much earlier and less supported than many young people leaving home. The importance of risk and responsibility needs to be recognised and young people need to be supported in decisions they make that may eventually prove to have been unwise. The concept of 'defensive caring' needs to be addressed (who is this really protecting?) as does the 'protecting' approach that many foster carers feel they have to adopt (the balance between caring and preparing).

Traditional sessions focused on particular issues, such as budgeting and health, are also important. It should be recognised that these sessions will have a greater impact if young people have had some experience of exploring or practising these issues and skills beforehand.

Many young people leave the care system and go on to be successful young adults. If we want more care leavers to succeed and to better manage the transition to adulthood, we have to focus on helping them develop the necessary skills and qualities right from the start. We need to ask young people where they think their strengths and weaknesses are, what help they think they need, and perhaps prioritise with them and target specific areas at different times.

We also need to look at preparation for leaving care in its widest context and be realistic and honest with young people about what they can expect when they've left care, challenge them when appropriate, and help them develop self worth and aspirations. Finally, we have to remember the early age at which these young people face independence and ensure that they are fully prepared and ready to leave care.

Resources

Buchanan, A. and Hudson, B. (2000) *Promoting Children's Emotional Well-being.* New York, Oxford University Press Inc.
Centrepoint, Department of Health, Department for Transport, Local Government and the Regions. (2002) *Care Leaving Strategies: A Good Practice Handbook.* London, Department for Transport, Local Government and the Regions.
Clarke, A. and Clarke, A. (2003) *Human Resilience: A Fifty Year Quest*, London, Jessica Kingsley.
Gilligan, R. (2001) *Promoting Resilience*, London, BAAF.
Woods, D. (2004) *Supporting Care Leavers: Developing Resilience*, Centrepoint final report, Unpublished.

Section Two: Nature and Level of Personal Support

Personal Support

Ann Wheal

Every young person who is leaving care should have a Pathway Plan and a Personal Advisor.

Pathway planning

There is a legal requirement (Reg. 8 of the Children (Leaving Care) (England) Regulations 2001) in preparing a Pathway Plan (PP) to set out in the plan, the manner in which the authority proposes to meet the assessed needs of the child, and the date by which, and by whom, any action to implement any aspect of the plan will be carried out.

There is also a legal requirement (Regulation 9) to review the plan if a child or young person requests it, if the local authority (LA) or the personal advisor (PA) considers it necessary, and in any other case, at a minimum of every six months. In reviewing the PP the LA must consider whether any change is necessary.

> *The Pathway Plan should be pivotal to the process whereby young people map out their future, articulating their aspirations and identifying interim goals along the way to realising their ambitions. It will also play a critical part in making the new arrangements contained within the Act work.*
>
> *The Authority should work to ensure that the Plan is owned by the young person and is able to respond to their changing needs and ambitions. It should look ahead at least as far as the young person's 21st birthday and will be in place beyond that where the young person is in a programme of education or training which takes them past that age.*
>
> Children Leaving Care Act Guidance, Chapter 5.

The content of a pathway plan

- Nature and level of personal support.
- Details of accommodation.
- Education and training (detailed plan).
- Employment.
- Support to sustain family and social relationships.
- Practical and other skills (programme).
- Financial support.
- Health needs – how are they to be met?
- Contingency plans.

Pathway plan

- Make it work for you.
- Understand what it means.
- Know what you can expect.

- Know how to make the most of it to help you prepare for adult life and how to manage when you are out there on your own.
- Get it updated and changed if you are not happy with it.

Pathway plans and good practice

- Young people must have the option to remain looked after until they are prepared and ready to leave.
- Pathway planning should run parallel to a young person's care plan and Integrated Children's Service (ICS) planning (previously LAC), including any personal education plan or Connexions plan.
- Pathway planning should take place early, recognising the need for structure and stability.
- All people with an interest in, or involved in, supporting the young person should be fully involved in the process.
- Pathway planning should be at the young person's pace and should ensure that they are fully involved and informed about the options available.
- Real choice is vital, as a young person's assessment of need will have identified which options will be most suitable and agreeable to the young person.
- Specialist leaving care teams must be involved at an early point in order to ensure that they offer specific knowledge to young people, and help focus the pathway planning process.

Personal advisors

Functions of PAs are also set out in the regulations (Reg. 12) and include: participating in the assessment and preparation of PPs, (where financial support should be set out); to liaise with the LA in the implementation of the PP; to co-ordinate the provision of services; take reasonable steps to ensure that the young person makes use of such services. In practice this means:

The role of the personal advisor:
- Exploring options, advising, providing practical support.
- Understanding the young person's needs.
- Preparing the Pathway Plan.
- Ensuring the Pathway Plan needs are met including sources of finance and arrangements for payment.
- Linking with the Connexions service or other similar services.
- Co-ordinating the provisions of services.
- Maintaining written records of contact.
- Keeping in touch.

Other people who might offer support.

All local authorities have leaving care teams and a young person must be allocated a personal advisor from that team or from the Connexions service. However, some times a young person prefers someone else from that team in whom to confide. Wherever possible this should be accommodated.

The Connexions and other similar services may also have personal advisors who help and advise on careers, educational matters and personal development.

Mentoring

Mentoring is about:
- companionship
- support
- friendship

Mentors are usually:
- People from the local community.
- Different from the person whom they are mentoring.
- Different from other adults the mentored usually meets.
- Good listener and communicator.
- Good community role models.
- Multi-talented individuals.
- Of high integrity.
- Open-minded.
- Kind and down-to-earth.
- Strong personalities.
- Not easily influenced or 'taken-in'.
- People with a broad experience of life.

The three stages of mentoring are:
1. Building a relationship of trust and getting to grips with the issues of the person concerned.
2. Helping the person to understand the basis of these issues and developing strategies to cope with the situation.
3. Evaluating the strategies the person uses, recognising what does and doesn't work, and helping the person to develop a new life plan.

Mentors are usually volunteers but may occasionally be paid workers. They may work with one person only or may have several clients. The mentoring may last a short time, say a few weeks, or may last for a year. Either party may stop the mentoring if they feel it is not working or they have achieved their goals. Mentoring should be time-limited and extended only if all parties agree.

Mentors:
- Have an awareness of themselves and how they function.
- Must be able to challenge their own strengths and weakness and areas for development.
- Should be able to relate to their own experiences objectively.
- Must understand that the relationship is task orientated.
- Must be suitably checked, trained, supervised, supported and monitored.

> *A mentor for a young person leaving care is a committed supporter, a private helper, who will look on the positive side of the young person's agenda and will move at the young person's pace.*
>
> The Prince's Trust mentoring scheme for care leavers

The benefits of mentoring to care leavers are:
- Advice and encouragement.
- Opportunities to learn new skills.
- Sign-posting to other sources of support.
- Increased self-esteem and self-confidence.
- Reduced isolation.
- Help to access grants and programmes.
- Individual time and attention.

How you get a mentor

Sometimes a young person hears about a mentoring scheme and contacts the mentoring organisation. Other people who might refer a care leaver to a mentoring project are:
- Social worker.
- Personal advisor.
- Foster or residential carer.
- Parent.
- Family.
- Friend.
- Counsellor.

However, even when someone else has made the referral, the young person must decide for themselves whether to apply to be part of a mentoring scheme.

Advocacy

There is now a great awareness of the need to provide independent advocacy for vulnerable children and young people so they have an effective voice in decisions affecting their lives. This is particularly pertinent for care leavers.

Young people themselves see access to independent confidential advocacy services as a key element in equalising the imbalance between powerful adults and bureaucracies and potentially vulnerable and isolated young people.

The Minister for Health, Lord Hunt, confirmed to Parliament during the passage of the Care Standards Bill that:

> *Advocacy is about effectively articulating the child's view, right or wrong. It is not about what the advocate thinks is best or in the child's welfare. Advocacy is grounded in Article 12 of the UN Convention on the Rights of the Child, which assures children capable of forming their own views that right to express those views freely in all matters affecting them.*

The Law:
- Children (Leaving Care) Act 2000 – empowerment and participation plus advocacy and why it is needed.
- The Children Act (1989) – involvement in decisions that affect young people's lives as well as complaints procedure.
- The UN Convention on the Rights of the Child – participation of children in decisions concerning their lives.
- Article 8 of the European Convention on Human Rights – includes the notion of procedural fairness in the decision-making process concerning private and family life.
- Human Rights Act 1998.

During the 1990s a wide range of advocacy services has been developed including local authority children's rights services and the appointment of a children's rights officer, although some of the advocacy work is contracted out to other agencies to ensure independence.

There are also specialist independent children's and young people's advocacy organisations such as Voice of the Child in Care (VCC) and National Advocacy Service (NYAS).

These organisations endeavour to ensure that they are free of all pressures or conflicts of interest that could prevent the advocate from being single-mindedly on the child's side. They also offer a significantly higher threshold of confidentiality to children than social workers or others in social services. Advocates will only breach children's confidences where circumstances are such that urgent action is needed to protect them or others from serious danger.

Other relevant organisations are:
- A National Voice (ANV) – run by, and for, young people who have been in public care.
- Naypic – similar to ANV, but in Northern Ireland and Scotland.
- Who Cares?
- Fostering Networks.

> *My first thoughts about an advocate were that they were very similar to social workers . . . Once I met her I realised straight away. She seemed to be really at ease with young people. My advocate explained*

her role and the issues she would be taking up for me. She was there for all my important meetings. When she saw that social services weren't looking after my needs, she made them TOTALLY aware of their faults.

Young person

Complaints, and redress, when things go wrong

The main source of redress is making a statutory complaint under the Children Act. Sometimes making a formal complaint is not necessary and with the help of an advocate a young person can negotiate with a local authority to reconsider their decision on a specific issue. At other times a mediation process can be set up where all parties can attempt to resolve the problem without the young person making a formal complaint:

The law covers children who are making a complaint, thinking of making a complaint or want to make 'representations' about something that is bothering them without this first being framed as a specific complaint:

- Advocates should be able to help at the earliest possible stage of the young person's concerns which may avoid the use of the complaints procedure at all.
- A range of publicity materials should be produced by local authorities.
- Management and funding of advocacy services should *as far as possible* be independent of the local authority.
- Children in authorities with in-house children's rights officers should be informed of alternative sources of outside help and the local authority should consider the young person's request carefully and think about what steps it might take to meet the young person's needs.
- Everyone who enters the care system must be given details of the complaints procedure for their local authority. The authority should ensure that the procedure is fully understood by the young person.
- If a formal complaint is made there is a time limit by which it must be dealt with; an independent person should be appointed to take part in the investigation and to sit on a panel that will review the complaint; local authorities should identify who is responsible for taking action to implement panel recommendations; complainants should be kept informed about progress; review panels should propose remedies they think appropriate.
- In extreme cases redress to the law may be necessary in which case legal advice should be sought from a lawyer on the Children Panel.

Using the web for support

Some leaving care teams have their own web sites that young people can access, the North West Regional Forum is a good example. Some young people's organisations also have web sites that can offer support such as A National Voice. There is also a site so contact can be made with family, friends and ex-foster carers called Care Leavers United. The web addresses are at the back of the book together with information about the groups.

There is also a site called SoNet (social networks) www.sonet.soton.ac.uk which is an independent site hosted by the University of Southampton and supported by Fostering Network.

It is aimed for use by any of the following:
- Young people leaving care and who have left care.
- Young people in care.
- Social work practitioners.
- Social work students.
- Foster and residential carers.

- Journalists.
- Academics.
- Adults who have been in care.
- The general public.

The forum has rules for users and for guests; it is moderated; it is easy to join and easy to use; membership is optional (i.e. it is possible to contribute to a discussion without giving any of your personal details) and it is easy to unsubscribe.

The most discussed topics so far are:
- Maintaining links with families.
- Should foster carers get paid?
- Experiences of care.
- Advice if things go wrong, including advice on debt.
- Education and leaving care.
- Entitlements, particularly for continuing in education.

However, most inputs from young people have been seeking advice for their particular circumstances. Responses have come from other site users, sometimes from the moderator and sometimes from members of the site project team. Young people have also been signposted to other organisations such as VCC.

UNICHAT closed site – www.sonet.soton.ac.uk/pt

This site is for care leavers going to any university and is supported by the University of Southampton and the Prince's Trust. It provides:
- Relevant information, such as what the different qualifications mean, a jargon buster, financial entitlements.
- Opportunity to have a discussion, both on the site and via emails, with other care leavers.
- A facility to ask questions and receive a variety of responses from people using the site.
- Support from trained and police-checked mentors.

Care leavers attending higher education clearly need some form of support especially in their first term at university. The scheme uses as mentors the services of people who have retired from employment who have a wealth of life experiences as well as the time to 'just listen'. Mentors may also be care leavers but the young people consulted were keen that the mentors should not be foster carers or social workers.

The mentors can also offer advice, if asked, and are generally available to respond flexibly. The set-up, recruitment, training and support for the mentors is almost identical to the existing successful Prince's Trust Mentoring Scheme.

How the scheme works

Care leavers from anywhere in the UK, having agreed to join the scheme, will get their details approved by the moderator. They are then able to access the 'room' in order to get help with any issues that may be causing them concern or that they wish to raise or discuss. The mentors, or other care leavers, will be able to see the query and decide whether or not to input any comments. At this stage there is no tie-up between the mentors and the care leavers – it is an open forum. The care leaver will see the various responses and can continue the dialogue in an open way or can contact an individual mentor if that is what they prefer to do.

Each mentor is provided with an email address or private messaging facility so they do not have to give their own personal details out unless they so wish.

Written guidelines including confidentiality issues are provided for both young people and mentors. A 24-hour telephone helpline for mentors is available in case of need on a rota basis similar to that provided by the SoNet scheme.

CareZone

CareZone is a range of secure online services for young people in public care which is managed by The Who Care's Trust. It gives access to national information about all aspects of the care system, including rights, education, the world of work, health and preparation for adult life. This information is presented in a variety of formats such as games or photo stories that can be accessed through different rooms within the CareZone, virtual world. Information about local services can also be accessed through local authorities own rooms within the site.

Users can communicate with each other through the moderated message boards, chat rooms, email and instant messaging tools as well as attend or host chat forums based around set themes, such as keeping healthy, how to budget, as well as topics of their own choosing.

All users also have their own room and vault where they can safely store personal belongings such as life story books, or photos.

To ensure the highest level of security, entry to the site is controlled using pin numbers and a small portable electronic device that is provided to a user by their local authority.

Conclusion

Some dictionary definitions of the word support are:
- sustain
- keep going
- back up
- contend for
- represent
- prop

Going out into the world as an inexperienced young adult would be daunting enough for any of us. Doing so without the support of our family and friends around us would be devastating. Many care leavers just do not have any close-knit support networks to help them so they must rely on professional help. They need someone to be there when needed, or to just telephone them to see how they are getting on, but most of all they need to know that there is someone out there who cares about them and is willing to support them through thick and thin.

Resources

Fostering Network, Greenwich Council, First Key (2003) *Preparation for Adult Life.* London: Fostering Network.
Wheal, A. (Ed.) (2002) *The RHP Companion to Leaving Care.* Lyme Regis: Russell House Publishing.

4
Young Disabled People Leaving Care: Pathway Planning

Julie Harris

This chapter has been written for use by residential social workers, foster carers or care workers, young disabled people, their social workers and personal advisors. Its aim is to guide the practitioner or young person through the pathway planning process exploring some of the key issues that arise for young disabled people in addition to those of care leavers in general, particularly concerning transition. It provides some tips for practice and signposts further reading or useful resources that may help in the day-to-day support of young people.

The approaches to practice described in this chapter are based upon the social model of disability. This is the description of disability, used by disabled people themselves, that focuses on the barriers that exist for someone with impairments, which prevent them from being equally included in society.

These barriers are both physical and attitudinal and deny disabled people equal opportunities; for example:

- In education.
- Getting a job.
- Using public transport.
- Having suitable housing.
- Having an active social life.
- Feeling part of the community.

This approach is in contrast to the medical approach which says that a person's impairment is what disables them. The social model moves the emphasis away from the person's impairment.

The use of the social model is especially important in terms of service and resource planning to ensure that there is capacity to provide the services that are needed. This model when applied to individual planning leads to a whole-needs approach. This focuses on overcoming barriers and enabling a person to do the things they want. It says that someone's impairment, whilst a part of them, does not define who they are and that they will have other needs, wishes, expectations and aspirations and equal rights to all the opportunities enjoyed by the non-disabled population.

It is essential that young disabled people be introduced to these ideas and approaches, especially as they begin to build an adult identity.

This chapter aims to show how such approaches can be built in to the pathway planning process for young disabled people who are leaving care, in order that it becomes a central tool for making the transition to adulthood one of confidence and growing self-determination.

What do we know about disabled care leavers?

The answer is not a great deal. There has only been very little research specifically exploring the experiences of young disabled people leaving care. In general, this is a group that has been omitted from policy on, and service provision for, those leaving care (Morris, 1995; Harris, Rabiee and Priestly, 2002). One research study however (Rabiee, Priestly and Knowles, 2001) identified that different issues arise for these young people than for other care leavers and that they are faced with significant additional barriers to social and economic inclusion, as they become adults.

More general research about young disabled people in the process of transition to adulthood points to issues and difficulties that are likely to be further compounded and exacerbated by the leaving care experience (see below under *Transitions for young disabled people*).

What do we mean by 'leaving care'?

One of the immediate difficulties lies in confusion about what 'leaving care' means in this context. It has led to the needs of young disabled people being almost universally overlooked. It arises because of the absence of clarity or agreement between mainstream and disability services.

The net effect is that eligibility for the Children (Leaving Care) Act is, more often than not, determined by the service the young person uses rather than by their legislative entitlement or level of need. Young people using disability services, for example, may go on to use adult services after the age of 18 but, because they are not using mainstream children's services and not necessarily moving on to 'independence', are not viewed as 'care leavers'.

The definition of young people 'leaving care' in the Children (Leaving Care) Act however is of 'ceasing to be looked after'. This occurs at age 18 when the local authority children's services no longer has responsibility to provide accommodation and care, regardless of whether a child is defined as 'disabled' or of the services they will use after care. In circumstances where 'leaving care' means moving on to adult services, every local authority should have agreements between the relevant services about resources and with roles and responsibilities clearly defined:

> ...to ensure that **all** young people are in receipt of all their entitlements under the legislation as 'care leavers'.

There is another group of young people for whom particular difficulties arise in getting the level of support and service they need. These are young people who have additional support needs but who, because of strict access to service criteria, are unlikely to be recognised as 'disabled'. Very often these young people are described as having mild to moderate learning difficulties and mainstream leaving care services often feel under-resourced or inadequately skilled to meet their needs.

Young people in both categories are likely to be placed in a variety of locations including fostering, residential or private care, residential schools and colleges, short break units, at home with parents (on care orders) in hospital or in secure units, etc. Good information and tracking systems are therefore fundamental in ensuring that they and their entitlement to leaving care services are not overlooked.

Research suggests that young black disabled people and those from minority ethnic groups are likely to face additional barriers in accessing statutory support services which include information about services in different languages and formats (Chamba et al., 1999). Young people and their families report feeling double discrimination because of ethnicity and disability (Baxter et al., 1990; Hussain, Atkin and Ahmad, 2002). In particular, low expectations by education professionals result in the young people being inadequately prepared for adult life (Bignall and Butt, 2000).

The pathway planning process introduced by the Children (Leaving Care) Act presents an excellent opportunity for strengthening the transition process for care leavers, so that it becomes less of a process of transfer between services and more about young disabled people and their transition to adulthood. If based upon the social model of disability and a human rights approach, pathway planning has the capacity to become a powerful planning tool that can aid the development of autonomy and self-determination as young disabled people leave care.

Transitions for young disabled people

Transition planning is a process involving numerous service providers and which is surrounded by a complex framework of legislation and public policy. It is intended to support the transition from school to adult life for young people with special educational needs, but very often represents the move from children's to adult services.

All young people with a Statement of Special Educational Needs (SEN) should have an educational review in Year 9 (aged 14 years) to assess their future educational needs. A representative of social services should be involved in this review if support from social services is anticipated when they leave school (Section 5 of the Disabled Person's Act 1986) as will be the case if the young person is 'looked after'. Generally, the leaving care service would not become involved with a young person until the age of 15½ to 16 years old but if transition and pathway planning are to be effectively dovetailed, age 14 is probably the best time for that involvement to begin with young people who are likely to remain 'looked after' until at least the age of 16.

Learning disability partnership board

In each local authority area the Learning Disability Partnership Board should be working on transitions issues for young people with learning difficulties but may also be addressing the needs of young disabled people in general. There should be a Transitions Champion on each Board. One of the roles of the Connexions service is to improve the transitions process and inter-agency collaboration. A Connexions representative must also be involved in the 14-plus review (SEN Code of Practice) and this person will then go on to oversee the transitions plan and should attend all the subsequent transition reviews.

Where a young person is going into further or higher education or training at age 16, the Connexions advisor will undertake an assessment under Section 140 Learning and Skills Act 2000. This will build on all the previous transition plans and identify an action plan, which includes all the services, and agencies that will need to be involved, outlining the nature of their support.

There is evidence to suggest that many young people with learning difficulties leave school without any transition planning (Heslop et al., 2001). A variety of research (see Bibliography and References) suggests that, as a process, young people and their parents or carers can find transition characterised by poor information, poor co-ordination between service providers, a lack of planning and decisions based on resources rather than need.

Very often changes of placement or service can happen very abruptly. Not surprisingly, these factors combine to create an often anxious and uncertain time for young people and their families. Young people say that often transition planning does not focus on the things that are important to them such as having friends and a social life, becoming more independent and having sexual relationships etc.

ⓘ **Tips for practice**

- Find out about the local transitions policy from the Children with Disabilities team, Transitions team or adult services.
- Find out about, and make contact with, the Transitions Champion located within the Local Learning Disability Partnership Board.
- Get involved with young disabled people who are likely to be 'leaving care' early in the transitional planning process at the Year 9 review.
- Make sure that pathway planning builds on existing assessments and plans, and that you have the professional and multi-agency links in place to enable you to undertake pathway planning effectively.

Personal advisors

Arrangements for the support of young disabled people will vary between local authorities and according to the services they use within an authority – usually determined by the perceived level or type of impairment and whether a young person is likely to qualify for adult services on reaching 18. In some authorities, staff skilled in working with young disabled people may work as part of the leaving care service. In others, personal advisors may be located in Children with Disabilities teams, Transitions or Adult teams. It is also possible that the role of the Connexions advisor within the transitional planning is rolled into the personal advisor under the Children (Leaving Care) Act or vice versa.

In any given scenario, it is important that as much flexibility as possible be built in to arrangements so as to be responsive to the needs and wishes of the individual young person. To reduce some of the disruption and uncertainty that we know young people experience in transition (see above) it is also vital to achieve continuity so that young people are given the opportunity to build positive, long-term relationships with adults they can trust.

All young disabled people who are eligible, relevant or former relevant (see Chapter 17: The Law and your Rights) will be entitled to the support of a personal advisor regardless of which service provides them with primary support.

ⓘ **Tips for practice**

In addition to the skills and qualities required of personal advisors in general, those acting as personal advisors to young disabled people leaving care should be trained and have an understanding of:
- Disability equality issues.
- The post-14 review process and transition issues.
- The role of Connexions in these processes.
- The principles of person-centred planning.
- Effective communication skills.
- Direct payments for 16-year-olds and those over that age.
- Self-advocacy, peer and citizen advocacy.
- Working with parents and carers.
- Changes to benefit entitlements that occur at 16.

Involving young disabled people

Some of the most significant barriers to involvement by young disabled people in planning for their future can arise through low expectations expressed by others. These may not be verbally expressed but are communicated by, for example, a failure to facilitate a young person's participation in meetings that are about them.

Research tells us that young disabled people leaving care and their parents or carers often feel excluded from decision-making, that they are talked over in meetings or not invited to them at all (Rabiee, Priestley and Knowles, 2001). This can have a devastating effect on a young person's confidence and sense of self-worth. The involvement of young disabled people and their families or carers can be time consuming and costly – it therefore needs to be anticipated in budgets and resource allocation, if it is to be undertaken properly.

(i) Tips for practice

In order to participate in meetings and other decision making processes young people and their parents or carers might need:
- Transport.
- Hearing equipment such as hearing loops.
- Accessible material such as symbol or Braille, parallel text.
- Specialist computer software or other equipment.
- Video or audio equipment to record discussion or decisions that have been made.
- A personal assistant or someone who is skilled in their form of communication: British Sign Language, Makaton etc.
- Access to an advocacy service.

They will **always** need:
- To feel that their opinion is valued and influential.
- Jargon-free information in a format that is useful to them.
- To exercise choice.
- Time to consider options and make decisions at their own pace.
- Space to take risks, make mistakes or change their minds.
- A clear record of decisions and plans in a format suited to their needs.

One way to ensure that the young person's wishes and feelings are at the centre of the planning activity is to adopt a person, centred approach to planning (see next section).

Person-centred approaches to needs assessment and pathway planning

All of the general headings used in the needs assessment and pathway plan will remain the same when planning for young disabled people. Both should, however, build upon the transitional review plans that have been in place since Year 9.

Pathway planning for young disabled people has the potential to be an extremely effective tool in co-ordinating services and addressing some of the difficulties that have been identified with transitional planning. Its greatest potential, however, lies in supporting the young person to develop the skills and confidence that they will need in order to make decisions and take control of their lives as adults. This can be achieved through the use of person-centred approaches.

Person-centred planning is a tool that has been promoted under *Valuing People: A New Strategy for Learning Disability for the 21st Century* (DoH, 2000) to help practitioners and service users engage together in more meaningful planning for the future. The five key features of person-centred planning are:

1. The person is at the centre.
2. Family members and friends are full partners.
3. Person-centred planning reflects the person's capacities, what is important to the person (now and for their future) and specifies the support needed to enable the individual to make a valued contribution to the community.
4. Person-centred planning builds a shared commitment to action that will uphold the person's rights.
5. Person-centred planning leads to continual listening, learning and action, and helps the person to get what they want out of life.

Taken from: *Valuing People: Towards Person-Centred Approaches. Planning with People: Guidance for Implementation Groups.*

Different styles and approaches have been developed towards person-centred planning, including, Personal Futures Planning, Maps or Essential Lifestyle Planning to reflect a range of need and circumstance. There should be training or guidance on the facilitation of these approaches available locally. Young people and their parents or carers with the appropriate training can also lead person-centred planning. Self-advocacy schemes can be especially effective in helping young people to take control of planning their futures in this way (see section below on Self-advocacy and Empowerment).

(i) *Tips for practice*

- Needs assessments should focus on the disabling barriers experienced by a young person and how to overcome them rather than on a young person's impairment.
- Find out about the approaches used towards person-centred planning in your local area and identify who can act as a facilitator of person-centred plans.
- Is there training available in planning centred approaches that you as key worker, personal advisor, young person, parent or carer could take advantage of to help with pathway planning?
- Find out about local self-advocacy schemes that the young person might like to become involved with.

Keeping in touch: communication and information

The Children (Leaving Care) Act places a duty on the local authority to keep in touch with young people up to a minimum age of 21 or beyond if they are involved in education or training as part of the pathway plan. Contact levels have been monitored through the *Quality Protects* target of four recorded contacts in the nineteenth year.

Special consideration will need to be given to young people living out of authority (see below).

Young disabled people, their families and carers are reliant on good information to be able to make choices, experience equality of opportunity and feel empowered to exercise some control within planning processes. Despite this, research shows that transition is characterised by poor information and families report having to struggle to get even the most basic information about services and options. This predictably leads to anxiety and uncertainty at a time when young people and their families and carers are already experiencing significant change as the young person approaches adulthood.

There are particular issues for black young people and their families who can be further marginalised by poor information giving, which fails to take account of different language and communication needs (Chamba et al., 1999).

Young disabled people are particularly in danger of missing out on information given to other care leavers about their entitlements and the services available to them under the Children (Leaving Care) Act. In order to tackle this, local authorities should produce the local 'leaving care' guide in accessible formats.

(i) Tips for practice

- Keeping in contact with young disabled people may require additional thought, effort, time and resources and this will need to be taken account of when planning service.
- In order for a young person's communication and support needs to be met, continuity and a long-term relationship based on trust and with the same personal advisor or other consistent adults, are essential.
- You will need to adopt a flexible approach to keeping in touch using different communication skills or information-giving approaches as necessary. These may include different formats for giving or recording information, and providing specialist equipment or software.
- Local disability services and minority ethnic groups should be able to help with producing information in different formats and languages to meet a range of needs.
- Significant people in a young person's life, such as friends or family, can be a valuable resource and may be able to facilitate your keeping in touch, in the young person's preferred manner.
- Keeping in touch is far more likely to be successful if methods and regularity of contact are negotiated with the young person.
- Information should be kept free of jargon.

Young disabled people living out of authority

Young disabled people are more likely to be placed out of the local authority area than other 'looked after' young people, very often in residential educational placements. These may be jointly funded by education and social services or health. Sometimes young people as young adults can be moved into residential placements away from home and family because there are few options for supported or sheltered accommodation locally. Research shows that these young people are in danger of becoming isolated socially, with the links with family and other support networks broken (Morris, 1995).

These young people are even more likely to be disempowered and alienated from the decision-making process and consequently, less likely to experience good transition planning. Their status as 'care leavers' is also more likely to be overlooked, depending on the efficiency of management information systems and the level of communication between disability and mainstream aftercare services.

ⓘ Tips for practice

You will need:

- A strategy for keeping in touch with each individual young person, identifying key people, frequency and type of contact.
- A strategy for ongoing contact between the young person and the significant people in their life e.g. parents, siblings and other family members, friends etc.
- Arrangements for emergency contact.
- An accessible route for young people to make a complaint about their care or services received under the Children (Leaving Care) Act 2000.
- Good and regular communication with care providers and other partners in pathway planning.
- The young person should have access to an advocate or independent visitor.

Self-advocacy and empowerment

Independent advocacy is important for young disabled people, particularly those with complex communication impairments, and plays a vital role not only in ensuring that young people's views are heard but also in keeping young people safe. Young disabled people often lose touch with those who act as natural advocates for them – a friend and peer service user, a teacher or a member of staff – when they move to a different service. In some cases these may have played a significant role in supporting communication and so a service move can leave young people feeling very isolated and frustrated.

Advocates and independent visitors have a very important role to play in this respect. Also, family or friends outside services can often act as advocates if appropriately supported in the role. It is important that staff working directly with young people receive training about the value of advocacy and are committed to it.

The potential role of peers is also increasingly acknowledged as more peer-mentoring schemes are established and self-advocacy groups prove a very successful tool in increasing young people's confidence, and sense of value and belonging.

Self-advocacy is particularly effective in empowering young disabled people to take an active control in determining their package of support in transition planning, through the use of person-centred approaches (see above). Self-advocacy schemes can provide young people with a social group that can empathise and share experiences. It is important that they meet other disabled people who are successful in managing personal assistance and exercising positive control over their lives.

ⓘ Tips for practice

- Check out local independent advocacy schemes – are they accessible to young disabled people leaving care?
- Make sure that there is an accessible complaints process and that young disabled people have the support to use it.
- Find out if the advocacy service for looked after children has links to self-advocacy schemes.
- If you can't find any local self-advocacy schemes for young people why not set one up? (There is information signposted below on how to do so).

The Leaving Care Handbook

- Find out if there are any mentoring or peer-mentoring schemes that support young people leaving care in general? If so, have they thought about making the scheme accessible for disabled care leavers or could you encourage them to do so?
- Check whether any schools in your area are using *Trans-active*, a multi-media-based transitions planning tool that involves peer supporters (see below).

Independent living

For most care leavers 'independence' is an aspiration as they approach adulthood and often having their own home and financial autonomy are likely to be significant goals of the pathway plan. Leaving care services place an emphasis on the development of independent living skills such as cooking, budgeting and the general preparation of young people for life 'after care'.

Whilst some young disabled people may share these expectations of living independently, others may interpret independence differently and have other aspirations and goals as they become adults. These may be more about making their own decisions, being supported to manage direct payments and identify their own support needs, employ a personal assistant, go out with their friends, access further education, employment, social and leisure opportunities and do the things they want to do.

Research also shows that minority ethnic groups may have different cultural expectations around disability and independence (Hussain, Atkin and Ahmad, 2002). It is important that assumptions aren't made about 'independence', or the goals that a young people should be working towards. All pathway planning should reflect the wishes, choices and pace of the young person.

Personal assistance can be an empowering and effective way for a disabled person to achieve the level of independence that they want. Managing personal assistance, being an employer and getting the relationship right with a personal assistant can be quite complex, however, and the young person will need training and support (see below). Local direct payment schemes should be able to help with supporting the practical administration matters, but also with developing some of the interpersonal skills required.

(i) *Tips for practice*

- Take the time to explore with the young person what independence means to them and help them to think about their goals and aspirations. You may find the use of aids helpful – such as videos or interactive CD ROMs (see Trans-plan above). From here you can find out their options.
- What levels of support will they need to achieve them and does this include adapted equipment or furniture?
- Think about what skills they will need to acquire to achieve their goals and have high expectations for them.
- Find out about local disability organisations that offer support and training to young people in managing their personal assistance. Such schemes should ideally be run by disabled people themselves.
- Build any plans for managing direct payments and personal assistance into pathway plans. These should include the appropriate training.

Financial packages and direct payments

The financial needs assessment and pathway planning package will be different for young disabled people who claim Disability Living Allowance, than for other care leavers, as they will continue to receive the benefit rather than a maintenance allowance under the Children (Leaving Care) Act. This is not the case with Housing Benefit however and the local authority has a duty to provide accommodation until the age of 18 as for other care leavers.

Even if young people are claiming Disability Living Allowance they will still be entitled to other financial assistance over and above the statutory levels as part of the pathway-planning package. They may need help with adaptations, special equipment, or financial assistance in accessing further education and employment opportunities etc. The Children (Leaving Care) Act places a duty on the local authority to meet these assessed needs.

Young disabled people aged 16 and 17 are entitled to use Direct Payments (Carers and Disabled Children Act 2000). This means that they can purchase their own services and in this way have more control and management of their own package of support. They may, however, need help to do this. Research shows that the barriers to using direct payments include young people's lack of knowledge about such schemes and concerns about the difficulties they might have in trying to access them.

There should be local schemes which can be contracted in to assist and provide support with recruitment and administration. Personal advisors and other staff should, nonetheless, receive training and be committed to the ethos of direct payment schemes.

ⓘ Tips for practice

- The first needs assessment should address whether a young person wishes to direct their own personal assistance and work should be undertaken with the young person to enable them to identify their support needs.
- Arrangements for young people to purchase personal assistance should be specified in subsequent pathway plans.
- Make sure the young person has appropriate access to support and training in identifying and directing their own personal assistance. Find out about local groups or services facilitating Direct Payments Schemes who can offer advice and support.
- Make sure the young disabled person has the full financial needs assessment to which they are entitled through the pathway planning process, as means tested benefits are unlikely to cover adequately all their support needs.
- Make sure the young person has a benefits check to ensure that they are receiving all their entitlements.
- Make contact with a Benefits Advisor who has detailed knowledge of child and disability benefits.
- Sometimes the advice and support of a Welfare Advisor can be very helpful in developing arrangements with benefit agencies to ensure that claims are processed quickly and efficiently.
- Support the young person and encourage the development of their budgeting skills by helping them to open and manage a bank account.

- Make sure there are clear arrangements and procedures about the delivery of the financial support package, including arrangements for direct payments.
- Check whether the young person may be entitled to a grant from the Independent Living Fund (see below).

Accommodation

Young disabled people aged 16–17 will not be entitled to Housing Benefit and it is the role of the local authority to provide accommodation until they are 18, so funding arrangements between services need to be agreed as early as possible.

Very often decisions made about a young person's living situation are based on resources or what's available rather than on the young person's wishes or needs. Young disabled people may end up living in residential care because it is a cheaper option than being supported in the community.

For young disabled people wishing to move into accommodation of their own there are typically few options and many more barriers. These include low levels of suitable accommodation in the private sector and limited options for support. Many supported accommodation projects are segregated and can leave young people feeling socially isolated; often transition housing, intended to help prepare for independent accommodation, does not lead to any real accommodation options (Hendy and Pascall, 2002).

Partnership working between social services and housing departments is often poor; however, there should be a housing strategy in place to which the social services departments has contributed, which recognises the needs of people with learning difficulties, including those who are care leavers. There will also be local Supporting People schemes providing various options for supported accommodation. These should take the needs of disabled people into account.

(i) *Tips for practice*
- Make sure that accommodation issues are identified early within planning processes to allow time for funding arrangements to be agreed and options to be identified. These should include the meeting of personal support needs.
- Make sure that plans have been made to cover accommodation during vacations if the young person is in residential further education, Children (Leaving Care) Act 2000 23B (8) (b)).
- Contact your local Supporting People team, who should be able to tell you about options in your area and financial support (see link below).

For information about Supporting People go to www.spkweb.org.uk/ This site will provide links to your local Supporting People team, which should be able to offer advice on financial support with accommodation.

Housing Options is an independent advice and information service for people with learning disabilities which aims to assist people with learning disabilities achieve greater control over aspects of their life and to provide more housing and support choices. Go to www.housingoptions.org.uk

Education, training, and employment

Research shows that outcomes for disabled people in education and employment are very poor:
- Disabled people are twice as likely as non-disabled people to have no qualifications. This difference is consistent across all age groups.
- Disabled people are only about half as likely as non-disabled people to be in employment. There are currently around 3.3 million disabled people in employment: they make up 12 per cent of all people of working age in employment.

(The Disability Briefing, May 2002).

The *Valuing People* strategy sets the following objective:

> As young people with learning disabilities move into adulthood, to ensure continuity of care and support for the young person and their family, and to provide equality of opportunity in order to enable as many disabled young people as possible to participate in education, training and employment.

Young disabled people are offered very few options and opportunities to attain their education and employment goals, despite the fact that their aspirations are the same as those of other young people (Ryan, 1997). Often further education or training is offered as a substitute for day care but rarely leads to increasing prospects of employment. Some young people move away from home into residential college in order to achieve independence but sometimes this can act to delay decisions about adult placements and the levels of support available.

The potential for young disabled people to manage their own personal assistance through Direct Payments opens up more opportunities to access further education, training and employment opportunities (see sections above).

(i) Tips for practice

- Pathway plans should build on previous assessments and plans in respect of education such as the Personal Education Plan and transitional reviews.
- Make sure that young people are in receipt of any top-ups they are entitled to if engaged in further education or training, also any grants such as the Educational Maintenance Allowance.
- Would personal assistance benefit the young person in accessing further education, training or employment? If so, this needs to be clearly identified in the needs assessment and arrangements specified in subsequent pathway planning.
- Check a young disabled person's entitlement to accommodation in the vacation (under the Children (Leaving Care) Act) if they are attending a residential college for further education or higher education. There may also be financial support available for this from the Independent Living Fund so it is worth checking out all the options.
- Check out that any further education or training courses are 'real' and will further employment opportunities.
- Find out if any of the local colleges offer support schemes to enable young disabled people to access mainstream further education more easily.
- Having the right equipment or a personal assistant could mean the difference between accessing opportunities in education, training or employment or not so it is important that these issues are identified early in pathway planning (and should have already been identified in transitional reviews).
- Very often having a good relationship with a direct worker who can see the possibilities and help create opportunities can instil young people with real confidence and a desire to achieve.

- On the ground, links with training providers or supported employers are invaluable. A little persuasion of the local council to provide opportunities for their 'looked after' children can also be very effective and good publicity for the local authority.
- Try to develop good links and communication with Connexions, the Learning Skills Council and Job Centre Plus.

Health

For some young disabled people, health needs arising from an impairment or a health condition can obscure wider health issues including a young person's emotional health and well-being, sex and sexuality, diet, drug or alcohol use etc.

Sometimes the specialist health care services that young people are receiving are terminated suddenly at 16 when paediatric services stop (Morris, 1999). Both young people and their families say that they find it hard to get information about medical conditions and treatment or the longer-term implications of a condition as young people move into adulthood.

Under the Children (Leaving Care) Act Regulation 4(a) the responsible authority must undertake an assessment of young people's health and development as part of the needs assessment, within three months of the young person becoming eligible or relevant. This should be a holistic assessment and should follow the guidance issued by the Department of Health in 2001 *Promoting the Health of Looked after Children* (Appendix 4, *Adolescence and Leaving Care*: 11–18).

ⓘ *Tips for practice*

- Find out what the young person feels about their health as part of the needs assessment or first pathway plan – they may identify wider health issues that they want support with.
- Are young people successfully accessing the primary health care that they need? Make sure they are registered with a GP.
- Find out about the continuation of any specialist or therapeutic health service after the young person reaches 16.
- Is the young person in receipt of any information needed to manage a health condition? Is any other help or support needed?
- Make sure that the young person is given accessible information about healthy living, sexual health and sexuality and mental health etc.

Family

As with other young people leaving care there may be any number of issues at play between young disabled people and their families at the time of transition to adulthood. There may be tensions around becoming an adult, taking risks, making mistakes and moving towards independence and autonomy of decision-making. Some families may feel more protective than they would towards a non-disabled child and consequently find this a very anxious time. The situation may be made worse by poor information giving by the authorities, a lack of options and choice, and the other characteristics of poor transitions.

For a young disabled person with the same aspirations as any other young person of having a social life and going out with friends, having sexual relationships, going to college, finding a job etc. this can be a frustrating and difficult time.

Young people may also have very mixed feelings about wanting independence from their family. It is important that the anxieties and feelings of all are acknowledged, and addressed, and a balance negotiated between a young person's need for independence and a family's natural concern. The purchase of personal assistance through direct payments can be very helpful in giving a young person the control over decision-making and also the more practical support in doing the things they want to do. It can also help to improve relationships with parents even when the young person is living at home.

For other young disabled people, continuing contact may be an issue, particularly if the young person is living in another local authority area. These issues will need to be addressed in the pathway plan and funding allocated if necessary to ensure that the appropriate level of contact can be maintained according to the wishes of the young person and their family.

The role of family members or of foster carers as advocates is also an important issue as research suggests that young people living at home or in foster care tend to benefit more from having someone to help them find out options and promote their choices, than do other young people who are reliant on service providers (Rabiee, Priestley and Knowles, 2001).

ⓘ *Tips for practice*

- Make sure that arrangements for contact between the young person and the family (including funding) are included in the pathway plan.
- Is there training available from local disability organisations or advocacy groups for family members wanting to act as advocates?
- Do you know how the young person feels about the family and the role they would like them to play in helping to support them into adulthood and 'independence'? Are their wishes reflected according in the needs assessment and pathway plan?

Friends and relationships, community and leisure

Having friends and relationships is identified by young disabled people, as one of the most important issues, as is likely to be the case for most young people in this age group (Rabiee, Priestley and Knowles, 2001). Despite this however, young disabled people say that it is hard to make friends outside of the services that they use and they may not get many opportunities for socialising with people of their own age group. Sometimes families can feel anxious about young people having an independent social life and there may be risk issues that need to be explored. In addition, there are access issues and other practical barriers to getting out and about, such as using public transport or going out at night.

In more mainstream or social environments young disabled people can often experience discrimination and bullying from their non-disabled peers leading to a real sense of social isolation. Making and maintaining friendships can therefore be a very significant issue in a young disabled person's life.

Where young people do have important friendships or relationships these can often be overlooked in transition planning, and decisions may be made about changes of services or placements without any regard to the impact that they could have on the young person's life.

Young disabled people say that they don't get enough information about sex and relationships or the chance to adequately explore issues of sexuality. Limited social opportunities and changes in service use make it difficult to form or maintain relationships (the Fostering Network, 2002). Young disabled people need much more active support in staying in touch with friends and family – this may include helping them to travel, arrange social events, and maintain an active social network etc.

(i) *Tips for practice*

- As part of the needs assessment, identify with the young person the important people in their life that they would like to be in contact with.
- The implications of a placement or service move on important relationships should be considered and plans made for continuing contact.
- Contact arrangements and social activities can be built into the pathway plan. Practical arrangements such as transport will need to be included.
- Joining a self-advocacy group can be good way to meet new people and tap into leisure activities.
- Find out if there are any locally produced access guides, which give information about accessible venues and activities.

Resources

An Easy Guide to Direct Payments, Giving You the Choice and Control. This is a pack containing a book, CD ROM and tape. Ref 33291.

Baxter, C., Poonia, K., Ward, L. and Nadirshaw, Z. (1990) *Double Discrimination. Issues and Services for People with Learning Difficulties from Black and Ethnic Minority Communities.* London: King's Fund Centre/CRE.

Bethell, J. in Harrison, M. (Ed.) *Our Life, Our Say! A Good-Practice Guide to Young Disabled People's Peer Mentoring Support.* Joseph Rowntree Foundation/Pavilion Publishing.

Bignall, T. and Butt, J. (2000) *Between Ambition and Achievement: Young Black Disabled People's Views and Experiences of Independence and Independent Living.* The Policy Press.

Chamba, R., Ahmad, W., Hirst, M., Lawton, D. and Beresford, B. (1999) *Minority Ethnic Families Caring for a Severely Disabled Child.* The Policy Press.

Department of Health (March 2001) *Family Matters: Counting Families In.* Available from www.valuingpeople.gov.uk

DfES *Get it Sorted* – Guidance on Providing Advocacy Services www.children.doh.gov.uk/adoption/advocacyregulations04.htm

Direct Choices: What Councils Need to Make Direct Payments Happen for People With Learning Disabilities. Ref: 33715/Direct Choices.

Direct Payments Guidance: Community Care, Services for Carers and Children's Services (Direct Payments) Guidance, England 2003.

DoH (2001) *Valuing People: A New Strategy for Learning Disability for the 21st Century.* London: HMSO.

Ensuring Entitlement: Sex and Relationships Education for Disabled Children. Forum Factsheet, National Children's Bureau, www.ncb.org.uk/sexed.htm

Harris, J., Rabiee, P. and Priestley, M. (2002) *Enabled by the Act? The Reframing of Aftercare Services for Young Disabled People.* In Wheal, A. (Ed.) *RHP Companion to Leaving Care.* Lyme Regis: Russell House Publishing.

Hendey, N. and Pascall, G. (2002) *Disability and Transition to Adulthood: Achieving Independent Living.* Brighton: Pavilion Publishing.

Heslop, P., Mallet, R., Simons, K. and Ward, L. (2001) *Bridging the Divide: The Experiences of Young People with Learning Difficulties and Their Families at Transition.* Bristol: Norah Fry Research Centre, University of Bristol.

Hussain, Y., Atkin, K. and Ahmad, W. (2002) *South Asian Disabled Young People and Their Families.* The Policy Press.

Mitchell, W. and Sloper, P. (2000) *User-friendly Information for Families with Disabled Children: A Guide to Good Practice.* York: Joseph Rowntree Foundation.

Morris, J. (1995) *Gone Missing: A Research and Policy Review of Disabled Children Living Away From Their Families.* Who Cares? Trust.

Morris, J. (1998) *Don't Leave Us Out: Involving Disabled Children and Young People With Communication Impairments.* York: Joseph Rowntree Foundation.

Morris, J. (1999a) *Move on up: Supporting Young Disabled People in Their Transition to Adulthood.* Barnardo's.

Morris, J. (1999b) *Hurtling into a Void: Transition to Adulthood for Young Disabled People with 'Complex Health and Support Needs'.* Brighton: Pavilion Publishing.

Morris, J. (2001) *That Kind of Life? Social Exclusion and Young Disabled People with High Levels of Support Needs.* Scope.

Morris, J. (2002) *A Lot to Say: A Guide for Social Workers, Personal Advisors and Others Working With Disabled Children and Young People with Communication Impairments*. London: Scope.

Murray, P. *Hello! Are You Listening? Disabled Teenagers' Experience of Access to Inclusive Leisure.* Joseph Rowntree/York Publishing Services.

National Foster Care Association (2002) *Rights of Passage: Young Disabled People: The Transition from Foster Care to Adult Life, a Study of People with Learning Difficulties.* NFCA.

Rabiee, P., Priestley, M. and Knowles, J. (2001) *Whatever Next? Young Disabled People Leaving Care*. Leeds: First Key.

Ryan, T. (1997*) Making Our Own Way? Transition from School to Adulthood in the Lives of People Who Have Learning Difficulties.* London: Values into Action.

On direct payments for 16 and 17-year-olds, *Living it Up!* is available free of charge while stocks last as a printed magazine and a CD from the Norah Fry Research Centre at 3 Priory Road, Bristol BS8 1TX. The magazine also appears on the Norah Fry website, www.bris.ac.uk/depts/NorahFry

Useful Websites

Access to Work Scheme www.jobcentreplus.com/cms.asp?Page=/Home/Customers/HelpForDisabledPeople/AccesstoWork

Also available on the site is the original document: *Valuing People: A New Strategy for the 21st Century.*

Connexions www.connexions.co.uk

For information about accessing the Independent Living Funds, go to: www.ilf.org.uk

Learning Skills Council www.lsc.gov.uk/national

National Centre for Independent Living www.ncil.org.uk

National Service Framework for Mental Health www.doh.gov.uk/pub/docd/doh/mhexsum.pdf

On the same site is a new document entitled *Adult Education and Valuing People* describing the sorts of further education opportunities available after people have left school.

Sex Education Forum (2001) *Ensuring Entitlement: Sex and Relationships Education for Disabled Children.* Forum Fact sheet, Council for Disabled People.

Teenage Pregnancy Unit www.teenagepregnancyunit.gov.uk

The government has written an action plan called *Pathways to Work: Helping People into Employment. The Government's Response and Action Plan*. Available from www.dwp.gov.uk

The National Institute for Adult Continuing Education www.niace.org.uk

The Disability Briefing: May 2002. Available at www.drc-gb.org

The *Valuing People* website has very useful information about direct payments and their administration, including information for service users, councils setting up direct payment schemes, and policy and guidance.

The *Valuing People* website also provides useful information about person-centred approaches. On the same site you will find the guidance *Towards Person-Centred Approaches: Planning with People* and a paper by Martin Routledge on person-centred planning and Transitions. www.valuingpeople.gov.uk/pcp.htm

Valuing People Support Team. *Learning Disability Partnership Boards: Information Pack for Transitions Champions*. Download from www.valuingpeople.gov.uk

The *Valuing People* website has a range of documents to help with employment issues, including a *Framework for the Development of an Employment Strategy* and a useful *Employment Resources Guide.* Go to www.valuingpeople.gov.uk/employment.htm

Valuing People has developed a toolkit for developing advocacy services. It is available at: www.valuingpeople.gov.uk/latestnews.htm

Valuing People has developed a website to help people make their information more accessible to people with learning difficulties. This can be found at www.easyinfo.org.uk

For all the above go to: www.valuingpeople.gov.uk/DirectPayments.htm or order from Department of Health Publications, email: dh@prolog.uk.com

Values into Action www.viauk.org

Young Minds – The Children's Mental Health Charity www.youngminds.org.uk/professionals

Useful tools

Action for Leisure have a list of useful publications on their web site www.actionforleisure.org.uk/salespub.html

Active Advocates: Self-Advocacy and Young People. Wyre Forest Self-Advocacy consists of youth aged 17–25 who support the rights of those at risk of being isolated as a result of disability. They have produced guidelines, which enable young people to set up their own groups and raise awareness about self-advocacy. The pack is called Active Advocates and consists of a video, book and facilitators notes. Contact: Wyre Forest Self Advocacy, Burgage Lodge, 184 Franche Road, Kidderminster, Worcs., DY11 5AD.

All Change: Transition and Young People With Learning Disabilities. An Information Guide. (2003) (Information pack for parents, professionals and young people.) Brighton: Pavilion Publishing or www.pavpub.com

Ask Us. CD-ROM. Copies are available at £5 each from the Children's Society, publishing department, Edward Rudolph House, Margery Street, London WC1X 0JL www.childrensociety.org.uk

Dorset Self-Advocacy has made a Person Centred Planning awareness training video. It is called *My Plan*. Contact them at 3, Princes Street, Dorchester, Dorset DT1 1TP. This information was taken from the Valuing People Website: www.valuingpeople.gov.uk/pcp.htm

The Employability Plus materials aim to increase the further education, training and employment prospects of young people with learning difficulties so that they can participate wherever possible in paid work and therefore lead more independent lives. The pack includes an interactive CD ROM to explore options and identify goals with young people. Contact: Jenny Robson, Director of Development: jenny.robson@thewhocarestrust.org.uk

The TransPlan CD-ROM, produced in the North East Region, is a comprehensive guide to the process of transition planning as it impacts on young people with special educational needs. It contains information for young people, parents/carers and services and agencies involved in the process of transition planning. The Department of Education and Skills and Department of Health have funded an evaluation of TransPlan – copies of both the full and summary reports are available to download as Word documents from the Connexions website: www.connexions.gov.uk or contact e-mail dfes@prolog.uk.com, quoting TRANSPLAN 1 for the CD-ROM.

TRANS-ACTIVE is a tool for inclusion, outlines the process of transition and is a good model for peer support. It links directly to Citizenship, PSE, IT and individual communication targets. It covers equality, rights, choices and advocacy. The process gives young people the opportunity to explore who they are, what is important to them now and what they might like for the future. Topics covered include: about me, advocacy, living, learning, work, leisure and having a say. More information about the project can be obtained by going to www.trans-active.org.uk or contact: trans-active@mencap.org.uk

Two Way Street: Training video and handbook about communicating with disabled children and young people – copies available at £55 each from NSPCC National Training Centre, 3, Gilmour Close, Beaumont Leys, Leicester LS4 1EZ. Tel: 01162347223. The work was led by Triangle and the NSPCC. Triangle offers training and consultancy on services for children with complex needs: www.triangleservices.co.uk

Working Together – Connexions and Leaving Care Services

Amanda Allard and Roger Clayphan

This chapter looks at the role and work of the personal advisor for a young person who is leaving care. The present system involves either a local authority leaving care team or a voluntary agency leaving care team and the Connexions service. Although there may be changes in titles and in overall service in the future, this chapter gives useful examples of how working together in partnership can be successful in helping young people.

In theory, the fact that development of the Connexions service and the new local authority duties towards young people were developed within the same time frame should have ensured that the two services worked seamlessly together from the start. However, whilst anecdotal evidence suggests that joint working is improving, seamlessness is by no means a given. NCH runs 26 leaving care services in England. Because the Connexions service was developed locally, and therefore differently, each NCH project has had to negotiate joint working with their Connexions partnership from the start. This means we have a number of different models of joint working operating. This chapter seeks to clarify the different roles of the Connexions and leaving care services, and their personal advisors, and to identify which aspects of joint working offer the best option for young people calling on the services.

Leaving care services

The Children (Leaving Care) Act 2000 sets out a framework for local authorities in relation to their responsibilities to provide a range of support services to young people leaving care aged between 16–21 years. This includes the requirement for a Young Person's Advisor to be allocated to each young person leaving care in order to assess their needs and prepare a pathway plan for them. Plans focus on the young person making a successful transition from being 'looked after' into adulthood; and issues of education, employment and training are addressed, along with accommodation, health, relationships and social skills.

Connexions service

First announced in the DfEE White Paper *Learning to Succeed* (June 1999), the Connexions service was the concept of the Social Exclusion Unit. In one of their early reports on young people not in education, training or employment (*Bridging the Gap*, July 1999) they identified institutional fragmentation of support within the then mechanisms of support for young people, especially those from disadvantaged backgrounds, or experiencing particular difficulties.

To address the identified shortcomings it was argued that a new support service was needed. It would provide support to young people aged 13–19. Building on the support provided by the youth and careers services it would ensure a smooth transition for young people from compulsory schooling through post-16 options. It would end fragmentation by ensuring that **one** professional

The Leaving Care Handbook

had an overview of the whole of a young person's needs, able to provide support directly and refer on if more specialist services were required.

The Connexions service is the embodiment of that vision. It promotes and provides an integrated information, advice and guidance service for young people. It aims to assist young people in engaging in learning, to achieve their potential and make a smooth transition into adult life. There are particular targets placed upon Connexions to ensure they engage with the 'hard to reach' group of young people Not in Education or Employment or Training (NEET).

Working with care leavers – a co-operative approach

Young people in and leaving care were identified as a group who were at particular risk of ending up not engaged in education, training or employment. In the same year that *Bridging the Gap* and *Learning to Succeed* were published the Department of Health had published *Me Survive Out There?* which set out the new vision for leaving care services and led to the Children (Leaving Care) Act. From the very beginning therefore, the importance of effective co-operation between the new leaving care service and the new, youth support service was acknowledged. It was seen as vital that young people didn't end up with an army of different personal advisors and thus a new kind of fragmentation.

Whilst there is a considerable area of overlap there is a difference in the remit of the Connexions and leaving care personal advisors. The leaving care personal advisor is expected to provide holistic support for the young people in their care. The primary focus of the Connexions personal advisor is to encourage engagement in education, training or employment, although they will have regard for young people's needs more generally, since these may need to be addressed in order for the young person to engage effectively.

The role of the leaving care personal advisor, is prescribed by the Children (Leaving Care) Act 2000, and includes the following elements:
- Providing advice and support, including practical support.
- Participating in the assessment, preparation and review of the pathway plan and liaising with the responsible authority over its implementation.
- Co-ordinating the provision of services and taking reasonable steps to ensure that the young person makes use of such services.
- Keeping informed about the young person's progress and well being.

The role of the Connexions personal advisor is set out in Connexions guidance and may include any of the following elements:
- Engaging with young people to identify and address their needs, offering information, advice and guidance on learning and career options and personal development opportunities, with a view to raising the aspirations of each young person.
- Utilising and supporting education and training institutions and employees in meeting the needs of young people.
- Working with a network of voluntary, statutory and community agencies, and commercial bodies to ensure a coherent approach to support for the young person.
- Working with parents, carers and families to support young people.

Having tried to distinguish between the roles, it is important to acknowledge that where working with clients with a similar profile, the roles of the Connexions and leaving care personal advisors

may be identical. For this reason the Department for Education and Skills has been keen from the start of the two services to make clear their distinct roles in relation to young people in and leaving care. They have outlined a number of principles which they expect to underpin joint working. In terms of young people in and leaving care, the two set out below are probably key:
- The Connexions service should not duplicate or replace the work of existing agencies, but should work closely with them to ensure cohesive service planning and delivery for 13–19-year-olds.
- The most appropriate worker should be identified to lead the young person's case management and ensure that the roles of different agencies are clearly agreed and followed. Where a child's name has been placed on the child protection register or the child is looked after, the social services department will have lead responsibility for implementing and reviewing the child's plan.

Guidance thus makes clear that where young people are already involved with social services departments, that department has primary responsibility, but that when a child reaches 13, or is between 13 and 19 when they come into contact with the service, they should discuss with the Connexions service and the young person how Connexions will fit in with the work the social service department is already doing, or the services they are providing, and agree how this will work. If a Connexions personal advisor wishes to refer a young person not already in contact with social services for an assessment as a child in need they should ensure that they decide with the social worker and young person how they will work together. The social services department has lead responsibility for undertaking the assessment.

The outcome of the 'child in need' assessment will in part determine which agency takes lead responsibility for implementing the resulting plan. Where a child's name has been placed on the child protection register or the child is looked after by a local authority the social services department will have lead responsibility for implementing and reviewing the child's plan. For children outside these categories the lead agency will depend on the nature of the child's needs and services being provided, but it could be social services, education, health or the Connexions service.

With a young person leaving care the *Working Together* guidance sets out two possible alternatives as to who should take on the mantle of primary 'personal advisor'.

The roles of a Young Person's Advisor and a Connexions personal advisor are broadly similar, which is why the Young Person's Advisor under the Children (Leaving Care) Act will also normally act as the Connexions personal advisor for these young people.

Alternatively, if the Connexions personal advisor understands the requirements and workings of the care system and the Children Act, they would be well placed to continue to advise the young person. They could therefore fulfil the role of the Young Person's Advisor as well as Connexions personal advisor, with the work of the Young Person's Advisor being subcontracted to Connexions. In this situation the Connexions personal advisor will need to be in close contact with the Leaving Care team to receive support and supervision over the preparation and implementation of the Pathway Plan. In addition, arrangements will need to be put in place for a possible transition at age 19, as the young person moves out of the Connexions service remit, but will still be entitled to support under the Children (Leaving Care) Act 2000, unless the work is subcontracted to the Connexions service. In this case the Connexions personal advisor could continue to act as the Young Person's Advisor until the young person reaches the age of 21, or for longer (up to the age of 25) if they remain in an agreed programme of education past this age.

The Children (Leaving Care) Act guidance states that the young person should be able to express a preference about who should act as their personal advisor and that these requests should always be taken seriously, and accommodated as far as possible. However, the guidance also states that in the end the final decision rests with the responsible authority who must ensure that the person chosen is suitable and able to carry out the role (Children (Leaving Care) Act 2000 Regulations and Guidance).

Partnership working

The potential overlap of responsibilities lends itself to partnership working. In fact, arguably it is the only way to avoid duplication and it has the benefit of maximising resources in order to improve outcomes for young people. But the fact that it is the best approach does not mean that it does not present challenges to those working on the ground.

In 2002 the NCH Public Policy Unit completed a survey of their services to young people leaving care in order to ascertain their experiences of working with Connexions across the country and feed this back to the then Children and Young People's Unit at the DfES. At that time although the experiences were varied a number of common themes emerged:

- Confusion over the role of the Connexions PA and the Leaving Care PA.
- The lack of a single Connexion service model and the local development of services (whatever its advantages) had resulted in the service developing differently across the country. Consequently, partnership working needed to be negotiated afresh in each area and the ability to draw on and learn from existing partnership arrangements was lessened. For a national organisation such as NCH there was no possibility of working out a good model which all leaving care services could utilise.
- A feeling that, both with Connexions and with the Children (Leaving Care) Act, insufficient resources were available to deliver on the two visions.
- Continued confusion over the issue of data-sharing.

Notwithstanding this, the survey also highlighted that a number of innovative joint working initiatives had been developed.

Partnership model 1

Connexions Personal Advisors (PA) and Leaving Care Young Persons Advisors (YPA) working within the same team providing a generic service to care leavers. All workers operate as both Leaving Care PAs and Connexions PAs.

The key features of this model involve negotiating a secondment of Connexions PAs into the leaving care service. The PAs do not require specialist education, training and employment knowledge or skills. Consideration needs to be given as to whether these workers are additional to the current staffing complement of the leaving care service or represent part of the existing complement. The Connexions PAs would be managed within the leaving care service. Regular liaison meetings between the leaving care manager and the manager responsible for the Connexions PAs are essential in dealing with any operational issues as well as ensuring that the arrangement is meeting the respective organisational performance indicators.

Strengths of model 1

- Potential for increasing staffing resources within the leaving care service.
- Opportunity to develop and strengthen working relationships between leaving care service and the Connexions service.

- Consistency of the values and ethos underpinning the service delivery.
- Broadening of the understanding by the Connexions service of the range and complexity of needs faced by young people leaving care and the barriers to Education, Training and Employment (ETE) that they face.
- Potential for sharing premises and service delivery points.
- Consistency of relationships between PA and young people from 16–21 plus.

Disadvantages of model 1

- Lack of specialist focus on ETE issues within leaving care service.
- Transition point between Connexions and leaving care service at 16.

Case study model 1

John had been in care since his early teens, had experienced a number of placement moves and had finally left care aged 16 from a residential placement with no formal qualifications. At the point of referral to the NCH leaving care service he was homeless and had already exhausted most of the local hostel-type accommodation options, and was not engaged in any ETE activity. He had had no previous contact with Connexions and had no further contact with social services.

He was allocated to the Connexions PA working within the leaving care team. The initial assessment highlighted a number of unresolved issues with his family, particularly his mum, and these manifested themselves in angry and violent outbursts. He had drug and alcohol problems and had a history of offending behaviour linked to his violent outbursts which were directed at women. Consequently the initial plan was to focus on developing a relationship with his PA in order to engage John in preparatory work to help stabilise him in accommodation and to then try to focus on ETE issues. Due to the risk assessment he was initially excluded (for the first 2–3 months) from group or drop-in services at the leaving care service and was offered individual work with his PA on anger management which involved working with him and his family on some of the unresolved issues around his feelings of rejection.

Now aged 21 John has just ceased to receive services from the leaving care team. His original PA has worked with John consistently for the past five years and although for the first three years John continued to experience a number of unsettled and difficult periods he has for the past two years become more stable. He has worked for a call centre for the past two years and is now team manager; his appraisals highlight his strengths as a team worker and he has a specific role in dealing with angry complaints from the public. He is in a long term relationship and has been settled in his own private rented accommodation for the past two years.

On leaving the service he sent his PA and the team a thank you card acknowledging the difficult behaviour he displayed at first and thanking them for the continued support they offered.

What the guidance seems to proscribe, but a model which seems to work well for service providers is where a young person's primary personal advisor is their leaving care personal advisor but where they also have access to a Connexions personal advisor for help and advice with education, training and employment issues. This is the case with models 2 and 3.

Partnership model 2

Connexions PAs and Leaving Care Team PAs working within the same team with the Connexions PAs, offering a 13–19 service. The 13–16 service is aimed at looked after children whose plan would be to

> *leave care and transfer to the leaving care service. The 16–19 service is aimed at young people receiving a leaving care service from PAs with specific ETE needs.*

The key features of this model require similar negotiations in order to agree secondment of Connexions PAs to the leaving care service provider organisation. The PAs require specialist ETE knowledge and skills. As the model provides an overlap between the looked after children (LAC) service and the leaving care service, the Connexions PAs require a clear remit with clear protocols to prevent duplication with other services. Communication between all key agencies is essential.

Strengths of model 2

- Provides additional resources to the LAC service and leaving care service.
- Offers a 'through care' model that assists the young person's transition into the leaving care service.
- Provides an ETE focus from aged 13 which can improve ETE outcomes.
- Specialist ETE service offered from 16 plus to care leavers.
- Opportunity to develop and strengthen working relationships between leaving care service and the Connexions service.
- Consistency of the values and ethos underpinning the service delivery.
- Broadening of the understanding by the Connexions service of the range and complexity of needs faced by young people leaving care and the barriers to ETE that they face.
- Potential for sharing premises and service delivery points.

Disadvantages of model 2

- Transition from Connexions service built in at 19 unless young people with special needs.
- Specialist role of PAs requires more than one worker to provide services to a young person.

Case study model 2

The Connexions PAs linked to the NCH leaving care service ran a five day course, *Stop, Look, Achieve* for a group of Year 11 students who were in care and planning to transfer into the leaving care service once they reached 16 years old.

The course was designed for those young people who it was thought were at serious risk of disengagement and of not making any positive transitions upon leaving school.

The aims of the course were to give the participants a more positive and confident approach to 'life after school' and to training and work in particular. Job search and interview skills were significant parts of the course with a built in element around self-appraisal.

Lifetime Careers had secured Objective 1 funding to deliver *Stop, Look, Achieve*. The course had been developed in South Yorkshire for several years but an amended course programme was developed to meet the needs of this specific group of young people. The course ran for one day a week over five weeks and took place in school time with the full support of the schools.

The course programme was amended to both include the job search and career action planning elements but to also include elements addressing issues of motivation, self-awareness, being part of a group, working as a team, developing self-awareness and self-esteem, problem-solving and communication skills.

The outcome of this course has been that all course participants have an ETE destination as part of their transition plan.

It is intended that these young people will be followed throughout their time with the leaving care service to monitor outcomes as it is hoped that this piece of work will impact on areas that include early discharge, ETE outcomes and stability of accommodation.

Partnership model 3

The Connexions PA is a specialist careers advisor, who is seconded into the Leaving Care Team and provides specialist advice to the Young Person's Advisors and direct services to young people where there are specific ETE issues.

The key features of this model require similar negotiations in order to agree secondment of Connexions PAs to the leaving care service provider organisation. The PAs require specialist ETE knowledge and skills. Any caseloads carried by this PA need to be managed to maintain the specialist role offered to all young people.

Strengths of model 3

- Specialist ETE service focus on 16-plus care leavers.
- Opportunity to develop innovative approaches to improve outcomes.
- Opportunity to develop and strengthen working relationships between leaving care service and the Connexions service.
- Consistency of the values and ethos underpinning the service delivery.
- Broadening of the understanding of the Connexions service of the range and complexity of needs faced by young people leaving care and the barriers to ETE that they face.
- Potential for sharing premises and service delivery points.

Disadvantages of model 3

- Transition to and from Connexions service built in at 16 and 19 unless young people with special needs.
- Specialist role of PAs requires more than one worker to provide services to a young person.
- Requires close liaison with ICS (previously LAC) to ensure smooth transition.

Case study model 3

John is 17 and had been working with the NCH leaving care team since leaving care at 16. He had achieved five plus GCSEs at C and above at school. He has been NEET for over a year due to mental health problems. He lacks confidence and is very self-conscious due to having a severe fungal infection on his hands. John had expressed an interest in joining the Army and was interested in engineering. However, he and his YPA were unable to progress past this point due to John's lack of confidence and health issues.

His YPA discussed this with the specialist Connexions PA within the team and it was agreed that they would get involved. After a number of meetings between the Connexions PA and John where they were able to focus specifically on John's aspirations and barriers to achieving these, it was assessed that a college course would be a good option for him initially because as well as advancing John's career aims, it would also give him the opportunity to gain confidence in mixing with his peers. The PA had developed positive links with a college and was able to support John through the initial stages and was able to negotiate a support plan for John that involved the college, his YPA and the PA to assist him in maintaining attendance through to completion of the course.

Partnership model 4

There are also projects where there is no embedded link with Connexions. There may either be a protocol or an ad hoc relationship. In some areas this is because of practicalities. For instance in Cornwall there are six district areas. If a single Connexions worker was seconded to the service they would spend the majority of their time on the road. In our experience as an organisation unless there is a specific reason such as rurality for not entering into a secondment arrangement then this is the one which works best for young people.

Taking an overview of the four models there seems to be one simple element which really adds value for young people leaving care. This element is additional resources and can be split into two factors, specialist expertise and quite simply, extra input.

1. Access to education, training and employment expertise

In one sense it doesn't matter how you draw these into the leaving care project, but because of the complexity of the world of education and training it is of real benefit to young people to have a specialist advisor who has the time to be completely up-to-date and the energy to focus on that aspect of the young persons' life. Even if that person is operating as a generic worker they are still on hand to advise other workers.

2. The benefit of two advisors?

The guidance may suggest that this is not ideal, but those working with young people suggest that often it is, particularly for young people with complex needs. Having a Connexions personal advisor focusing on education, training and employment leaves the leaving care personal advisor free to concentrate on other aspects of the young persons' life.

Particularly for chaotic or volatile young people there can be a real benefit in having two workers. It opens up the option of one taking a 'firmer line' with a young person who is not engaging, whilst lessening the risks since the other can mediate if the strategy backfires.

There are two possible drawbacks to having two personal advisors. Firstly, that both workers think an issue is being covered by the other and it gets left undone. However, this danger is minimised by the specialism of the Connexions worker, and can be further reduced by the two workers sharing a line manager as happens in models 1, 2 and 3. Secondly, if either or both workers bring any personal inadequacies to work with them you can get competition for the young person's affections, which isn't necessarily in the best interests of the young person. However, again this danger is far less likely to go unaddressed if both workers share a line manager.

Most working partnerships experience teething problems. The relationship between Connexions and leaving care personal advisors was probably made more sticky by the extreme overlap between the two roles, and the insistence that young people should only have one personal advisor – either leaving care or Connexions, but not both. This meant that, rather than initially welcoming the Connexions service as an additional resource, leaving care workers tended to view its advent with suspicion and its workers as rivals. The individual nature of the Connexions partnerships meant that leaving care managers in each area had to forget their own relationship with their Connexions partnership, and many Connexions partnerships were initially so busy setting themselves up that some were not initially proactive at making links with others working in the field until much later on.

Having said all of this, time has passed, and anecdotal evidence suggests that relationships between the leaving care and Connexions services are very much moving in the right direction and that this is good news for young people.

We can only hope that any changes which are made to Connexions partnerships in the future are made in such a way as to ensure that the hard won lessons of the present partnerships are retained.

Resources

Children (Leaving Care) Act 2000.
Children (Leaving Care) England Regulations 2001 (Statutory Instrument 2001 No. 2874) and Guidance.
Department for Education and Employment (1999) *Learning to Succeed*. DfEE.
Department of Health (1999) *Me, Survive Out There? New Arrangements for Young People Living in and Leaving Care*. DoH.
Department of Health, Connexions (2001) *Working Together: Connexions and Social Services*. Connexions Service National Unit.
Social Exclusion Unit (1999) *Bridging the Gap*, SEU.

Section Three: Accommodation

Accommodation

Jane Murphy and Rachel Strahan

This chapter looks at the legal situation relating to accommodation and young adults who are in, or who have left care. It covers:

The Local authority's duties and powers to help young care leavers
- The local authority's duties and powers to help young care leavers.
- The housing department's duties and powers to help young care leavers.
- A flowchart detailing how to make a homeless application.

The Different types of accommodation
- Types of housing, what they offer young people and issues to consider.
- The average length of stay.
- The types of tenancy agreement.

The Eviction process from private and local authority housing
- Why a landlord would want a tenant out of their property.
- How can a landlord get his property back?
- Determining status of occupation.
- Action needed to legally evict an occupier.
- The possession procedure.
- What are the possible outcomes of a court hearing?
- When a landlord does not follow the correct eviction procedure.

The Local Authority's Duties and Powers to Help Young Care Leavers

Local authorities have duties to ensure that:
- Young people do not leave care until they are ready.
- They receive support once they have left.
- They are provided with somewhere appropriate to live.

Local authorities are responsible for housing and supporting most care leavers aged 16 and 17 years old but they also have duties and powers to support care leavers who are 18 or over.

Accommodation

The law categorises care leavers into four main groups:

Eligible children and Relevant children

Eligible children are 16 and 17 year olds who are in care and have been in care for a total of at least 13 weeks after reaching the age of 14.

Relevant children are 16 and 17 year olds who were in care for a total of at least 13 weeks after reaching the age of 14, including at least one day when they were 16 or 17, and who are no longer in care

Former relevant children

Former relevant children 18 to 21 years old (or older, if still receiving services listed in their pathway plan), who left care after 1st October 2001 and who were either an eligible or relevant child before they became 18.

Relevant Students

Relevant students are under 24 years old who are former relevant children and are still in full time education. This definition needs to clarify whether it covers only qualifying young people or only former relevant young people . . . if it is 'former relevant', are they sure that its only up to the age of 24 because the local authority's responsibilities to former relevant young people can continue past the age of 24, depending on the Pathway Plan. In the case of qualifying young people, the local authority's responsibilities extend only to the age of 24. See Figure 6.1 and 6.2, pages 48–9.

The housing department's duties and powers to help young care leavers

Care leavers aged 18 or over who are homeless should go to the LA's homeless persons unit or section (usually part of the housing department) to make an application as a homeless person (Figure 6.3, see page 50). The LA has a duty to give help and advice, but the amount of help it has to give depends on an individual's circumstances.

Most young homeless care leavers will be in 'priority need' and be eligible for help. Priority need status is given to people who are viewed as being more vulnerable than others. The council should decide that someone is in priority need if they are homeless and are:

- Aged 16 and 17 years old (except care leavers to whom social services has a duty).
- Care leavers aged 18, 19 or 20 years (except those to whom social services has a duty).
- Responsible for a child or children.
- Pregnant (or the partner with whom they live or want to live with, is pregnant).
- Homeless because of a disaster, such as a fire or flood.
- 'Vulnerable'. This means that they are more at risk than other people. For instance, they could be vulnerable because they are disabled or have serious physical or mental health problems, or are escaping violence or threats.

The council may also find young people in 'priority need' if they are vulnerable because they:
- Have been in care in the past.
- Are leaving, or have recently left, a young offenders' institute.
- Are leaving, or have recently left, the armed services.
- Are at risk of violence or sexual abuse.
- Are at risk of alcohol or drug abuse or prostitution.

The Leaving Care Handbook

Figure 6.1 *Local authority's duties and powers to help young care leavers*

Legal definition	Duties and powers (generally as laid down by the Children Act 1989 with amendments under the Children (Leaving Care Act) 2000
Eligible or relevant children	A local authority personal advisor should help the young person find, secure and maintain suitable accommodation through practical, emotional and financial support. The type and level of support should be agreed as part of the young person's Pathway Plan and contact maintained beyond their 18th birthday.
Former relevant children	A personal advisor should remain in contact, offering emotional and practical support as detailed in the Pathway Plan. The young person can claim benefits to help pay for accommodation. If they were accommodated under Section 20 of the Children Act, and if they were 16 or 17 and looked after following a court order, they are exempt from the single room rent restrictions until their 22nd birthday.
Relevant students	A personal advisor should help the young person find, secure and pay for vacation accommodation.
Qualifying children	Social Services departments should give the young person advice and assistance which can include accommodation, or help to access it, such as the cost of a deposit and rent in advance. They can also help with the cost of education and training up to the age of 24.
Under 18 unaccompanied asylum seekers	Social Services departments should help the young person find, secure and maintain suitable accommodation through financial, practical and emotional support. *(It's not clear whether they are referring to care leavers or young people still in care. Almost all young people in this group would stay in care until they are 18. Like any other young people, they could be relevant or qualifying, depending on the length of time in care and the age at which they left. The references to the Children Act 1989, as amended by the C(LC)A 2000 would be different depending on whether they were relevant, former relevant or qualifying children).*
18 to 21-year-old unaccompanied asylum seekers	The duty to accommodate the young person passes to the National Asylum Support Service (NASS) but Social Services departments should help with costs beyond the normal financial limit on NASS assistance (see last sentence in my note to above category). The young person should not be moved from the area they were formerly living in.

It is important to give the council enough information about how someone may be vulnerable or less able to fend for themselves than other homeless people. Once the council has carried out an interview and decided that someone is homeless, eligible and in priority need, it has to provide emergency accommodation while it makes enquiries into the rest of their circumstances. If they are a relevant child, they may refer them back to social services. Where possible, the council should inform the young person of their decision within 33 working days.

A young person's application for permanent housing may fail if they are found to be intentionally homeless. This means the housing department believes the young person had done or has failed to do something that has caused them to become homeless. If the young person does not have a local connection to the area they may be referred to an authority where they have a local connection but they should be provided with accommodation whilst this is happening, and they have the right to remain in temporary accommodation for another 28 days. Decisions can be

Accommodation

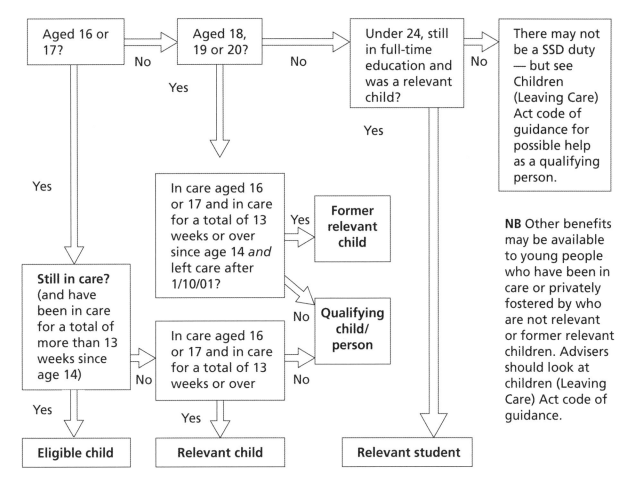

Figure 6.2 *The status of care leavers and those still in care (excluding private fostering)*

challenged through a review process. This is a difficult and lengthy process so it is best to seek specialist advice.

The different types of accommodation

Types of housing available to young people vary enormously. It is important to know what each offers as well as the issues to consider. The amount and standard of housing for young people will differ from area to area.

A **tenant** has exclusive use or possession of their accommodation (this can include a single room in a house where the rest of the premises are shared).

A **licensee** has permission to occupy somewhere (only a personal right); the accommodation is usually not in separate, self-contained units and meals or communal cooking facilities are provided. See Figure 6.5, pages 52–4.

The eviction process from private and local authority housing

Why would a landlord want a tenant out of their property?

It could be for a number of reasons, including:
- Owing a high level of rent arrears.
- Playing loud music.

The Leaving Care Handbook

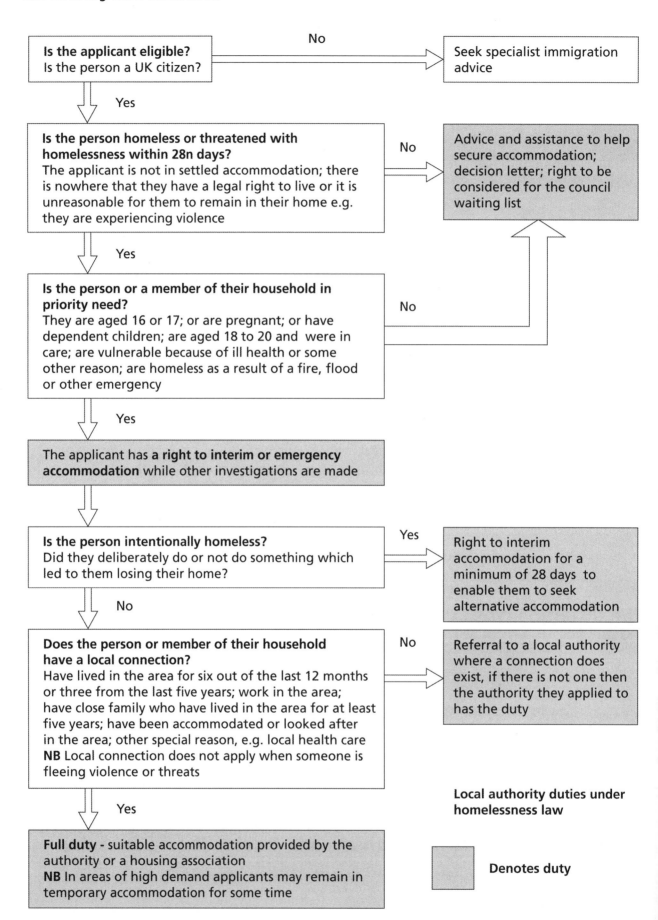

Figure 6.3 *Making a homeless application: a quick reference flowchart*

Accommodation

Figure 6.4 *The Housing Department's duties and powers*

Age group	Duties and powers (generally under the Children Act 1989 as amended by the Children (Leaving Care) Act 2000 and the Homeless Act 2002)
Under 18 care leaver	The housing department may provide a tenancy, but if they're a relevant child the responsibility to provide support lies with social services. Joint protocols between the two departments would allow a more co-ordinated approach to meeting the young person's needs.
18, 19 and 20 year-old care leavers	The housing department should provide somewhere for the young person to live at least temporarily while their situation is looked into. Their status as a care leaver means they are in 'priority need' of housing.
21 year-old and over care leavers	The housing department must provide temporary accommodation whilst looking into the young person's situation, and help to find permanent accommodation if they have reason to believe that the young person is 'vulnerable' as a result of being in care and therefore 'in priority need'.

- Anti-social behaviour by the tenant or any of their visitors.
- Illegal activities.
- Damage to the property.
- Breaking the terms of the tenancy agreement.
- End of a fixed term tenancy.
- The landlord wants the property back for himself or a family member.
- The landlord wants to sell the property.

How can a landlord get his property back?

Eviction is the legal process that a landlord has to follow to remove someone from his property. The legal procedure they have to follow depends upon the type of tenancy agreement of the young person. Figures 6.1 and 6.4 can be used to determine the status of occupation.

Action needed to legally evict an occupier

Determining who the landlord is and when the tenancy began, identifies which piece of legislation provides protection and the action needed by the landlord to legally evict an occupier. If the landlord does not do this they could be committing a criminal offence. See Figure 6.8, page 57.

The grounds for possession are reasons that a landlord could use to try to evict someone from a property. These can be mandatory or discretionary.

Mandatory grounds: if the landlord is able to prove one ground as their reason for eviction, then the court must give a possession order immediately.

Discretionary grounds: even if the landlord can prove a reason for wanting eviction, the court does not have to automatically grant a possession order. They can consider personal circumstances of both landlord and tenant to make their decision.

The greatest level of protection from eviction is given to secure, assured and protected tenancies. Other agreements have no protection from eviction provided the correct legal procedure has been followed.

The Leaving Care Handbook

Figure 6.5 Types of housing

Type of housing	What it offers	Issues to consider	Length of average stay	Tenure
Night shelters	A bed in a shared dormitory, open to anyone in need. Some are free, others charge a nominal fee.	Young people may feel unsafe and dislike the lack of privacy and long term security.	One night or any number.	Licence
Night stops	A room in the home of a trained or approved volunteer host for one to three nights. A bath, an evening meal and a listening ear are available.	This is only a short term solution and is one that is not open to young people with drug dependencies or severe mental health issues.	One to three nights with one host.	Licence
Hostels	A single or shared room. Residents pay rent either from their wages or by claiming housing benefit. Emergency hostels and direct access hostels are for shorter stays and offer minimal support. Others offer more support on developing independent living skills.	Young people may feel unsafe and dislike the lack of privacy and long term security. Some only take referrals from the council or are for specific groups of people.	Varies from one night to a number of months or years.	Licence
Bed and breakfast hotels	A single or shared room in a house run by private owners. Rent is charged (housing benefit can be claimed).	Young people may feel unsafe and dislike the lack of privacy and long term security. Some take people at the door, others only take referrals from the council. Some ask for rent in advance and not all accept people claiming housing benefit. Housing benefit may not cover all the rent. Residents share bathrooms and there are often no cooking facilities or living areas.	Varies from one night to a number of months or years.	Licence
Women's refuges	A room in a shared house for women, with or without children, who have had to leave home because of violence or threatening behaviour. Rent is charged (housing benefit can be	Young people may feel unsafe and dislike the lack of privacy and long term security. Residents share cooking, bathroom and living facilities.	Varies from one night to a number of months or years.	Licence

Figure 6.5 Continued

Type of housing	What it offers	Issues to consider	Length of average stay	Tenure
	claimed). Workers are trained to offer support on domestic violence issues as well as practical help. Addresses are kept secret and in most cases male visitors are not allowed.			
Foyers	A single room or a flat in a unit housing only young people. Tenancies are linked to education, training and employment opportunities, as residents sign a contract agreeing to attend training or to look for work. Rent is charged (housing benefit can be claimed).	May not offer a high enough level of support needed by some young people.	Up to two years.	Licence or assured shorthold tenancy
Supported lodging schemes	A single room within a household, usually only for 16 to 18-year-olds. Can be a way for young people to remain with their foster carers beyond the end of being looked after (payment of carers will continue). Support workers should keep in touch with the young person and the householder.	The family environment may not be appropriate for all young people. In legal terms' people who live with their landlord have less rights.	Up to two years.	Licence
Supported housing schemes	Covers a wide range of schemes offering young people their own tenancies. Housing benefit can be claimed to cover the rent.	It's important to find out about each scheme and the different type of accommodation and level of support on offer.	Minimum of six months.	Assured shorthold tenancy

Figure 6.5 Continued

Type of housing	What it offers	Issues to consider	Length of average stay	Tenure
Private rented accommodation	A room in a shared house, a bedsit, or a flat owned by a private landlord. Housing benefit can be claimed but it may not cover all the rent. Rent levels vary according to the size, condition, location and if it's a shared property.	Most young people will need support to access and maintain a tenancy. A deposit and a month's rent in advance are usually required before moving in. Some properties are rented out furnished, others are unfurnished. Private tenancies offer little security.	Minimum of six months.	Assured shorthold or assured tenancy
Council and housing association tenancies	A flat or house owned by the council or housing association. Rent levels vary according to the size, condition, and location of the property but tend to be more standardised than renting privately and usually cheaper (housing benefit can be claimed).	Most young people will need support to access and maintain a tenancy. In areas of high housing demand, there may be very few places available.	Ongoing.	Most councils offer secure tenancies, some use introductory tenancies that only become secure after a specific length of time. Housing associations offer assured or assured shorthold initially.
Floating support schemes	Support for young people living in their own tenancy. Workers visit young people in their homes and offer support with the practical and emotional side of independent living (housing benefit can be claimed).	May not offer a high enough level of support for some young people.	Ongoing.	Depends on whether the tenancy is with a private landlord, a council or a housing association.
Buying or owner occupation	Taking out a mortgage to buy a property. Can be cheaper and more secure than renting as long as mortgage repayments are made.	The high costs involved means it is not an option for most young people.	For as long as mortgage is paid.	Owner occupier rights apply.

Accommodation

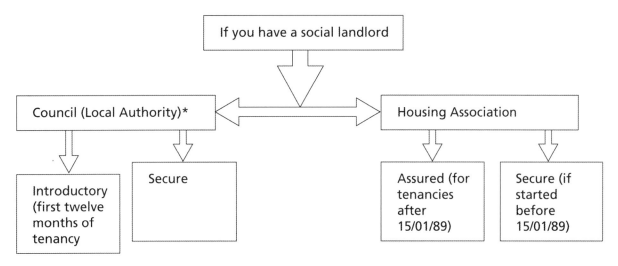

*The council can also provide a non-secure tenancy if a person is accommodated by them in interim self-contained accommodation following homeless application.

Figure 6.6 *Determining the status of occupation: social landlord*

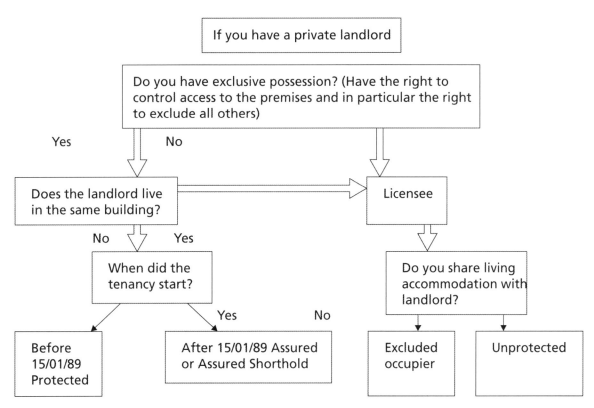

NB. These are only a rough guide to determining tenancy type. If in any doubt seek advice.

Figure 6.7 *Determining status of occupation: private landlord*

The possession procedure

Landlords start the procedure which always follows the same order except in the case of excluded occupiers; it is just the detail of the notice and grounds that change depending on the tenancy type. Figure 6.9 (see page 58) shows the possession procedure.

What are the possible outcomes of a court hearing?
- The proceedings are stopped.
- The proceedings are adjourned to a new date.
- A suspended order for possession is made (delays possession on certain conditions such as payment of weekly rent plus a sum off the arrears).
- An outright order for possession is made (states a date when eviction of the occupier will go ahead).
- The conditions of an existing suspended possession order are altered.
- A warrant for possession made in a previous court hearing is suspended (tenant does not have to leave property but must keep to new conditions of suspended possession order).

When a landlord does not follow the correct eviction procedure

A landlord cannot just throw someone out of privately rented property. It is a criminal offence if a landlord does not follow the procedures set out above. Action taken by a landlord or another to prevent an occupier having access to all or part of their accommodation without following the correct legal procedures constitutes illegal eviction (s1(2) Protection from Eviction Act 1977).

Examples of illegal eviction
- Occupier being told to leave without having correct notice served.
- Locks changed and occupier's belongings put in the street.
- Occupier being denied re-entry.
- Occupier being physically removed from the property.

Illegal eviction is most common in the private rented sector, but other occupiers could also be subjected to illegal eviction.

Possible reasons for illegal eviction
- Landlord's ignorance of the law.
- Prejudice against the occupier.
- Landlord's frustration with process of law.
- Landlord's hope of financial gain.

How you can deal with illegal eviction is determined by status of occupation. An eviction without a court order is illegal unless the person is an excluded occupier. Protected, assured, secure and assured shorthold tenants have legal rights to remain in their home unless they break the terms of the tenancy. There are steps they can take to prevent their landlord illegally evicting them.

Other residential occupiers including excluded tenants up until the expiry of the notice they are given, are protected from illegal eviction under the Protection for Eviction Act 1977. This Act only covers accommodation let as a home and not temporary accommodation provided by a local authority.

If illegal eviction has taken place, legal advice should be sought to consider what civil action can be taken (injunction against the landlord to allow tenant to stay in the property and to get damages

Accommodation

Figure 6.8 *Action needed to legally evict an occupier*

Tenancy/licence	Form of notice	Grounds for possession	Court order needed?
Introductory	Notice (s.128 Housing Act 1996)	Grounds for possession not needed (s.127 Housing Act 1996). Landlord guaranteed possession if procedure followed correctly.	Yes
Secure	Notice seeking possession (s.83 Housing Act 1985)	Discretionary grounds for possession. Grounds 9–11, court must be satisfied that suitable alternative accommodation is available (Schedule 2, Housing Act 1985). Landlord not guaranteed possession.	Yes
Protected	Notice to quit	Mandatory and discretionary grounds for possession (Schedule 15, Rent Act 1977). Landlord not guaranteed possession on discretionary grounds.	Yes
Assured	Notice seeking possession (s.8 Housing Act 1988)	Mandatory and discretionary grounds for possession (Housing Act 1988). Landlord not guaranteed possession on discretionary grounds.	Yes
Assured shorthold (end of the fixed term, usually 6 or 12 months)	Notice requiring possession (s.21 Housing Act 1988)	Landlord guaranteed possession of the property if valid notice served.	Yes
Assured shorthold (during the fixed term)	Notice seeking possession (s.8 Housing Act 1988)	Mandatory and discretionary grounds (Schedule 2 Housing Act 1988). Landlord not guaranteed possession.	Yes
Unprotected	Notice to quit	No grounds needed, landlord will obtain possession if valid notice served.	Yes
Excluded	Reasonable notice	No court order necessary, no grounds to prove. Landlord will obtain possession.	No

as compensation for their landlord's actions) and possibly what criminal offences may have been committed. In most cases the local authority has a Tenancy Relations Officer who can investigate complaints about illegal eviction.

The Leaving Care Handbook

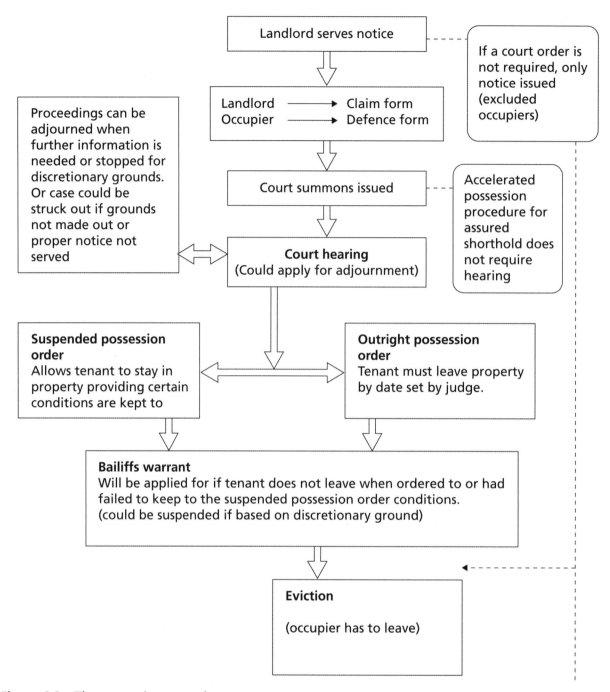

Figure 6.9 *The possession procedure*

Accommodation

Resources

Shelter: 88 Old Street, London EC1V 9HU. 020 7505 2000. Shelterline: 0808 800 4444. A 24 hour national freephone housing helpline. Minicom and interpreting services available. Website provides online advice and information about practical solutions to common housing problems. The site contains information about Shelter's publications including good practice guides and educational materials such as *The Housing Game*, and the *Runaways Teachers Guides*. Details of Shelter's training courses can also be found on this site. www.shelter.org.uk

Shelter Scotland: 4th Floor, Scotiabank House, 6 Charlotte Street, Edinburgh EH2 4AW. 0131 473 7170. www.shelterscotland.org.uk

Shelter Cymru (Wales): 25 Walter Road, Swansea, West Glamorgan SA1 5NN. 01792 644844. www.sheltercymru.org.uk

Centrepoint: housing young people at risk. Belway House, 2 Swallow Place, London W1R 7AA. 020 7629 2229. www.centrepoint.org.uk

Childline: 0800 1111. www.childline.org.uk

Commission for Racial Equality: St Dunstan's House, 201-211 Borough High Street, London, SE1 1GZ. 020 7939 000. www.cre.gov.uk

Connexions Service National Unit: Department for Education and Skills, Moorfoot, Sheffield, S1 4PQ. www.connexions.gov.uk

Connexions Direct: www.connexions-direct.com

Equal Opportunities Commission: Arndale House, Arndale Centre, Manchester M4 3EQ. 08456 015901. www.eoc.org.uk

Foyer Federation: 2nd Floor, Humatt House, 146-8 Clerkenwell Road, London EC1R 5DP. 020 7833 8616. www.foyer.net

Get Connected: 0808 808 4994. A national helpline open from 1pm–11pm all year round and a website for young people who might be thinking about running away. www.getconnected.org.uk

Housemate: offers online information and awareness-raising exercises for young people about housing and homelessness. www.housemate.org.uk

Law Centres Federation: Duchess House, 18-19 Warren Street, London W1T 5LR. Tel 020 7387 8570. www.lawcentres.org.uk

Lesbian and Gay Switchboard: 020 7837 7324. www.llgs.org.uk

Message Home: 0800 700 740. A freephone 24 hour helpline for people who have left home or run away. Enables callers to leave messages.

National Association of Citizens Advice Bureaux: Myddleton House, 115-123 Pentonville, Road, London N1 9LZ. 020 7833 2181. Online advice. www.adviceguide.org.uk

National Missing Persons Helpline: 0500 200 700. A freephone 24 hour helpline providing advice, practical help and support for missing persons and their families.

Refuge: 24 hour domestic violence helpline: 0808 808 999. www.refuge.org.uk

Refugee Council: 3 Bondway, London, SW8 1SJ. 020 7820 3000. Adviceline 020 7346 6777. www.refugeecouncil.org.uk

Runaway Helpline: 0808 800 7070. Help and advice to young people who have run away from home or care or been forced to leave home. www.runawayhelpline.org

The National Youth Agency: Online information toolkit for young people, includes a section on housing. www.youthinformation.com

Who Cares?: 0500 564 570. A freephone offering information and support to young people who are or have been in care. Open 3.30 pm-6 pm Monday, Wednesday and Thursday.

Women's Aid National Helpline: 0345 023468. www.womensaid.org.uk

Youth Access: 2 Taylor's Yard, 67 Alderbrook Road, London, SW12 8AD. 020 8722 9900.

Youth Net UK: Contains information about housing, employment and managing your finances. www.askthesite.org.uk

Section Four: Education, Training and Employment

Education in School, in Further and Higher Education

Ann Wheal

Education is not just about the '3 R's' but about helping the care leaver as a person in all aspects of their development.

This chapter highlights some of the difficulties young people have told us about and contains information and ideas to enable care leavers to achieve their academic potential.

The chapter begins with important background information taken from a research project – 'Guidance and Support for Care Leavers in Post Compulsory Education' (Berkeley et al., 2000). This research project was carried out at Southampton University Summer School and involved 150 young people from inner city areas who had competed year 11 at school. 25 of these young people were care leavers. The young people who attended were planning to go into further education the following September.

The chapter then explains how the education system works in the UK and attempts to unravel the many and varied qualifications and entitlements that are available for young people who wish to further their education. It explains how to go about continuing or getting back into education and what the options are. The chapter ends with a university jargon buster.

Introduction: care leavers and research

Neither the researchers nor the statisticians knew the status of any of the young people. The statisticians were given a completely free hand to look at the data contained in the measurement tool that all the young people were asked to complete. It was they who came up with the differences in responses between the young people who lived with their parents and the ones who did not. In fact, one of the statisticians said:

If they don't have parents to contact who do they speak to? I ring my mother all the time.

The measurement tool comprised three parts:
- A questionnaire completed by the young people.
- Evaluation of the young people's work during the summer school by the facilitators who worked with them.
- Observations of selected young people by the researchers.

Education in School, in Further and Higher Education

The objectives of the research project were to discover:
- What are the attitudes and aspirations of care leavers towards post compulsory education?
- What is the nature of their problem when facing post-compulsory education?
- What do care and education professionals need to do in order to help care leavers into post-compulsory education?

The following is a summary of the practical ways for education and care professionals to support care leavers with their education – in school, in further education and in higher education:
- Recognising success.
- Helping to change their behaviour and attitudes.
- Flexibility in the curriculum.
- A new environment for learning.
- Practical support.
- Pastoral support.
- Other support including financial.

What the care leavers said about the week at the summer school:

It was a life changing experience for her.

Leaving care worker

I felt I could walk along the road and hold my head up high.

Care leaver

If it takes me until I'm 40, I'm going to get to university. I don't want to be just another statistic.

An unemployed single parent care leaver

Thank you for helping me. I feel so much more confident now.

e-mail from a care leaver some three months later

Findings from the research indicate that care leavers experience problems making new relationships with adults and peers as a result of low self-esteem and poor communication skills. They often report low aspirations for their future lives, and are less motivated to work for long term goals. The following is a brief summary of some of the outcomes:

(a) **Students who do not have parents as next-of-kin** experience problems communicating with adults. Compared with students with parents as next-of-kin, students with other persons as next-of-kin agree *more* frequently that:
- Some teachers ignore them.
- Teachers do not understand their individual needs.
- They do not like to admit to a teacher that they do not understand instructions or are having difficulties with academic work.

(b) **Students who do not have parents as next-of-kin** experience difficulties working in a group and establishing new relationships with their peers. Compared with students with parents as next-of-kin, students with other persons as next-of-kin agree *more* frequently that:
- They are not good at working in a team.
- They find it difficult to confide in their peers when they are experiencing problems.
- They find it difficult to listen to instructions and information.
- They need help to meet more people of the same age and background.

(c) **Students with parents as next-of-kin** have higher aspirations for education and are able to motivate themselves to attend school and college. These students reported *more* frequently that:

- They attended school, colleges and training courses regularly.
- They feel confident at school, college and training.
- They believe that more study will help them to go further in their lives.

(d) **People who think study *will not* take them further** in their lives are much more likely to:
- Truant from school, college and training courses.
- Give up when school, college and training courses become difficult.
- Say they are not getting a chance to say what they mean.
- Say they do not have any real ambitions for the future.

(e) **Students who do not have parents as next-of-kin** report a lower self-esteem and express negative attitudes towards mental, physical and sexual health. Compared with students with parents as next-of-kin, students with other persons as next-of-kin agree *more* frequently that:
- They feel generally unconfident.
- They report greater dislike of their self-image and lack of confidence as a result of negative self image.
- They feel drinking and substance abuse can cure depression.

Problems communicating with adults and peers

Students who have not lived with their parents report high levels of concern over their communication skills. This may relate to specific special educational needs relating to reading and writing, as was observed in students who had experienced disrupted schooling and long periods of absence from school (more than 10 per cent of the academic year). These students were very loath to deal with verbal and numerical written information during the summer school, although they were more prepared to manipulate information that was presented using computer-based IT.

These students often reported concerns over contributing to discussion and communicating their viewpoints. Discussions with individual care leavers indicated that the opportunity to express their opinions was extremely important for them. However, many of these students did not contribute to group discussions, and often remained taciturn or were very talkative. Some of them subsequently commented that they were not prepared to speak to the others in the group for fear of ridicule. Some felt they lacked sufficient knowledge about the subject being discussed and were anxious not to appear ignorant. A particular group of care leavers in one subject area entirely rejected the idea of group discussion as worthwhile commenting that they set little store on the opinions of others, having learned that:

> *You have to look for number one when you are in care.*

Care leavers also appear to have difficulty in expressing themselves clearly, particularly in front of other people, and most especially in front of people that they do not know. Dealing with new people at the summer school was an initial concern for all the young people, but the need to communicate and work with new people appeared to remain a particular source of concern for many of the care leavers in the sample. They also described themselves as not being good at listening to instructions and finding it difficult to gather and process information. Communicating with adults appears to be particularly difficult for these students; 60 per cent felt that teachers ignored them, compared to only 24.1 per cent of students who lived with their parents.

Good verbal and oral communication skills are essential for educational achievement. Without the confidence and experience to use language in research and discourse these students may not be able to devise appropriate strategies for developing and using their communication skills to

Education in School, in Further and Higher Education

progress beyond Level 2 of the National Framework for Qualifications. However, observation and facilitators' reports indicated that with appropriate support and guidance, many students who reported low confidence in communication were able to make demonstrable progress during the summer school. It was gratifying to note that most care leavers were fully involved in presentation of work and chairing discussions in the final sessions of the summer school.

Problems forming new relationships and working with others

When presented with hypothetical problems with relationships with teachers and other students, most young people are able to supply realistic and practical solutions to these everyday challenges. They appear to have a realistic understanding that they are operating within a social network in school or college, and generally seek to form positive relationships with teachers and with peers. They appear to recognise that their behaviour contributes to forming a positive social environment in school, and that negotiation and compromise are a necessary part of interactions with others. They indicate the need to work positively with most people and to adapt themselves to a working situation. They report that the positive relationships they have formed with fellow students are a major motivational factor in performing well at school.

Care leavers appear to be less adaptive when formulating working relationships with peers and adults. This may stem from anxiety about meeting and getting to know new people. Only 26.7 per cent of students who did not live with parents felt they worked well in a team, compared to 60.3 per cent of other students. When challenged to identify solutions for dealing with problems when working in a group, most care leavers suggested refusing to participate or arguing with other group members as effective solutions, whereas other young people suggested more productive means of achieving good team work. Care leavers value good relationships with other people very highly, but tend to describe relationships with others in terms of the support that the other person provides them. For example, they report that they work better for teachers who are nice to them and do not impose harsh rules.

Analysis indicates that students who live with their next-of-kin are far more likely to recognise that they must take some responsibility for managing their own learning, and report self-determination and self-organisation as major factors in academic success. It is significant that care leavers regard natural ability as being a more important factor in academic success than motivation or hard work, suggesting that they do not have as good an understanding of their responsibility for managing their own learning.

The responses of students who lived with their parents indicated that their views on working with others are most likely to be related to their character and personality. The vast majority of these students reported that they felt confident when working with others, and could decide when it was the most appropriate time to seek help. The majority of care leavers feel that they cannot make academic progress without specific and individualised help from teachers. This group also reported that they are far less likely to admit that they do not understand things in school and college, partly because they are too shy to speak to a teacher about their difficulties, and were not confident about speaking out in class and to their peers. Many students in this group reported negative experiences of learning in school and some cited this as the reason for their diffidence.

However, reports from facilitators, and observation, indicated that a lack of self-confidence in care leavers does not automatically translate into quiet and withdrawn behaviour. Some care leavers were reported as being noisy and difficult to manage in group work, several were described as being over sensitive to changing their ideas, and touchy about working with people that they had not met before. This suggests that a care leaver's anxieties about working with others in an educational setting may be expressed in bravado and argument.

Achieving aspirations

All the students in the sample had aspirations and expressed clear ideas about continuing in education and training, before progressing onto employment or further education. They understood they could achieve significant lifestyle changes through the increased earning power available to them if they continued with their education. However, comparison between students who live with their parents and care leavers indicated that parental influence is a significant factor in enabling these young people to determine strategies for achieving their goals.

Consistently, young people value the advice and support of teachers, friends and parents, but care leavers rate the advice of friends and professionals far more highly. Care leavers also report consistently that they would rely on the help and support of others in order to achieve more challenging long term goals, whereas other young people report self-determination and self-organisation as being ways of achieving such long term goals. Whilst it is not surprising that a care leaver might rely more on carers than parents, this may also be an indication that the experience of living in care makes these students far more reliant on those around them than students who live with their parents.

Students who want to study do so as they have clearly defined ambitions. Discussions with young people indicate that those who live with their parents generally regard education as a gateway to further employment, and many regard it as an essential hurdle before achieving long term lifestyle and career goals. Students who do not live with their parents demonstrate a greater antipathy towards the idea of further study, and reported more frequently that they did not believe that study would get them further in their lives. They are also much more likely to say they do not have any real ambitions for five or ten years hence, and that they do not feel that they could be successful in a job or at university.

Where care leavers do articulate their long term aspirations, cross tabulation indicates that they may not have a realistic perception of the self-management required to achieve them. This situation was also evident in observations and conversations with care leavers. One care leaver expressed an intention to take performing arts GNVQ in order to become a singer and dancer, but also commented that she hated the college as she found the work hard and thought the teachers too strict as she received low grades for her work. She frequently truanted from college. She did not apparently see the connection between her low achievement and frequent absences from college.

Self-esteem and self-image

Examining the correlation between students who live with their next-of-kin and self-image indicates that those who have not recently lived with their parents are generally less self-confident. In addition, in both groups, males generally report that they are more confident in school or college than females. Students who do not live with their parents report worries about their looks, being overweight and not having enough friends. Having people talking about me behind my back and making a fool of myself in front of my friends is a particular concern for these students. One care leaver at the summer school was particularly anxious that other students should not find out she was living on the dole, as she thought the others would *call me a waster*.

Education in School, in Further and Higher Education

She wanted people to know she was attending a course in ICT at college in order that she would be able to find employment.

It is evident that the low self-esteem of students who do not live with their parents influences their behaviour in school and college. Of students who lived with their parents, 83.9 per cent described themselves as being confident at school compared to only 60 per cent of students who lived without parents. Students who do not live with their parents were less likely to attend school, college or training courses regularly. These students are also less able to suggest positive strategies for organising themselves when studying, and several suggested that 'giving up' and 'not doing it' were ways of coping with work they found challenging. This suggests that the high incidence of truancy and low academic achievement of care leavers and looked after children in education may be, in part, due to lack of self-belief and self-worth.

Research conclusions

This research project indicates that care leavers who plan to enter post-compulsory education are likely to face a number of educational and emotional difficulties which they must overcome in order to be successful. This section presents a number of practical ways in which education and care professionals can support these young people.

It is essential to engender positive aspirations for education in the care leaver. All young people need confidence, motivation and determination to succeed. For the care leaver who may be living alone, who may lack the support network of family and friends, and who may be obliged to provide for themselves financially, the discipline needed to succeed seems immense. Research reiterates care leavers require 'joined up' support from carers, social workers and teachers in order to create and maintain a supportive base from which to initiate their careers. A stable home base is essential, and it must be a stable base that the young person can control if they are to develop the personal skills and experience to become an independent adult. Success at home and in work and education is mutually reinforcing:

> *They tell you at school that it doesn't matter if you don't do well in your exams, and that you can always do them again another time. But when I left school I found they were wrong, and now I am having to study and work, and bring up my daughter at the same time and it's hard. They should tell you the truth: if you don't get your exams when you're at school you're nowhere.*
>
> Care leaver

This research project indicates that care leavers may have a negative image of their potential as learners and low aspirations for attainment through education, related to real or perceived low attainment in earlier school experience. The care leaver needs to be challenged to overcome these fears. Some young people are sceptical about changing their personal situation, especially if their experience is that change is destructive and damaging. The professional must challenge the young person's perceptions of schooling in order to puncture these views, and provide practical and pastoral support as the care leaver takes responsibility for shaping their future. Positive aspirations will build from positive self-belief and evidence of success.

Changing behaviour and attitudes: care leavers and education

If a care leaver has experienced a disrupted education, it is likely that they will have become disaffected with education. Care and education professionals must work with the young person to help alter attitudes and behaviours. Opportunities for the young person to be successful in the early stages of their chosen educational programme are important to establish positive perceptions of education in the mind of the young person. The young person may need support in learning to be successful in personal and social aspects of educational life such as achieving good attendance and actively participating in group activities as well as in academic work. Feedback from other care leavers in education may be useful to the young person in providing an opportunity to discuss common challenges and to identify strategies for dealing with these matters.

In order that the young person can begin to take responsibility for their own learning, they must develop strategies for self-organisation and independent management of time and resources. The young person may need help to understand that long term goals such as academic qualifications take time to achieve. One care leaver commented that his biggest problem at college was getting out of bed in the morning. Once he was at college he found his work interesting, but was beginning to fall behind with coursework as he was absent too frequently.

Care leavers should be able to rely on professional help and support throughout their education. Care leavers value a good relationship with teachers and other professionals very highly, and do not appear to thrive in a situation where they feel the teacher to be uncaring, arrogant or disinterested in their personal case. This research indicates that care leavers may only be able to work effectively with adults to whom they are personally attached. They may require counselling in order to learn how to establish the more detached and objective relationships with their teacher which are typical of education in further and higher educational institutions.

Flexibility in the curriculum

The care leaver should be made aware of the possibilities that are open to them in the post-16 curriculum. There should be close liaison between schools, colleges, the Connexions or similar service and social workers to ensure accurate and helpful advice is available.

A number of education pathways are available to students in the current framework, which enables students to combine academic and vocational qualifications with employment. The National Framework for Qualifications recognises the need to provide entry routes into Levels 2, 3 and 4 for students without traditional qualifications and provides stand-alone qualifications in key skills and mathematics for such students. This may be a more attractive prospect for a care leaver than being obliged to repeat qualifications.

Practical and pastoral support

The transfer from compulsory education into further education normally coincides with leaving the care environment. The young person must cope with the logistics of independent living, in addition to the demands of a training or education programme. It is precisely at this point in their training and educational career when a care leaver needs specific and focused support from education and care professionals to enable them to develop the self-determination and self-organisation required to be successful in education.

All young people experience frustrations and disappointments during their academic career, and all require pastoral support from family, friends and teachers. It is essential that the care leaver has a readily available network of people in easy contact when such times occur. Regular pro-active monitoring and review of a care leaver's progress in education is essential and all the education and care professionals concerned must maintain close and regular contact with one another.

A lack of continuity in care and schooling and consequent lack of continuity in care providers and teachers can engender distrust between the young person and adults who are in authority. If a care leaver has undeveloped communication skills they may find it difficult to express their feelings with others, particularly adults they don't know. The care leaver needs time to build relationships with familiar adults who they trust to advocate for their needs in education.

The higher than average incidence of special educational needs among care leavers indicates that a programme of learning support should be devised at the start of a course of study. The review and monitoring process should focus on the progress of the care leaver set against these targets.

All those responsible for the care leaver must be aware of warning signs of disengagement and non-achievement in the early stages of all educational programmes. If a care leaver is returning to education, they are likely to need support and guidance in developing good study habits. Evidence of poor punctuality, non-attendance, and submitting work late may be indications of the young person failing to thrive in education. Prompt action in dealing with these issues before they develop is extremely important.

One very important point that was evident was that many of the areas where the care leavers perceived that they had problems or experienced difficulties were overcome during the week of the summer school. This indicates that with not a great deal of work and support it is possible for care leavers to attain similar levels of achievement as other young people. This was particularly true in areas such as team working, communication and presentation skills, self-esteem and self-confidence and would indicate that opportunities should be provided as a priority for care leavers to develop these skills.

A newly qualified teacher said that once she realised that, when a young person said:

This is . . . or,

This is boring, or,

You don't expect me to do that, do you, or,

Missed your lesson because I didn't get up in time.

what they really meant was, they didn't understand, and didn't know what to do, or didn't know how to tell her they didn't understand, so she could help them.

Many local authorities provide financial incentives to persuade care leavers to attend further education college. This is fine. But it may be that if more work was done on finding out what extra help a young person needed and then providing that extra help, then these incentives may not be quite so necessary.

Personal Education Plan (PEP)

Every child and young person who is in the care sector should have a personal education plan which should have been completed with them by the designated teacher in school who is responsible for looked after children.

As well as providing factual information on key stages and other educational achievements, people involved with the young person and factors affecting education progress, a PEP also provides information on the student's views and aspirations and the carer's, parent's or social worker's views and the teacher's plans and proposed actions to help the young person.

PEPs should be kept up-to-date and reviewed regularly; it is a good idea if at all possible, and the young person agrees, for the PEP to be sent to the FE or 6th form college as this will enable the institution to know what additional help a young person may need (say the young person is dyslexic) as well as ensuring that the young person is recommended to take a course appropriate for their ability.

Most further education establishments have designated tutors for care leavers and it is anticipated that higher education establishments will also have a designated tutor in the future.

Most local authorities now have specific education support services for children in care and care leavers and these should be involved in all aspects of the education of looked after children and work closely with the different agencies to help to ensure all care leavers achieve their educational potential if at all possible.

How the education system works: a guide for young people

Young people in care and those who have just left care are given advice about which courses and exams to take. However, sometimes because of their circumstances and occasionally because they are given the wrong advice from people who don't understand their situation, they may choose courses that may not be in their best interests. Sometimes young people choose a course simply because their friends are going to do that course.

Having said that, no learning or education is ever wasted. With the modern way of giving a points rating to exams it is now possible to use any qualifications achieved to help work towards the qualifications a young person actually wants and is capable of achieving. The following should help to clarify the situation.

School

In the UK everyone is required by law to have a formal education from age 5 to age 16. During this time they will be taught a set series of subjects in a set way. This is called the National Curriculum.

At age 16 when you leave school you will have been tested and will leave with, hopefully, some qualifications – at present called GCSEs.

After school: further education

From age 16 onwards the choice as to whether or not you continue to study is yours. If you decide to continue studying you move into what is called further education (FE) normally at a further education college although sometimes in a 6th form, normally at entry level. At an FE college you may re-sit exams you failed to pass whilst at school or you may take further exams such as A-levels. Also in FE you may study non-academic subjects such as music or plastering. You can attend an FE college at any age and regardless of whether or not you did well at school. Depending on your circumstances you can attend an FE college on a full-time basis or, if you have a job, on a part-time basis – possibly at an evening class. There is no age barrier to joining an FE college so even if you have not studied for many years you can enrol on a course. All FE colleges have advisors who can help you decide on the best course for you.

After college: higher education?

Depending on your aims and your achievements in your chosen subject, you may progress to what is called higher education (HE) levels. Normally this means going to university full-time and

Education in School, in Further and Higher Education

studying for a degree – but it is possible to stay in a job and study part-time to achieve a qualification that is equivalent to a degree. Figure 7.1 shows approximately how the various qualifications in the UK compare in terms of value. (The chart is approximate because it is not possible to *definitively* relate one qualification to another as various examination bodies are responsible for different aspects of measuring and assessing qualifications and they do not work together at present).

To get into FE at entry level (see What are the various levels? below) requires no previous qualifications – hence the name.

To begin a course of HE study at a higher level will only be possible if you can demonstrate to the college that you have already met a required standard. Usually this means that you will have obtained the required GCSEs whilst at school. Other qualifications that you may have obtained years ago – GCEs for instance or any NVQs that you have – can also be valid. The HE college admissions staff will value these qualifications using University and Colleges Admissions Service (UCAS) tariff points. They have produced a tariff calculator (see www.ucas.com/info/index.html) that most HE establishments refer to when deciding whether or not to accept a student for a particular course.

As all HE qualifications are awarded by universities you will need to apply to the university responsible for the subject that you propose to study. Again, each university will have its own requirements in terms of entry qualifications (UCAS points). As with FE colleges the universities have admissions staff who can help if you have any queries.

Alternatively you can continue with higher education whilst staying in your job and some of your work experience *may* count in your favour.

Just to confuse matters, when you are doing HE, the unit of measurement (or currency), changes to CAT points. CAT stands for Credit Accumulation Transfer and its purpose is to credit you with any studies that you successfully complete so that, if you need to change universities, or if your job or family circumstances mean you have to move, the credits stay with you and can be transferred when you re-start your studies – even several years later. Typically each successful year of a degree course gains you 120 CAT points.

Going to college: what might be different?

- Calling the tutor (teacher) by their first name.
- No-one calling the register.
- No-one apparently noticing if you turn up late or don't turn up – they **do** notice, they just don't make it so obvious.
- Being expected to manage your own time, including free time.
- Lots of people of different ages, from all walks of life and from many different races and cultures.
- Often a much larger building.
- More friendly, relaxed atmosphere.
- Being more responsible for your own study.

Fortunately, in the UK, it is possible to enter or re-enter the education system at any age. There are many examples of retired people going back to study – even going on to university. The following sets out the options available to anyone wishing to kick start their education.

Let us assume that you left school or expect to leave school with no paper qualifications whatsoever. What are your options?

1. Do nothing. Get the best job you can – or live on benefits. Use your wits. Duck and dive. You may make it to the top. But remember – **most people don't make it!**
2. Get some form of qualification at whatever level. No matter that your qualification may be at the bottom rung of the ladder – it will show a prospective employer that you are doing something to improve yourself – and you will enjoy the sense of achievement.

Getting qualified

A qualification is a passport to a better job. Even for what you might think are ordinary jobs, it is becoming increasingly necessary to have a qualification to be allowed to do the job. There may be issues about health and safety, and issues about being able to prove you are competent. It is no longer simply about being able to do a job; it is having the qualification to prove that you can do it. Sometimes an employer wants the evidence that you can do the job and sometimes this is required by a customer or prospective client.

Almost any job that you want to do will require you to have some form of qualification. To progress and get promotion in almost all jobs you need a qualification, even if the employer you work for knows your skills and experience. What if you want to change jobs? Better to get the qualification now rather than have to wait to get a qualification between leaving one job and getting another.

What are qualifications?

There are many types of qualifications you can get from learning. Some of these are ones that people usually get at school, but you can get **any** of these qualifications as an adult too. There are a lot of qualifications that are **nationally recognised**. These are:

- GCSEs, A-levels and A/S-levels.
- Degrees and Access courses.
- NVQs and GNVQs.
- BTECs, HNCs and HNDs.
- City and Guilds awards.

Note! Not all courses give you a qualification. Many give you a **certificate** or **diploma** when you have completed the course. These certificates might not mean anything to an employer or another learning institution.

A tip: For an overview of what qualifications mean, visit the Qualifications and Curriculum Authority's website at www.qca.org.uk. The QCA website also has information on entry level qualifications for those people new to learning.

What qualifications can I get?

There is a wide range of courses and qualifications towards trade and professional qualifications and a variety of pre-university to post-graduate qualifications. Most qualifications are made up of a number of units or modules. Individual units and modules can be studied separately and you can get a certificate for passing each one.

This scheme can also give you a flying start onto a major qualification. The most likely types of qualification are either; Higher National awards, Foundation degrees or National Vocational Qualifications (NVQs). Foundation degrees in particular are aimed at those working and studying at the same time.

Education in School, in Further and Higher Education

Framework for Higher Education Qualifications		National Qualifications Framework (revised - Implemented from spring 2004)		National Qualifications Framework (previous)
D	(Doctoral) Doctorates	8	Vocational diplomas	5 Higher levels
M	(Masters) Masters degrees, postgraduate certificates and diplomas	7	Vocational certificates and diplomas [NVQ 5]	
H	(Honours) Bachelors degrees, graduate certificates and diplomas	6	Vocational certificates and diplomas	4 Higher levels
		5	Key skills Vocational certificates and diplomas [NVQ 4]	
I	(Intermediate) Diplomas of Higher Education and Further Education, Foundation Degrees, Higher National Diplomas	4	Vocational certificates and diplomas	
C	(Certificate) Certificates of Higher Education			
		3	Key skills Vocational certificates and diplomas A levels [NVQ 3]	3 Advanced
		2	Key skills Vocational certificates and diplomas GCSE (Grades A*-C) [NVQ 2]	2 Intermediate
		1	Key skills Vocational certificates and diplomas Basic skills GCSE (Grades D-G) [NVQ 1]	1 Foundation
		Entry	Basic skills Certificates of achievement	Entry

Source: National Qualifications Framework, Regulatery Authorities Awarding Bodies website.

Figure 7.1 *What are the various levels?*

If you want a major qualification you will still have to study and be assessed in some modules by the standard methods. This may include exams. But your existing knowledge can give you a head start.

Where do I start?

You will need to enrol at a Further Education (FE) college. If you have a job you will need to enrol at an evening class or, if you are lucky, an employer may give you day-release to study. If you are not working, you can enrol for a full-time course.

What should I study?

This depends on what you want to do in life and the level you are at now. All FE colleges have advisors trained to assist you in deciding what is the best course for you. They will also advise you of the level you are at now and the level of course that you should be taking to progress.

What are the various levels?

Entry level

If you have few or no qualifications at present you will be advised to take what is called an entry level course. Entry level qualifications recognise basic knowledge and skills and the ability to apply learning in everyday situations under direct guidance or supervision. Learning at this level involves building basic knowledge and skills and is not geared towards specific occupations. Qualifications are offered at Entry 1, Entry 2 and Entry 3, in a range of subjects.

Level 1

Alternatively, you might be steered towards a Level 1 course. Level 1 qualifications recognise basic knowledge and skills and the ability to apply learning with guidance or supervision. Learning at this level is about activities that mostly relate to everyday situations and may be linked to job competence. *Examples* of Level 1 qualifications include:
- NVQ 1.
- Certificate in Plastering.
- GCSEs Grades D to G.
- Certificate in Motor Vehicle Studies.

Level 2

If you already have Level 1 qualifications then you can start at Level 2. Learning at this level involves building knowledge and or skills in relation to an area of work or a subject area and is appropriate for many job roles. *Examples* of Level 2 qualifications are:
- NVQ 2.
- GCSEs Grades A* – C.
- Certificate in Coaching Football.
- Diploma for Beauty Specialists.

Level 3

Learning at this level involves obtaining detailed knowledge and skills. It is appropriate for people wishing to go to university, people working independently, or in some areas supervising and training others in their field of work. *Examples* of Level 3 qualifications include:
- Certificate for Teaching Assistants.
- NVQ level 3.
- A levels.
- Advanced Extension Awards.
- Certificate in Small Animal Care.

Level 4

Learning at this level is appropriate for people working in technical and professional jobs, and/or managing and developing others. Level 4 qualifications are at a level equivalent to Certificates of Higher Education. *Examples* of Level 4 qualifications are:
- Diploma in Sport and Recreation.
- Certificate in Site Management.
- Certificate in Early Years Practice.

Level 5

Learning at this level involves the demonstration of high levels of knowledge, a high level of work expertise in job roles and competence in managing and training others. Qualifications at this level are appropriate for people working as high-grade technicians, professionals or managers. Level 5 qualifications are at a level equivalent to intermediate Higher Education qualifications such as Diplomas in Higher Education, Foundation and other degrees that do not typically provide access to postgraduate programmes. *Examples* of Level 5 qualifications are:
- Diploma in Construction.
- Certificate in Performing Arts.

Level 6

Learning at this level involves the achievement of a high level of professional knowledge and is appropriate for people working as knowledge-based professionals or in professional management positions. Level 6 qualifications are at a level equivalent to bachelors degrees with honours, graduate certificates and graduate diplomas. *An example* of a Level 6 qualification is:
- Diploma in Management.

Level 7

Learning at this level involves the demonstration of high level specialist professional knowledge and is appropriate for senior professionals and managers. Level 7 qualifications are at a level equivalent to Masters degrees, postgraduate certificates and postgraduate diplomas. *Examples* of Level 7 qualifications include:
- Diploma in Translation.
- Fellowship in Music Literacy.

See also AimHigher web site at https://www.aimhigher.info/registration.cfm?fromhow=PREGCSE

Level 8

Learning at this level involves the development of new and creative approaches that extend or redefine existing knowledge or professional practice. *An example* is:
- Specialist awards.

The system of levels is designed to encourage learning throughout life. It is flexible, you can progress at your own speed and move in and out of learning as and when it suits you. In addition, you can build your credits towards an award if you wish.

Work-based qualifications

These are assessed by a college or employer. The FE college part is delivered through block- or day-release from work.

The Leaving Care Handbook

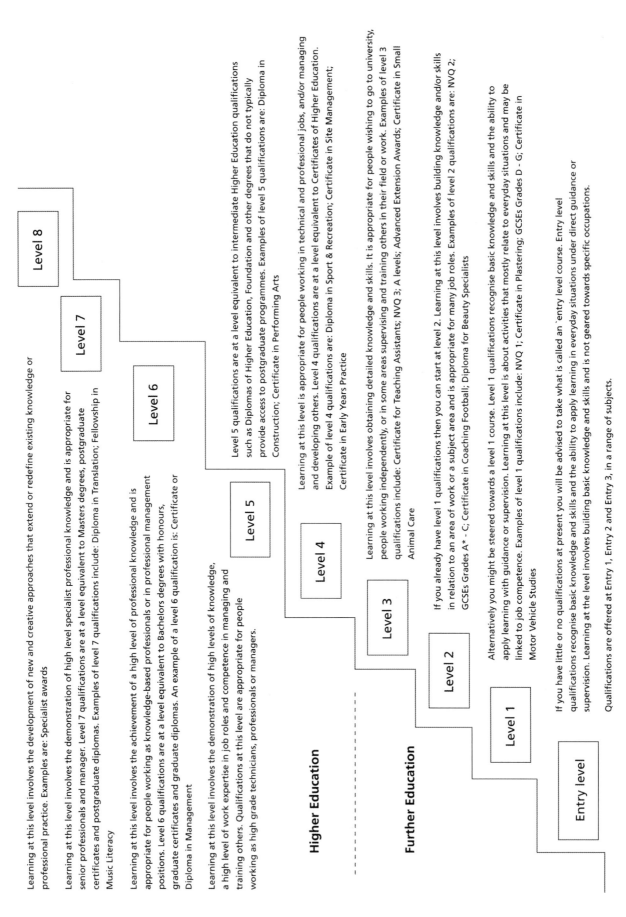

Figure 7.2 Chart with examples showing different qualifications and approximate levels

Education in School, in Further and Higher Education

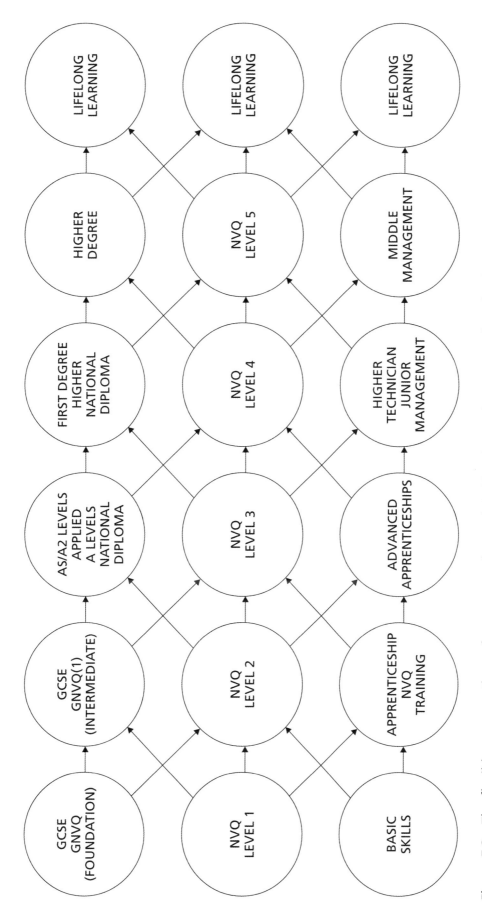

Figure 7.3 *The flexible career pathway for your way forward @ 16+ Connexions, West of England*

Although many work-based qualifications are recognised qualifications this is not true of all employers, some of whom offer their own forms of accreditation. For example, a young man applied for a job as a bus driver, having got a clean driving license and several years experience. He was successful, but for the first week he didn't see a bus since he was at the training centre, and at the end of the week he sat several exams. He passed them and soon became a bus driver. However, the exams he passed were only approved by the bus company for whom he worked.

There are three main work-based training programmes in operation offering work experience and qualifications:
- Modern Apprenticeships.
- National Traineeships.
- New Training (Youth credits).

Modern Apprenticeships

Modern Apprenticeships (MAs) are aimed primarily at those in the 16-19 age group who have the ability to gain high level skills and qualifications. Funding is available up to a person's 25th birthday.

The programme of training is to NVQ Level 3 and the training is usually employer-led with the trainee starting as an employee. As a rule of thumb an entrant will require some good GCSEs in order to be considered for a MA.

National Traineeships

National Traineeships are designed for people aged 16–24 who have a job, and want to gain a job-related qualification. Usually it is possible to study to NVQ Level 2. The training would normally last two years. Training costs are paid by the employer.

New Training (Youth Credits)

This is usually called Network Training – the programme may have a different name in other areas. It is aimed at people 16–18, who don't have a job, and is designed to give those young people the opportunity to gain valuable training, qualifications and work experience. They are a combination of work experience in a preferred field which amounts to about four-fifths of the time. A college qualification is usually completed on a day-release basis.

Most trainees aspire to NVQ Level 2 although other qualifications can sometimes be offered, depending on the chosen work area.

These three are the main government-sponsored training programmes, but many young people continue to do post-school qualifications such as Indentured Apprenticeships, for example, organised by their employer's trade association or professional body.

Qualifications for people with learning difficulties

All local colleges offer courses for young people who may have special needs. These courses have various umbrella names such as 'discreet' and are designed for young people for whom NVQ Level 1 or Foundation (see above) is not deemed appropriate. There are three main levels: pre-foundation; towards independence; and vocational access.

Pre-foundation

This course lasts one year and often includes sheltered work-experience. Students capable of doing so should move onto a Foundation course.

Education in School, in Further and Higher Education

Towards independence

These courses have little academic study and concentrate on teaching life-skills. Students with severe learning disabilities would often be on these courses.

Vocational access

These are work-experience college-based courses for young people with learning difficulties. They often contain elements of Mathematics and English but are essentially practical. Vocational access courses are offered in a range of skill areas including: Catering, Information Technology, Carpentry etc.

Thinking of going into higher education?

Choosing a course

If you are not sure which university to choose then the Guardian *University Guide* may be able to help as it gives advice on:

- A ranking system for subjects which can be studied at UK universities.
- League subject tables that are designed with student experience in mind.
- Expert advice from academics and students on how to find the best course at the right university for **you**.
- Full and frank advice on the application process, from form filling to asking the right things at interviews.
- Honest assessments from students on what life is really like at each university.

This book should be available in libraries, Connexions/careers offices and in colleges.

What help students need

The research report *By Degrees, The First Year from Care to University* (Jackson et al., 2003) makes the following recommendations based on interviews with students who are care leavers:

- Support provided must be flexible and appropriate and tailored to the individual.
- Education must be valued, encouraged and supported by all.
- Maximum stability in home circumstances necessary – **no** to independent living at 16, or ending foster placements at 18.
- Advisor must be well-informed and available for frequent advice including in the early stages. Students from overseas need special consideration.
- Financial support must be based on actual costs and agreed in writing.
- Living accommodation both during term and during holidays must be appropriate to the student's needs.
- Policy on student loans needs to be clear and known to the student in advance.
- Advice on budgeting may be needed and emergency help if they get into debt.
- Students may need help to get to university at the start of the course and help with settling in.
- A named person must keep in regular touch, show interest in their progress and send congratulations if results are good, or comfort and encourage if not.
- This person should also help with planning for the next steps in the student's life.

One young person who is studying at a university posted a message on the independent SoNet web site (www.sonet.soton.ac.uk/pt) that is hosted by the University of Southampton, saying:

> *Care leavers should have a named person they can talk to, at a time when best suited for them. Social workers are only available 9–5 and that's if they're not busy dealing with something else. Most students*

have the option of calling their parents when they want to, care leavers don't. Someone should make regular calls to the young people in the same way many parents call their child to see how they are, especially in the first term. Care leavers shouldn't be made to feel left out and should receive calls so they feel cared about.

From this, and other discussions with young people, a new closed web site has been made available called www.sonet.soton.ac.uk/pt for care leavers at university and for those thinking of going to university. It offers:

- Relevant information, such as what the different qualifications mean, a jargon buster, financial entitlements.
- Opportunity to have a discussion, both on the site and via e-mails, with other care leavers.
- A facility to ask questions and receive a variety of responses from people using the site.
- A mentoring service, supported by the Prince's Trust Mentoring Scheme, where people from different walks of life, experience and age groups can support the students. Initially the contact is via e-mails but if both sides agree contact may be via telephone calls and face-to-face meetings.

The site is open to care leavers preferences and to the trained and police-checked mentors.

Preparing the ground

In addition to the above, anyone going to university will need practical information about budgeting, form filling, cooking, study skills and just what being at university is really like.

Preparing the ground, and providing support for such things as attending summer schools, and open days, are as important as understanding the jargon and having high but realistic expectations. Celebrating their successes and having someone there to help when things don't turn out well is equally important.

Local authorities are required to make financial provision for care leavers who are going, or who are at university. Finances play a huge part in how easily and well a student settles at university. They need to know:

- How much money a student will get.
- When they will get it – this needs to be negotiated to ensure it fits within the requirements of the university and the needs of the young person.
- That they will get it regularly and on time.
- What it covers.
- How extras that may be needed for specific courses, will be paid for.
- What the situation is on student loans.
- What the situation is on part-time working.
- What finances they will get during the vacations.

NLCAS, Rainer produced a fact sheet in September 2004 on which the following is based.

Grants, loans and other financial help

What is the Higher Education Grant?

New students from September 2004 may be eligible for the new Higher Education Grant. This annual grant is to help with the costs of living and studying. The amount of help available will be assessed on a student's, or their household's, income and this grant does not have to be repaid.

The Higher Education Grant is means-tested. Care leavers will receive the highest amount.

Education in School, in Further and Higher Education

For other students, the level of Higher Education Grant available will depend on their, or their household's, income.

Is this the same as the Care Leavers Grant?

No. The Care Leavers Grant is available to care leavers in higher education, to help with accommodation costs during the long summer holiday. It is administered by the LEA and is paid directly to the student or, if they prefer, their landlord. Care leavers can apply for this grant via the student loan form.

Additional help available to certain groups of students

Parents Learning Allowance

The Parents Learning Allowance is to help with course-related costs for students who have dependent children. How much is available depends on household income (including that of wife, husband or partner). The LEA will be able to advise individual students on their entitlement. The grant does not affect entitlement to benefits.

Child Tax Credit

Students with dependent children are eligible for the Child Tax Credit (CTC) from the Inland Revenue. Students receiving the maximum amount of CTC are entitled to free school meals for their children.

Students with children will be entitled to claim CTC, which is paid to parents whether they are working or studying. To qualify for CTC you must be:
- Aged 16 or over; and;
- Responsible for a child under 18 or someone aged 16–19 in relevant (full-time, non-advanced) education, or who is registered with the Careers Service or equivalent.

A parent will receive a higher amount of CTC if their child, or one of their children, is less than one year old, or has a disability. The money available depends on the parents' circumstances. Parents can find out if they are eligible for CTC by calling 0800 500 222 or visiting www.inlandrevenue.gov.uk/taxcredits

Childcare Grant

The Childcare Grant is available to full-time students with dependent children in registered or approved childcare. The amount available depends on actual childcare costs and household income. Any help received has no effect on other benefit entitlement.

Adult Dependents' Grant

If an adult member of the student's family is financially dependent on them, they may be eligible for the Adult Dependents' Grant. The amount depends on the student's income, and that of the adult dependents.

Disabled Students' Allowances

Disabled Students' Allowances (DSAs) are available to help disabled students with costs they incur in attending their course, as a direct result of the disability. They are available to full- and part-time students with disabilities, although part-time students must be studying for at least 50 per cent of a full-time course.

DSAs are available to both undergraduate and postgraduate students. The amount available does *not* depend on the student's income, or that of their household, and unlike a student loan, this assistance does not have to be repaid. Extra support, depending on individual need, could include specialist equipment, a non-medical helpers allowance, help towards the additional costs of travelling to college etc.

Help after starting a course

Access funds

Access to learning funds (known as Financial Contingency Funds, in Wales) are available through individual colleges and provide help for students on a low income who may need extra financial support for their course and to stay in higher education.

These funds are for full-time and part-time students (studying at least half of an equivalent full-time course). Students will be assessed according to individual need. However, the following groups of students are a **priority** for help from the Access and Hardship fund:

- Students with children, especially lone parents.
- Other mature students, especially those with existing financial commitments.
- Students with low-income families.
- Disabled students.
- Students who have been in care.
- Students in temporary accommodation such as foyers or who are homeless.
- Students in their final year.

Payments are usually given as grants, and do not have to be repaid, although sometimes they can be given as short-term loans. The college will also decide whether to make the payment in a lump sum or in instalments.

The welfare office of the college or student's union will be able to provide more information and advice.

University Jargon-buster

It can be very off-putting not knowing some of the university language. Here are some examples of a few together with their meaning:

Accreditation – Approval by a specific body, can be university or professional body, so that an undergraduate programme is accepted as a degree and as a professional qualification. For example, a degree in social work is accredited by the General Social Care Council. This means that a student studying social work will obtain a stand alone Bachelor degree and that degree means they are entitled to be called a Social Worker.

Alumni – Former student.

Bachelor – Award of first degree.

Campus – Geographical location in which the university is situated, this can include buildings used for teaching, administration and halls of residence. One single university may have several campuses or several different geographical locations.

Chair (professorial chair) – The term is usually followed by a subject or list of subjects e.g., Professor Joe Bloggs, Chair of Mechanical Engineering. It derives from historical times when 'readers' (see below) could read in the library but did not have a designated chair.

Dean – Usually an academic member of staff who has designated managerial responsibilities relating to a sub-set of the whole organisation e.g., Dean of the Faculty (see below).

Dissertation – In some respects an extended essay in terms of word length. This can be presented in the form of a systematic literature review, i.e. reading all the available literature on a subject, or a full-scale empirical study (see below).

Emeritus professor – Someone is usually given this title on retirement from a university in recognition of their services to the university at which they were a professor.

Empirical study – Collection and analysis of data, carrying out research and then analysing your results.

Faculty – Many universities choose to structure their institution into faculties as sub-sets of the whole organisation. These can be several in number but are very much specific to an institution. For example, Southampton University now has three large faculties which recently replaced a larger number of small faculties. Faculties are generally organised around a broad set of common disciplines, e.g. Arts, Science, Applied Science.

Fresher – A new undergraduate student.

Module – A specific part of a course programme. It can be taken as an integral part of that programme or it may stand alone. It is often associated with a number of credits awarded under CATS system (see *How Education Works – A Guide for Young People* section). Each module has specific aims and objectives and must have an assessment.

PhD (A Doctor of Philosophy) – One of several awards at doctoral level.

Post graduate is anyone who has obtained their Bachelor degree and is studying for a higher award, e.g. 'Masters'. Roughly, the progress through qualifications obtainable at university is **Bachelor**, **Masters** and **PhD**.

Reader – A senior academic appointment awarded in recognition mainly for research achievements. Often referred to, particularly in other countries, as Associate Professor.

Refectory – Dining hall.

Sabbatical – Time off for study or travel.

School of . . . – A sub-set of the whole organisation. 'Schools' often focus on one discipline e.g. School of Management or a group of related disciplines or subjects-e.g. School of Social Sciences.

Semester – Now largely replaces the idea of terms in a university year. By definition there are two semesters in a year. A university degree is usually based on six semesters as against nine terms which was previously the case.

Tutorial – Each student has a personal tutor who is a reference point during their programme of study. Tutorials consist of face-to-face contact between the student and tutor. These can be conducted individually or in groups. Increasingly the notion of e-learning is being introduced into tutorials.

Undergraduate - Anybody studying a programme which can lead to a first degree, e.g. Bachelor degree.

Vice chancellor – Like the chief executive of a company, or the head of a management team, this person is answerable to the university council, who are elected members of the university.

Visiting fellow – Not a member of staff, although they may have been. Usually, someone who has an association with the university.

Conclusion

Education is not just about qualifications, it is about achieving potential, about raising self-esteem and about feeling good about yourself, and knowing you have done something worthwhile.

The many examples of care leavers who achieve in education, despite their circumstances, is very encouraging. It is of paramount importance that everyone has equal opportunities to achieve their potential. This may mean:

- Initially supporting them to get to college or work on time.
- Being there if things go wrong.
- Maintaining contact even when things look as though they are going well.
- Ensuring they obtain any specific requirements they need such as drugs for a particular health condition, e.g. ADHD.
- Ensuring they have appropriate equipment for their situation, e.g. a laptop computer if they are dyslexic.
- Ensuring that financial arrangements are in place, so that payments are made on time, consistently and correctly.

We should support, guide and help anyone who wishes to continue with their education. We should also **celebrate their success** and help them plan for the next stage in their life.

Resources

Berkley, R., Wheal, A. with Beissel, G., Bodelon-Maceiras, M. and Tzavidis, N. (2002) *Guidance and Support for Care Leavers in Post-Compulsory Education.* Southampton: University of Southampton.

Connexions (2004) *Your Way Forward: Options @ 16+.* Connexions West of England.

DfES Booklet (2004) *Financial Support for Higher Education Students: Guide for 04/05*:
   www.dfes.gov.uk/studentsupport/uploads/FSS-Purple-guide-04-05.pdf

Also available from directly from LEAs or from the Information Line: 0800 731 9133.

Jackson, S., Ajayi, S., Quigley, M. (2003) *By Degrees: The First Year from Care to University.* London: The Frank Buttle Trust.

Leach, J. (Ed.) (2006) *The Guardian University Guide 2006.* London: The Guardian.

Office of the Deputy Prime Minister (2003) *A Better Education for Children in Care.* London: The Social Exclusion Unit, HMSO.

National Union of Students: www.nusonline.co.uk

Aim Higher, the HEFCE website: www.aimhigher.ac.uk/student_finance/index.cfm

DfES website: www.dfes.gov.uk/studentsupport/students

8

Training, Employability and Work Experience

Linda Daniel and Ena Fry

Introduction

In line with Government targets and objectives, the majority of young people now remain in some form of further or higher education post-16, including more care leavers. This development is discussed in Chapter 7 on Education. Although recognising that there is an overlap between training and employment, for example some employers offer 'day release' for young people to attend job-relevant courses at local colleges, the focus of this chapter is mainly on training and employability, particularly on work experience as a way of increasing and improving educational and employment opportunities for care leavers.

Currently the government seems to show a lack of recognition of the progress that can be made outside of main stream education. This work with care leavers will eventually lead to employability skills, to work itself or to a return to education. So, work experience plays an important part.

Broadly there are two groups of care leavers discussed in this chapter.
- Care leavers for whom work experience is part of education and training.
- Care leavers who are currently not engaged with either education or training.

This chapter is in two parts. The first part sets out the context in which young people are leaving care and entering the job market. The second part provides ideas, tips and pointers that may help you help young people to achieve success and assist in engaging more young people so they do not become the long-term unemployed and unemployable.

Training, employability and work experience

For young people leaving care, this is a time of challenging transition. Depending on the route they take, they will encounter diverse risk factors, and protective factors:

Protective factors are:
- Attending a FE establishment.
- Undertaking training.
- Being in some form of employment.
- Having stable accommodation.
- Having a firm relationship with carer, family or other adult.
- Being unlikely to become a parent.

Risk factors are:
- Having no daytime activity.
- Lacking advice and support for the future.
- Lacking in motivation and confidence.
- Irresponsible sexual behaviour.
- Misusing substances.
- Suffering mental health issues.
- Being isolated.
- Being involved in crime.
- Suffering a breakdown of placement.
- Being homeless.

From experience with young people leaving care, we need to acknowledge that some are not sufficiently stable to undertake any training scheme, college course or employment. Young people really appreciate understanding and the consequent reduction in pressure, while they build themselves a foundation on which to move forward. We need to help them build that. Young people do understand the need for qualifications but find the long-term vision too difficult. They need consistent, flexible support and plenty of reassurance. More importantly, they benefit from a relationship with someone who can be a role model, be trusted and be reliable.

Why do we need to be concerned?

The following statistics show why we need to be both concerned and proactive. They are based on personal experience as well as from *When Leaving Home is Also Leaving Care* (DOTT, 1997):

- Seventy-five per cent of care leavers leave school with no formal academic qualifications.
- Up to 97 per cent of care leavers leave school without qualifications that employers would recognise as achieving basic schooling.
- Seventeen per cent of young women leaving care are pregnant or already mothers.
- Care leavers are two years behind their peers in maths and one year behind in reading.
- Fifty per cent of care leavers are still unemployed two years after leaving compulsory education.
- Children in care, and care leavers, are ten times more likely to be excluded from school.
- Fifty per cent of children in care are absent from school on any one day.
- Between 28 and 40 per cent of children in care will be assessed for Statements of Special Educational Need.
- Twenty-three per cent of adult prisoners and 38 per cent of young prisoners have been in care.
- Thirty per cent of young single homeless people have been in care.
- Only one in three care leavers go to university compared with 40 per cent of their peers.

The world of work today

In today's labour market investment in plant and machinery seems to have been abandoned in favour of investment in workers who can adapt to advancing technology and new working patterns. Apprenticeships tend to require high skill levels and qualifications. Flexible working patterns, particularly in the service sector, tend to mean that older candidates, e.g. women returnees, are favoured in job appointments. Consequently, people without skills are left behind – stuck in precarious jobs that are poorly paid and unreliable. Three quarters of employers find it difficult to recruit due to skills shortages. One in five people lack basic skills and the competition for unskilled work is high. Most jobs require maths and IT skills. Therefore, those who would be employed have to meet the demands of the labour market; and young people who have underachieved at school have to acquire employability skills and qualifications to ensure their social inclusion. Young people formerly in care are often grouped with other disadvantaged groups such as ex-offenders, those who are homeless, those with alcohol and substance problems, and those from ethnic minorities. Employers prefer people without these 'disadvantages' – businesses are not willing to carry passengers!

The minimum requirements sought by employers, regardless of the lack of qualifications, are enthusiasm, reliability and motivation. Proof of some work experience to validate these qualities is evidence of employability.

As we have already established, young people who are in stable care and who are motivated and encouraged to continue in education are most likely to go on to further education and employment. However, those who undergo a more difficult, chaotic time in care will more often experience poor attendance at school, and temporary or permanent exclusion. It is not unknown for young people to have not attended school from year 10 onwards. This period of drift is now being vigorously addressed because of its negative long-term effect.

It is this cohort of looked after NEET (post compulsory education but **N**ot in **E**ducation, **E**mployment or **T**raining) who, in addition to their peers, are the cause of great concern to leaving care teams, the government and to all who work with them. The majority of the NEET young people leaving care will say:

I just want to work; I want to earn money and look after myself.

I can't help my behaviour – I get angry 'cos there's nothing out there for me.

All the jobs need qualifications but I don't want to go back to school.

What's the point in getting up – some days I can't be bothered.

Where are we now?

We have come a long way since 2001 and the implementation of the Children (Leaving Care) Act. With the advent of designated teachers, Personal Education Plans (PEPs), Pathway Plans, earlier interventions to prevent disaffection, increased financial support for those in education and for those post-19 in further education, the picture is improving. Connexions has had a huge impact on the services provided to young people. Personal advisors in schools, colleges, youth offending teams, leaving care teams, careers offices and the voluntary sector; all these offer an advice, guidance and personal development service on a one-to-one basis. They particularly target those young people 'at risk' of social exclusion. They ensure they receive full careers guidance and track them thereafter to monitor progress or to implement interventions if necessary. Connexions has connected local agencies together and, because of gaps identified in resources, has been influential in the educational and training provision delivered via the Learning Skills Council (LSC). The LSC is responsible for the funding and planning of further education and training for post 16 plus.

The LSC has stated that we need to unlock exclusion from work by tackling problems in the education system, equipping the unemployed and boosting the employability of individuals in work. The needs of the individual and the local, regional labour market must dovetail.

Tip: every personal advisor should have a copy of *Connexions NEET – A Resource Pack for Personal Advisors Working with Young People not in Education, Training and Employment* available from Connexions.

Outside of 'regular' post-16 further education, modern apprenticeships, network training (work-based with day release to college) etc. those in the NEET group of care leavers also have access to:

- Changing Places – an in-house work experience scheme initiated by Futures, London Borough of Hounslow and adopted by other local authorities.
- Teenagers to Work – an annual government-led scheme where local authorities offer two weeks work experience placements to young people.
- Prince's Trust – now delivered locally, for those 16 to 25.
- Outward Bound programmes.
- Summer Schools and Positive Activities for Young People – delivered during school holidays.
- Fairbridge – offering a programmed scheme for those 13–25.

- YCTV – short courses in drama, camera work, sound editing and first aid.
- Young mums projects: for example, computer club plus crèche.

More recent innovations are:
- More supported courses for those with learning difficulties and special educational needs delivered at local colleges.
- *Care to Learn* local college courses offering free childcare to young mums under 19.
- E2E government-led pre-NVQ training with paid weekly allowance for attendance. Includes tasters, construction skills and hands on music.
- Small-scale creative schemes such as JUMPSTART (part of E2E) – two small, highly supported classes of 8 incorporating work experience with basic and life skills which is accredited. Delivered in a small unit off site of community school.
- A new curriculum for pupils 14–19 providing more flexibility to suit the needs of individual pupils, focusing on vocational learning leading to vocational GCSEs, and allowing for achievement being measured at 19 rather than 16.

So – What Are the Barriers to Meeting Government Targets and Young People Leading a Rewarding, Independent Life?
- Non-attendance at school.
- Insufficient help or opportunities to catch up.
- Instability – unplanned moves of placements and schools – more the exception than the rule now.
- Insufficient educational support in and out of school – being actively addressed now.
- Insufficient help to overcome personal individual trauma.
- Schooling given low priority when moves organised – now being addressed.
- Low expectations of workers, teachers and carers – now being addressed.
- Low self-esteem of child.
- Non-identification of special needs (Looked after children are 6-8 times more likely to have special needs but this is often missed due to erratic attendance).
- Young people suffering from emotional stress or depression.
- 77 per cent of care leavers assessed had basic skills needs which affected employability.

(Taken from *First Key. Putting Young People at the Centre*)

Earlier interventions are beginning to take root and will improve the life chances of those coming through the care system now. We need to make school a positive experience and move away from the traditional poor attainment outcome. Attitudes of schools, foster carers and residential units are changing, so increasingly education is being given more priority.

Work experience

Employers today demand more and more from employees, and competition for jobs is huge. Minimum expectations from employers are often GCSE's in English, Maths and maybe a science subject too. Communication skills, both written and verbal, plus IT skills, need to be reasonably good, but the very least expectation is some evidence of work experience to persuade an employer that the young person is employable. Employment requires work disciplines and stamina. Some young people leaving care lead chaotic lives, suffer loneliness and poverty and have few negotiation skills for team work. Work experience can help to address some of these issues.

Training, Employability and Work Experience

The purpose of work experience is to improve the post-16 education, training and employment outcomes of those youth in and leaving care by developing their skills, confidence and motivation to enable them to access opportunities otherwise unavailable to them.

Care leavers form a significant proportion of the NEET group because they have fallen out of mainstream education, often for a year or more. Few care leavers look ahead to their lives in five years time and few regard education as an achievable long term option. The majority of young people develop skills and qualities through observations of daily life with parents, extended family, other adults, in school and leisure. This process of socialisation, learning and development is less evident than those in public care, particularly with regard to their acquiring positive feelings of self-worth, self-esteem and aspirations towards educational achievements and career. Also, previous negative educational experiences make these young people resistant to, and unable to sustain, main stream provision – they have developed a negative attitude and have little or no work ethic.

Work experience is about change, not just a piecemeal couple of weeks with any employer who will take a young person. It should be an aspirational stepping stone with educational and personal support.

Work experience schemes: three models

In-house schemes

Changing Places is an in-house Local Authority scheme formulated by the London Borough of Hounslow, and winner of Community Care Award 1998/99.

Outline:
- Acquisition of work experience placements within council departments, supported by the chief executive, council members and departmental directors.
- Planned and managed by the education officer of the leaving care team.
- Small – only six young people per year.
- Programme – roll on, roll off approach.
- Three days per week, expenses paid.
- Example of placements: parks and gardens, mail room, porters, administration, reception.

Current situation:
- Some placements were never taken up especially where the first week or so required work on health and safety – considered too cerebral.
- Administrative work was not found to be particularly attractive, especially by young men (often experienced as boring).
- Lack of payment was a disincentive – why get out of bed when you can get the same allowance for doing nothing. Allowances are now paid.
- Childcare – no budget until this year so young mums were previously excluded.
- Privatisation – many departments are now independent businesses and taking on a young person who will need time and attention is not always cost effective.
- Staff streamlining or shortages means staff are overworked and unable to spare the time to help and offer support.
- The young people are often unreliable. Placements have been lost most often because of unreliability and lack of enthusiasm on the part of the young people. This is often a result of, or cover for, the young person's insecurity or lack of confidence.

Changing Places was very successful in its early years because the young people involved had a higher level of skills. Despite their periods of drift all the *Changing Places* participants went on to further education. However, the client group has changed in recent times and their needs are far more complex and their behaviour more challenging. Forms 1–8 are examples of forms used on this scheme which may be adapted for use elsewhere:

Changing places forms

All young people who are interested in our work experience scheme are asked to complete these registration forms, which do demand a lot of information! The reason for this is that the more is known about the skills, experience, their likes and dislikes, the more likely it is that we can find the right placement for the right young person, although the intention is for them to experience a variety of placements.

Teenagers to Work (TTW)

This is an annual local government scheme introduced in 2000 which aims to provide two weeks work experience for care leavers. In Hounslow, it has been successful primarily because it has been 'waged'. The most successful placements are practical, out and about, or busy ones where someone works alongside the young person, taking them under their wing. One of our young men had resisted engagement in any educational provision but after TTW, and terrific support from his supervisor in painting and decorating, he is now enrolled onto a Jumpstart programme and doing well. In the past, some more able young people enjoyed working in Reception and IT but four years on, these young people are now more likely to be in college, and on an educational path, and so less needy of work experience as a first stepping stone. Also, TTW happens at the end of the school/college summer term, so departments are often a lot quieter than normal and struggle to provide a varied, interesting programme. Forms TTW 1–6 are examples of forms used on this scheme which may be adapted for use elsewhere.

Employability – building futures for young people in and leaving public care

This is the title of a resource pack produce by the Who Cares Trust funded by the Department of Health. It contains videos and CDs together with an information booklet. There is also a programme for young people with learning difficulties called *Employability Plus* which was funded by the Baily Thomas Charitable Fund, the Camelot Foundation and the Diana Memorial Fund.

The overall aim of the Employability Programme is to improve the post-16 education, training and employment opportunities and outcomes of young people in and leaving public care by:
- Working with young people in a creative way to increase their access to education, training and employment opportunities.
- Developing young people's skills, confidence and motivation to enable them to access the opportunities available to them.
- Developing a partnership culture of multi-agency working across social services and the whole authority which acts as the corporate parent.
- Linking with local businesses and other agencies to increase the opportunities for a range of training and employment initiatives.

The areas covered in the pack include: Communication skills; personal qualities and social skills; numeracy and literacy; and problem-solving skills. Local authorities who have used the pack have reported very successful outcomes.

How to get help when things go wrong

1. Ensure everyone involved has received the message that 'educational success leads to better life chances' and that 'it is the second most important factor after health'.
2. If the young person has not had a one-to-one careers guidance session with a personal advisor whilst they were at school, arrange it as soon as possible so that future direction has some foundation that has had proper involvement with the young person.
3. Find out what is not working for the young person; what are their anxieties. Listen to them, listen to what's not being said. Check out changes in behaviour/attitudes, mood swings, changes in friends, changes in relationships with carers, family etc. Question whether previous expectations were set too high, whether there are any health issues, or accommodation problems. Give the young person **time**.
4. Try to talk with the young person regularly so that problems can be pre-empted before they become a crisis.
5. Check that they have good leisure time.
6. Offer rewards for sustaining training/employment.
7. Link with youth services (part of Connexions) to access their services and resources.
8. Praise and encourage even the smallest positive moves. Focus on their progress so far and their future potential (this can be monitored and reflected back to the young person by APIR or Pathway plan). Should work experience not work out successfully for the young person, do your utmost to find a positive for them – perhaps ask the placement supervisor to write a letter or a card wishing them well for the future or praising them for the work done on however many days they managed to attend. Ask the young person how work experience felt for them – what was good or bad. You will learn a lot from their feedback. Photograph (with their permission) all the young people in their workplace, give them their own framed photograph and include them all in your borough newspaper. It is great for their self-esteem.
9. Reassure the young person that they are cared for and that their future is important to you.
10. Discuss resilience – how they can flourish and succeed despite being in care.
11. Inspire their move-on by using role models: Bruce Oldfield, Neil Morrisey etc. who were in care but who did not let it hold them back.
12. Look at short term goals if the young person has disengaged from education, training or employment.
13. Try to have a contingency plan to avoid periods of inactivity or disengagement.
14. Advocate for the young person; access educational and revision support.
15. Be sympathetic but firm – whatever our role, we *are* the corporate **parent**.

Work experience gives young people an insight into the expectations of the world of work and what they need to get there. At the end of this chapter is a section looking at some practical tips on helping anyone to access employment.

Money Box
In compliance with the Children (Leaving Care) Act 2000, Hounslow's leaving care service provides every care leaver with a written copy of Guide to Financial Support (Hounslow) which clearly outlines all their entitlements and discretionary payments available.

At the time of writing, 16–18s, not in foster or residential care, receive a living allowance of £44 per week. Hounslow tops this up by £24 per week if the young people are attending further education or training. At 18, those in education sign up for income support until their 19th Birthday, when they have to sign on for Job Seekers Allowance. This is complete bureaucratic nonsense, and is an issue which is currently being addressed by the Department for Work and Pensions (DWP). It causes distress and places pressure on young people who are engaged in study as they have to sign on fortnightly and undertake jobsearch in order to satisfy JSA requirements and entitlements.

It is always advisable to have a personal contact at the Job Centre Plus who deals specifically with care leavers. It saves time and frustration for both the worker and young people. Also, they have useful leaflets about earnings allowances.

Looked after children are a vulnerable group, and can sometimes qualify for hardship payments pending a new JSA claim.

Work experience programmes allow local authorities to give work expenses weekly which are not counted as earnings.

Conclusion

Every local authority acts as a corporate parent to care leavers so all departments have a responsibility to work together to improve outcomes. What we need is a much wider range of council and community based work experience placements which should be able to offer employment in some instances. This is the first thought of many of the NEET group – 'I just want to work, I need the money' but they have so little to offer and end up taking casual, exploitative dead end jobs with no future. Their emotional landscape and physical needs have a huge impact too on their employability. Some are 16 or 17 living semi-independently on a minimum income with little support other than from social services departments.

Realistic placements for the NEET group should be initially low skilled, practical, varied and mentored. The lack of work experience and a work history is a significant barrier to the long term unemployed and inactive. Surely we can do more now to help expand provision ensuring it is meaningful, motivational and aspirational. If we can achieve this, we would go a long way towards addressing the current imbalance.

Changing Places 1: Personal Information

Surname .... First names ....

DOB .... Male/Female (*Please delete*)

Address ....

....

Daytime Tel. No. .... Home Tel. No. ....

Where do you live:
- With foster family — Yes/No (*Please delete*)
- In a residential home — Yes/No
- Semi-independently — Yes/No
- Independently — Yes/No
- Other (e.g. B&B, hostel) — Yes/No

Is there someone in your family or where you live whom you would like us to contact about your choice to register on this scheme? Yes/No (*Please delete*)

If Yes, please give names ....

Relationship to you ....

Address (if different from your own) ....

....

Are you a registered disabled person? Yes/No (*Please delete*)

If yes, please give number (if known) .... Expiry date ....

Your National Insurance No. ....

Do you have an allocated social worker or key worker Yes/No

Please give name and location ....

....

Name of contact for Changing Places ....

Date of registration ....

Source: *The Leaving Care Handbook*. Russell House Publishing, 2005.

Changing Places 2: Record of Education and Training

Name .... DOB ....

School ....

Name and address of senior school From To Qualifications/other training

_____

_____

College

Name and address of college From To Course of study/qualification

_____

_____

Changing Places 3: Personal details

(I do/do not consent that this information may be passed on to the placement supervisor) (*Please delete*)

Special dietary requirements ....

....

Physical/health restrictions ....

....

Details of any medication ....

....

Any other information which we may need to be aware of? ....

....

Signed .... Date ....

Source: *The Leaving Care Handbook*. Russell House Publishing, 2005.

The Leaving Care Handbook

Changing Places 4: Agreement for young person in placement

Name .... DOB ....

Male/female (*Please delete*) Ethnicity ....
Placement identified

What skills/abilities can you bring to this placement?

What would you want to achieve in this placement?

Are there other placements that you are interested in?

I am willing to take part in Changing Places and have identified the area or work that I am interested in.

Signed .... Date ....

Changing Places 5: Agreement for department/section

Name of department: ....

Contact names: .... Tel. No. ....

Description of role/duty/area of specialisation ....
....

Special equipment required   Yes/No (*Please delete*)
Health and Safety checked   Yes/No (*Please delete*)

This department/section is willing to undertake the work experience programme and offer this young person a placement.

Name of young person .... DOB ....

Agreed number of days, e.g. three per week over a period of one month

Date of start: .... to end ....

Named supervisor if differs from above contact ....

Signed .... Date ....

Source: *The Leaving Care Handbook*, Russell House Publishing, 2005.

Changing Places 6: Monitoring information

This information can be used to make sure that everyone receives an equal service. Please can you tick the box which best describes you.

Age group   16–17   18–21

Ethnic Origin   White UK   White European
                   White other   Indian
                   Black Caribbean   Black African
                   Pakistani   Bangladeshi
                   Chinese   Mixed race
                   Other   (*Please specify*)

Gender: Female   Male (*Please delete*)

Are you a registered disabled person or do you have a disability? Yes/No (*Please delete*)

If your placement supervisor wanted to know in what way you are disabled what would you want us to say?

....

There are certain jobs which people who have been in trouble with the police are not able to do. This is why we ask the next question.

Have you ever had to attend a magistrates court in relation to a criminal offence? Yes/No (*Please delete*)

If yes, please give details ....
....

Please note, this information may have to be passed on to the placement supervisor.

Source: *The Leaving Care Handbook*, Russell House Publishing, 2005.

Employment – Getting a Job; and Keeping it

Changing Places 7: Placement evaluation (to be completed by supervisor)

Young person's name ....

Placement Title .... Location ....

Supervisor's names ....

Main duties allocated to young person ....

Any additional duties ....

Equipment used ....

Training given ....

Level of support needed ....

Young person's apparent likes or dislikes about the work, displayed or verbalised
....

Relationship with colleagues ....

Any other comments ....

Date placement started .... Ended ....

Reason for finishing ....

Signed: .... Date ....

Position ....

Source: *The Leaving Care Handbook*, Russell House Publishing, 2005.

Changing Places 8: Evaluation form to be completed by young person

Name ....

Job Title .... Location ....

Name of Supervisor ....

Main Duties: ....

Additional Duties ....

Equipment Used ....

Training received ....

Skills learned ....

Level of support needed ....

Relationship with colleagues ....

Likes or dislikes about the work ....

Date placement started .... Ended ....

Reason for finishing ....

Signed .... Date ....

Source: *The Leaving Care Handbook*, Russell House Publishing, 2005.

The Leaving Care Handbook

TTW 1: Work placement details

Job/placement title: ....

Duties: ....

Department: ....

Placement address: ....

Manager: .... tel: ....

Supervisor: .... tel: ....

Place to arrive if different from above: ....

Person to ask for: ....

Dress code: ....

Lunch arrangements: ....

Does the young person need to bring anything with them: ....

Number of people in the team: ....

Job description available/similar role: ....

Time the day will finish: ....

Any other information: ....

Please return to: ....

Source: *The Leaving Care Handbook*, Russell House Publishing, 2005.

TTW 2: Monitoring information

This information will be used to make sure that everyone receives an equal service. Please tick the box that best describes you:

Age: 16–17 18–21

Ethnic Origin: White UK White European
  White other Indian
  Black Caribbean Black African
  Pakistani Bangladeshi
  Chinese Mixed race
  Other *(Please specify)*

Gender: Female Male *(Please delete)*

Are you a registered disabled person or do you have a disability? Yes/No *(Please delete)*

If your placement supervisor wanted to know in that way you are disabled, what would you want us to say?

....

....

There are certain jobs which people who have been in trouble with the police are not able to do. This is why we ask the next question.

Have you ever had to attend a magistrate's court in relation to a criminal offence? Yes/No *(Please delete)*

If yes, please give details

....

....

....

Please note this information may have to be passed on to the placement supervisor.

Source: *The Leaving Care Handbook*, Russell House Publishing, 2005.

Employment – Getting a Job; and Keeping it

TTW 3: Young Person Profile

Name: ....

Date of birth: ....

Address: ....

....

School or college: ....

Currently studying: ....

Qualifications: ....

Languages spoken: ....

Interests: ....

Career aspirations: ....

Any other relevant information – medical/health issues etc:

....

Emergency contact: Name: .... Telephone number: ....

Source: The Leaving Care Handbook, Russell House Publishing, 2005.

The Leaving Care Handbook

TTW 4: Young Person's personal information sheet

You will be working at (organisation's name in full): ....

Address: ....

....

Telephone number: ....

Supervisor/person to report to: ....

Date of your work experience: From .... To ....

Your working hours: From .... To ....

Dress code:
Uniform   shirt/tie   smart
Overalls   boots   casual
                                  other
(Please delete those not applicable)

These will be provided by:
Me   the company   work experience project manager

You should **not** wear: ....
(Please delete those not applicable)

Travel arrangements: ....

In order to get to your place of work on time, you need to leave home at: ....

I will travel by: ....

Tea/coffee breaks:

Time .... how long: ....

Lunch arrangements: ....

My lunch break is: for .... hour(s) from .... time to: ....

Packed lunch   canteen   lunch provided   other:
(Please delete those not applicable)

Health and Safety	Yes	No
Have you had a tour of the work area and welfare facilities?		
Action on discovering a fire – do you know what to do?		
Means of escape – have you checked exits?		
Fire warning system explained – by employer/supervisor?		
Do you know where the fire fighting equipment is?		
Can you find your way to the assembly point if there is an evacuation?		
Are the gangways/corridors clear of obstruction?		
Can you identify first aid facilities and first aiders?		
Are Health and Safety precautions followed, e.g. chemical/electrical/mechanical hazards?		
Lifting and handling – has this been explained to you?		
Use of personal protective equipment – is it needed?		
Can you identify your supervisor?		
Has a 'Be Safe' booklet been given to you?		
Who is responsible for accident report procedures?		

Name ....

I have received and understood the instruction/training/information as shown above.

Name .... Signature ....
(Please print)

Job title .... Date ....

Employer .... Signature ....

Young people should complete this form, with the help of their employer/supervisor to check they have understood the health and safety training on the first day of their work experience.
Supervisors, please return form to ....

Source: *The Leaving Care Handbook*, Russell House Publishing, 2005.

Employment – Getting a Job; and Keeping it

TTW 5: Young person's evaluation form

This form is to be completed by ....

before you leave your placement and are sent to ....

Your name ....

Name of company .... Department ....

Name of supervisor ....

How did you do?	Excellent	Good	Fair	Needs improvement

Communication skills

Talking and listening

Expressing own ideas

Recording clear messages

Using telephone, fax, e-mail, IT

Communicating confidently

Personal qualities and social skills

Respecting equal opportunities

Dealing with the public

Developing good relationships with colleagues and supervisor

Being responsible and reliable

Time keeping and punctuality

Dressing appropriately

Ability to accept praise

Ability to accept criticism

Hardworking and willing to learn

Motivation and enthusiasm

Ability to understand and follow instructions

Honesty

Equipment

Use of telephone

Use of fax machine

Computer packages – Word

Excel

Other

E-mail

Filing

Photocopying

Other work related equipment and skills
(Complete as appropriate)

Numeracy and literacy skills

Using numbers

Reading, e.g. for research

Writing

Problem solving

Overcoming problems

Using own initiative

Being able to ask for help

Would you recommend this placement to another young person?   Yes/No

Did you receive enough support?   Yes/No

What would have made this better, (if anything)?

Please add any other comments you may wish to make about your work experience. You can include anything you wish to record, e.g. 'I've done really well' 'Hard work but worth it' etc.

Name .... Signature ....
(Please print)

Date ....

Please return to ....

Source: *The Leaving Care Handbook*, Russell House Publishing, 2005.

97

The Leaving Care Handbook

TTW 6: Supervisor's evaluation form

This form is to be completed by ....
date and sent to ....

Name of young person: ....

Name of company: .... Department ....

Name of supervisor: ....

How did the young person do?	Excellent	Good	Fair	Needs improvement
Communication skills				
Talking and listening				
Expressing own ideas				
Recording clear messages				
Using telephone, fax, e-mail, IT				
Communicating confidently				
Personal qualities and social skills				
Respecting equal opportunities				
Dealing with the public				
Developing good relationships with colleagues and supervisor				
Being responsible and reliable				
Time keeping and punctuality				
Dressing appropriately				
Ability to accept praise				
Ability to accept criticism				
Hardworking and willing to learn				
Motivation and enthusiasm				
Ability to understand and follow instructions				
Honesty				
Equipment				
Use of telephone				
Use of fax machine				
Computer packages – Word				
Excel				
Other				
E-mail				
Filing				
Photocopying				
Other work related equipment and skills (Please complete as appropriate)				
Numeracy and literacy skills				
Using numbers				
Reading, e.g. for research				
Writing				
Problem solving				
Overcoming problems				
Using own initiative				
Being able to ask for help				

Please add any other comments you may wish to make about the young person placed with you.
....

Would you be willing to take a young person again for work experience? Yes/No

Any other comments regarding this scheme?

Name of supervisor .... Signature ....
(Please print)

Date ....

Please return to ....

Source: *The Leaving Care Handbook*, Russell House Publishing, 2005.

9

Employment – Getting a Job; and Keeping it

Linda Daniel and Ena Fry

This chapter has been written specifically for young people and their helpers.

Here are some points to help young people who are thinking about training and employment.

ⓘ Tips on applying for a job

Things to consider when applying for a job which has been advertised in a newspaper:
- Do you have the relevant qualifications being asked for?
- Do you have any relevant work experience being asked for?
- Check if there is a closing date. The sooner you apply the better!
- Is it within travelling distance for you?
- Do the hours of work suit you?
- What is the pay like?
- Is there any mention of training being offered?
- Remember there can be different names for the same job. Make sure you read the job details carefully.
- If you are unsure if the job is for you, send for a job description if one is available.

If you are making a telephone call, it is important to remember that the person on the other line is judging you by the way you talk. That doesn't mean using a 'posh' accent, but it does mean speaking clearly and to the point. Make some notes before you start if the call is important.

When you ring up about a job vacancy, always have the advert beside you so that you know:
- The number you want to ring.
- The extension number, if one is given – this is the number you ask for when the switchboard operator answers.
- The name of the person you need to speak to, or the department, usually personnel or human resources. If no name is given, you can say, I'm ringing about the job advertised for a . . ., and let the person at the other end put you through to the correct extension.

If you ring from a call box:
- Have plenty of coins – or use a phonecard that's well in credit – so that you don't get cut off before you've finished your call. If you use your mobile phone try it out first to make sure the reception is OK and check that the battery is fully charged.
- Have a pen and paper, or your diary, so that you can write down details (time, place, name of the person to see) if you are offered an interview.

You will probably have to provide basic personal details or you may have to leave your details in response to an answerphone message.

Prepare yourself before the call with:

- Information about yourself.
- Information about your qualifications and experience and why you want to apply.

Don't forget, first impressions count so:
- Be calm.
- Sound enthusiastic.
- Have all your personal information to hand.
- Give concise, informative answers.

Other things to think about are:
- The way you walk – think about the impression you give if you slouch, walk with your hands in your pockets or scrape your feet along the ground.
- The clothes your wear for an interview may need to be different from the ones you normally wear. Get some advice, talk it over with others.
- If you are at an interview or meeting, for example, and are offered a cup of tea with a saucer and also a biscuit, how should you respond? Often it is better to refuse rather than make a mess of things. It is perfectly acceptable to politely say 'no thank you'.
- In Britain, people often shake hands as a sign of greeting or when they are introduced to someone new. Think about this – a too firm handshake is really off putting but equally a wet, floppy handshake is just as bad.

But only you can decide what you wish to do, or how you wish to behave.

Job application forms

When you see a job advertised in the paper often the next step is to fill in an application form; the advertisement will tell you how to get the form. Remember, this is the first chance you have of impressing the employer!

Filling in job application forms – IMPORTANT!
- Read through the whole form before you start to fill it in. It is a good idea to photocopy the original and use this as your first draft.
- Follow the instructions on the form carefully – e.g. if asked, use BLOCK CAPITALS.
- Sometimes it is possible to download the form from the Internet – check the instructions to see whether they are happy for you to word-process your answers or whether they wish you to hand write the form.
- If you need to fill in the form by hand, write clearly and use a pen, preferably with blue or black ink – **never** complete a form in pencil.
- Try to answer all the questions. If something does not apply to you write *NA* (not applicable).
- Include all relevant information. Make sure you tell them about *all* your achievements and interests. Never sell yourself short!
- Make sure your form is neat, tidy and well presented.
- Check that your form is accurate and has no spelling mistakes. Ask someone to double-check it for you.
- Remember to sign and date the form.
- Take a photocopy of your completed form before sending it off. If you are called for an interview you can refer to this copy to refresh your memory.
- Return your form promptly – there is often a closing date for receipt of application forms and if yours arrives late you will **not** be considered for the job.

Employment – Getting a Job; and Keeping it

Writing a letter of application

- Always write neatly and clearly – it's a good idea to make a practice copy first. You can wordprocess your letter if the advert does not ask for a handwritten reply.
- If writing, use black or blue ink – a fountain pen or a fine roller-ball pen, rather than a biro. Use white, cream or a discreet pale coloured paper. Paper should not be lined. If you can't write straight, use bold lines under the paper to guide you.
- Make sure your spelling is correct – get someone to check it for you.
- If you start 'Dear Sir/Madam', you should end 'yours faithfully'. You use 'yours sincerely' only if you are writing to somebody you know.
- Make sure your signature is clear and print your name underneath.
- Apply for a job as soon as you hear about it.
- If you name people who will give you a reference, make sure you ask their permission first.
- Always say which job you are writing about and where you saw the advert – one firm may have several vacancies at the same time.
- Take a photocopy of your completed letter.

If the job advert says 'write for further details' or 'write for an application form' do just that! If the advert says 'apply in writing' you should give full details about yourself and your reasons for applying for the job.

Sample covering letter

John Smith
10 Flowerpot Road
Up-the-Garden-Path

20th September 2010

Hilary Jones
The Personnel Manager
Make-it-quick
Swamping Sands
Bournemouth

Dear Madam

Lathe Operator
Advertisement in Bournemouth Echo, 19.9.10

I am interested in the above job that was advertised in the Bournemouth Echo. I enclose a copy of my CV from which you will see that I have experience using a lathe during my woodworking lessons at school.

I have had the same Saturday job since October 2009 which shows I am reliable.

I can attend for an interview at any time except on Wednesdays when I am at college.

Yours faithfully

John Smith

Enc:
(This means you are enclosing other papers (CV, etc.) with your letter)

Writing a curriculum vitae

When you are applying for a job, you are sometimes asked to send a *curriculum vitae* (CV) which is an outline of your career to date. It is also a useful way of presenting skills and experience when applying to employers 'on the off-chance'.

Always enclose a covering letter explaining your reasons for applying for that particular job, without just repeating what is already in the CV or application form.

Preparing a curriculum vitae

A CV should be presented on a sheet of paper separate from any covering letter – preferably not more than two sides of A4. If possible word-process it so that it is easy to read, and ready should you need it again, amend and update it when necessary.

CV stands for *Curriculum Vitae*. The term is Latin. The dictionary definition says a CV is the course of one's life. Many companies and organisations ask for a CV when you apply for a job or you could send it to a company to see whether you are suitable for any job they may have. A CV is a way of telling an employer about yourself in a simple and easy to read way. The important thing about a CV is that it must be:
- Accurate, without even the smallest 'white lie'.
- Up-to-date.
- With no spelling or typing/writing mistakes – always get someone else to check it for you before you send it out.

You will need to ask one or two people to act as referees on your CV – you should ask a teacher, a social worker, your doctor, or someone for whom you have worked before – people who know you reasonably well, and who you think will speak positively and honestly about you. They may be asked to comment on your character, and your suitability for the job you are applying for. Every time you give the names of the referees when applying for a job, you should tell the people concerned, giving brief details of the job you have applied for.

Always keep a copy of your CV so you can:
- Read it before an interview.
- Up-date it when necessary.
- Use it as a help when filling in a job application form.

There are many different ideas about the best way to write a CV. The sample CV at the end of the chapter is just one example.

Ensure that you include all relevant information.

Don't sell yourself short, **but** be truthful, otherwise you will soon be found out!

Mention if you have any transferable skills such as a first aid certificate or a guide/scout leaders award.

Make sure your CV is clearly and attractively presented: use headings and bullet points to make it easy to read.

Photocopy your CV so that you can use it over and over again.

You could include a photograph of yourself on your CV if you wish.

If you do not have much work experience to quote, emphasise the abilities you have which will be of use in the job. These may be ones learnt as part of your hobby, such as being a team player, collecting the subscriptions, making posters etc.

You can adapt the order or the format of a CV to draw attention to your individual strengths or to suit a particular job that you are applying for.

If you are successful and asked for an interview, some interview questions might be:
- Why did you apply for this job?
- What do you feel you can bring to this job?
- What is your definition of working within a team?
- Although we are looking for a part-time worker, will you be flexible about any additional hours that may need to be covered?
- What particular skills do you feel that you can bring to this job? What evidence can you show of this, e.g. which things have you done so far illustrate it?
- What do you see as your major strength?

Think about how you might answer these questions beforehand and be ready.

Conclusion

Getting a job and keeping a job is not an easy experience for most of us. It requires care, trouble and hard work to **get** it and it requires care, trouble and hard work to **keep** it. Take advice from other people, learn by your mistakes and you will succeed.

Resources

DOTT (1997) *When Leaving Home is also Leaving Care: An Inspecting Service for Young People Leaving Care.* Yorkshire.
First Key *Putting Young People at the Centre: Developing Services for Care Leavers.* First Key.
Lifelong Project (2002) *Risk and Response.* Update, No. 6, 17–19, Manchester.
The Prince's Trust *Leaving Care*. Fact sheet.
The Who Cares? Trust (2002) *Employability: Building Futures for Young People in and Leaving Public Care.* London: The Who Cares? Trust.
Wheal, A. (2003) *Young People in Foster and Residential Care.* Lyme Regis: Russell House Publishing.
Hounslow Leaving Care Service: various documents including forms from Changing Places and Teenagers to Work schemes.

Sample curriculum vitae

Samantha Brooks   Age 15   DOB 23rd June 1989
26 St. John's Avenue
Fareham
Hampshire
PO25 1XX   Telephone 0123 0000

Education and Training
1999–2003: Ballharbour School

I will be taking the following exams in June:

Subject	Type of Examination
English	GCSE's
Mathematics	GCSE's
Geography	GCSE's
Biology	GCSE's
Music	GCSE's

I have also gained my bronze life-saving award.

Employment and Work Experience
I have worked in Newswell newsagents on Saturdays since November 1998.

Interests
I enjoy badminton and swimming and I also help run the school aerobics club. I am a member of the school choir and I play the piano to grade 3 standard.

Referees

Mrs. P. Green, Head of School   Mr. S. Singh Manager
Ballharbour School   Newswell
Smarts Lane   42 Station Road
Fareham PO23 2YZ   Portsmouth PO1 1ZZ
Tel. 01234 567890   Tel. 01987 65321

Section Five: Support to Sustain Family and Social Relationships

10

Family and Friends: Getting in Touch and Staying in Touch

Shelagh Beckett

Introduction

Leaving care may feel like a new and exciting stage in a young person's life but for many it can also be scary and daunting. At any time when we are faced with a major transition or big change in our lives, we can feel very vulnerable. Leaving care presents new opportunities, perhaps also new freedoms but some of these also carry the potential for risks and disappointments alongside the hope of forging rewarding lasting relationships.

This chapter aims to help staff and young people to think more about individual needs by focusing on each care leaver's family and other significant relationships. Worksheets provide opportunities to think about a young person's current relationships, future relationship needs and how contact may or may not meet these. For example, young people should have an opportunity for reflective space to consider the advantages and possible disadvantages of re-establishing contact.

The aim throughout is to encourage young people to feel entitled to make informed decisions and choices that take account of their emotional well-being.

The process of becoming looked after and the experience itself may, for many children and young people, mean many changes of many things, including the starting and stopping of placements. Whilst recent government initiatives have stressed the need to promote placement continuity, sadly this will not have been the experience of many young people leaving care today.

The need to enter public care is usually, though not always, related to pre-existing difficulties within family relationships. As Clayden and Stein wrote:

> *For most young people the acquisition of life skills is a gradual process beginning in childhood and progressing with increasing age and development. It is also a supported process usually taking place in the context of close and stable family and friendship relationships. And it is a participatory process involving family discussions, negotiations, risk taking, making mistakes and trying again. Looked after children are very likely to come from families where this kind of steady progress in acquiring self-care and life skills is not always found.*
>
> (Clayden and Stein, 1996)

Relationships between children and their family may subsequently improve but for many young people being looked after can contribute to further fracturing and fragmentation in family ties.

The experience of placement moves is all too common and tends to create additional difficulties for young people not only in respect of learning relationship-building skills but also having the opportunity to practise and develop comfortable, trusting relationships. Experiences will vary enormously. Each individual is likely to be influenced by their cumulative experience that will play a part in how they approach making and sustaining relationships both now and in the future. This has been well summarised by Howe:

> *Adverse relationship environments upset children's ability to develop social understanding and to cope with other people. Feelings of self-esteem and self-efficacy are likely to be low as a result of such experiences. Children who fail to develop a good understanding of their own emotional make up, other people and the social situations in which they find themselves, find social life difficult.*
>
> (Howe, 1998)

Whilst relationships between some young people and their parents may be fraught, other family relationships may have provided continuity. The reported experiences of young people leaving care has emphasised the significance of brother/sister relationships:

> *Siblings were a particularly important source of emotional support and for some of the young people their closest and most supportive relationships were with brothers and sisters.*
>
> (Biehal, 1999)

Some young people preparing to leave care may feel completely satisfied with the relationships that they already have in their lives and consider that these relationships are well-established in their day-to-day life. For other young people, leaving care may create uncertainty about who to keep in touch with, and raise questions about re-starting contact. Care leavers' closest friendships may typically be with other young people in the looked after system (Ward, 1995; Quinton et al., 1993).

Research on the use of assessment and care records has shown that although most looked after children were said to have some close friendships the majority of these were with other looked after young people. This fact may be positive in many respects – such as shared experience of adversity and awareness of difference – but may also carry inherent limitations, such as socialising with others who have low self-esteem and possibly low expectations.

At the point of leaving care young people may also experience an additional sense of fragmentation in their lives if they move on, whilst friends remain looked after in foster or residential care.

The prospect of making new friendships with others who have little knowledge or understanding of 'care' may be a huge challenge. For example, care leavers may be wary of how much to share about their personal circumstances and this may be perceived by them, and perhaps by others, as a barrier to making new relationships. Worksheets 1 and 2 (Appendix 10) are for the young care leavers to complete.

Self-esteem, relationships and contact

How you feel about yourself is likely to influence the decisions you make. Young people can benefit from safe opportunities to think about how their own view of themselves might influence what they are seeking from contact. This can be especially important when they want to re-establish contact with someone who has not treated them well in the past.

Young people can also be helped to think about what they can do that makes them feel happier. This might include identifying leisure activities, sports and physical exercise as well as opportunities for close emotional relationships.

Having high self-esteem and feeling good about yourself is made up of lots of things – it's not only about what you have achieved, it's also about knowing that there are some people to whom you are important and that you can show warmth and concern for people that really matter to you.

Relationships with friends, relatives or others that you can rely on, are important to think about and to take care of – spending time with people you like and who also like you, is something we all need and makes a big contribution to how happy we feel.

Trust, and keeping confidences: who can I talk to?

One of the things that helps us to get closer to other people is sharing our personal thoughts and feelings about our past as well as our hopes and plans for the future. You can probably think of times when friends have shared personal information with you and you have felt pleased that they trusted you enough to do this. Hopefully you have also had some good experiences of sharing some of your innermost thoughts with people that you trusted.

Sadly, most of us have also had some mishaps – times when we shared private and personal information that we trusted the other person to respect and they let us down.

When we are faced with making important-to-us decisions, it can help to talk about the possible advantages and disadvantages with someone you trust. To make the best decisions for yourself, you need to think carefully about who you can trust. For example, ask yourself questions such as:
- How long have I known this person?
- Do I really know them well enough to trust them?
- Have I shared private information with them before? If so, do I feel happy with the way that they dealt with this – were they helpful or unhelpful?
- If I haven't talked to them in depth myself, do I know whether they have been a trusted and helpful person to others?

If you're unsure how much to trust someone then take your time to get to know them better before you share too much information. Remember that once you have shared personal details about yourself or your family background, you can't take this back.

Taking care of my own needs

One of the most important choices is that of deciding to take care of yourself; to think about what helps to make you happy, or what might upset you, or put you in situations where you don't feel safe.

If you don't feel confident that you can make decisions that will keep you safe, then it is probably best to give yourself more time to work on this before, for example, deciding to re-establish contact with someone. Think about the following and perhaps discuss these in more depth with a trusted person:
- It's OK to think about my needs and what will make me happy.
- My safety is important – if I care about myself I won't deliberately put myself in situations where I'm not safe.

- Making any decision carries consequences, some of which might not be intended.
- Looking after my needs might mean that sometimes I make a decision that upsets or angers one or more people.

All on my own: alone or lonely?

Some young people say that one of the biggest hurdles they faced when they left foster or residential care was coping with feelings of loneliness. Being 'independent' can sound exciting and it may be great in lots of ways but most people also enjoy being part of a group at least sometimes. We all need to feel that we matter and that someone would notice if we were unwell or didn't turn up for work, at college or perhaps just the local pub! There are ways that you can promote links with people you like and people who want to maintain contact with you. For example, make sure that you let trusted friends and adults have details of different ways to contact you:

- address
- landline telephone
- mobile number
- e-mail address

You might want to think about getting some cards printed with your contact details on – why not ask your support worker about whether they could help you do this? Remember to let your social circle and support network know if you change your telephone number or move address.

Like any major change or transition, leaving care can provide an opportunity to re-think and re-evaluate who is important in our lives. No longer being in care, might mean that we feel completely free to resume contact with family and others who we have lost contact with. Perhaps you have lost touch with a foster carer or would like to re-connect with a young person that you used to know and got on with really well.

Thinking about re-starting contact: pointers to consider

- What do I know about why contact ended? Do I need to know more about why this happened before I decide to try to re-start contact?
- What am I hoping to gain by re-starting contact?
- How will I feel if this person doesn't want to re-start contact?
- Are there any risks that I need to think about so that I can protect myself?

Remember that 'risks' aren't just about things such as being physically hurt. They could also include being sexually abused or exploited or just feeling used. Ask yourself questions such as:
- Has this person encouraged me and helped me to feel good about myself?
- Has this person done things or acted in ways that have made me feel happy?
- Has this person acted in ways that made me feel angry, sad or upset?

If your answers to these questions raise doubts in your mind, think about who you can talk to before deciding whether to re-start contact. Although it can be tempting to think *and* hope that someone may have changed and might treat you better than they did in the past, try to be realistic and listen to what you feel inside. If friends or others urge you to be careful about resuming contact with someone, then remember that they have your interests at heart. They care about what happens to you. Other questions to ask are:

- What practical help do I need? For example:
  - Do you have an up-to-date address and telephone number for the person you want to contact?
  - Who can help you if you need to do some searching to find out a relative or friend's current whereabouts?
- Who can I talk to about how I feel? Think about who you trust to listen to you, someone who will respect such personal and private information.
- What sort of contact would I like? Think about this in stages – for example, would it help to have more information about what's happening in your relative's life before you decide to meet up? Beginning with sending a letter, card or making a telephone call might be a good way of re-starting contact with someone that you haven't seen for a long time.

Thinking about the above aspects might lead you to decide that you want to proceed with making contact, **or** might lead you to decide that the time is not right for you to go ahead at this stage.

Example

When Mariah was 18 she thought about resuming contact with her mother. Mariah learned that her mother was working as a prostitute and had long-standing problems with alcohol abuse – she had recently been offered a six week detoxification placement but had left this in the first week. After a lot of thought, Mariah decided that she needed to wait until she felt strong enough in herself to cope with seeing her mother again.

Building new relationships

Meeting new people and starting to get to know them not only involves spending time together but often includes sharing information about you and your life. It can be helpful to think about the extent that you want to confide personal information and with whom. Sharing private details about your history may feel like the right thing to do and may encourage you and a new friend to feel closer to one another. People tend to feel pleased if they know that they are trusted enough for another person to share such personal information. On the other hand, we've all had the not-so-good experience of having trusted someone and later wishing that we hadn't. This is one reason why most of us take time to 'build up' friendships and to get to know someone before sharing very personal and private details about ourselves, our families and earlier experiences in life.

Key things to ask yourself:

- What information about myself do I feel comfortable sharing? For example, do I want to talk about:
  - my own family experiences?
  - why I became looked after?
  - what it was like then and now?
- What do I put into this relationship?
- What do I get from this relationship?
- Is there 'give and take' or is it really too one-sided? For example, how would you answer the following:
  - If we go through a difficult patch am I prepared to work at things?
  - If 'Yes' also ask yourself: Do I think that the other person is also prepared to make a similar effort?

The Leaving Care Handbook

Example

Tom had lacked confidence in his ability to make and keep friends. Between the ages of 13 and 16 years, Tom had moved three times. He got into a pattern of thinking that he could only make friends or that people would only like him, if he bought them drinks, shared snack items or gave them items belonging to himself that he knew they liked. Tom was so desperate to have friends that he even stole some things that he thought would help him to be liked more within his group.

At the age of 18, Tom and his social worker recognised that whilst Tom had now learned a lot more about how friendships were formed, he was still vulnerable to being exploited. They spent time working out how Tom could gradually develop new relationships at work. With his worker's help, Tom set out some personal targets for building his confidence and getting to know new people. He and his worker agreed to meet every few weeks over the next few months to review how this was working. Tom was also encouraged to keep in touch with staff and friends at the residential unit he was leaving.

Valuing important people in our lives, and feeling valued

Relationships tend to become deeper and more important to us, when they have weathered the test of time and seen us through difficult as well as happy times. We may be able to make some friendships quickly – perhaps feeling an immediate 'connection' with people who share a similar outlook or those who have been through a similar experience to ourselves. There is also something special about people who have supported us over many years, through the bad times, as well as the good.

Keeping in touch with people that you feel close to can make a big difference to your life as well as to theirs. It usually helps us to feel better about ourselves if we know that there are people who have been and remain really interested to know how we are getting on. Think about the friends, relatives and previous foster carers in your life who 'champion your corner' and want the best for you. For example, ask yourself:

- Whose opinions and views matter to me?
- Who do I ask for advice, ideas or suggestions?
- Who makes me feel that I am likeable?
- Who do I enjoy spending time with?
- Who has helped me to feel that I am worthwhile – whether I am feeling 'upbeat' or 'down'?
- In the past, who has been pleased when I have done well or succeeded in some way – this could be at a sport, in a competition, at school or in some other area of my life?
- Who remembers special occasions in my life – birthdays or significant events, including any cultural or religious occasions that are important to me?

People might show their interest and belief in you in different ways:

- Making time to find out how you are feeling.
- Telling you that you're a great person.
- Praising and encouraging your efforts.
- Celebrating your achievements by buying you a card or present.
- Perhaps taking you out for a meal or to enjoy a favourite activity.

Similarly there are – or will be – people in your life for whom you want to make that extra effort. You care about how they feel and want to let them know this. You don't have to spend money to let people know that you care. Often, just telling them matters far more. Making a card, copying a CD, sending a photograph or a letter, and, if you enjoy cooking, baking a cake or similar treat might be a lovely way to say 'thanks for being there.'

Re-connecting with people who were once important to you but with whom you have lost contact, can also prove hugely rewarding. Sharing memories and filling in any gaps regarding past events in your life can help you to make better sense of earlier experiences. For example, you may not have a clear understanding of why a relative could not care for you or why you had to move from a foster carer that you liked and in whose home you felt happy. If you don't already have the necessary information to contact former carers, your support worker should be able to obtain details for you or perhaps ask a former foster carer to make contact with you directly. Fresh opportunities to ask questions and to gain a better understanding can help you to feel more whole as a person. Most foster carers will be delighted to hear from young people that they have cared for in the past. If you have lost contact with family members, re-connecting with parents, siblings and other relatives can make a big difference to how you feel about yourself and help you to make better sense of earlier experiences.

Families are all different and there are no guarantees – so it's important to try to be realistic. If you re-establish contact and are finding this upsetting or unhelpful then you need to take steps to protect yourself as outlined earlier. However, parents, as well as you, may have changed a great deal since you were last in touch.

Example

Surinder had become looked after at the age of 11. She had made allegations of sexual abuse against her father which her mother had found difficult, if not impossible, to accept. Eventually, Surinder's father had discouraged contact between mother and daughter so that by the time Surinder was 14-years-old she had completely lost contact with her mother. By then, Surinder was settled in a long term foster placement some distance away from her family home and felt she had little need of her mother, towards whom she felt angry and resentful.

As she matured, Surinder became more aware of the pressures that had been exerted on her mother, and learned that she had been scared of her husband who had physically assaulted her for many years.

At the age of 18, Surinder became reconciled with her mother who was now living independently and felt tremendous guilt at not having been more supportive of her daughter. Mother and daughter were able to talk openly for the first time about their individual experiences, and to start to re-build their relationship.

Surinder found that this was difficult sometimes, because she felt that her mother 'should somehow have been stronger'. However, she also recognised that her mother had continued to love her even when they were not in contact with each other. Looking back, Surinder says that she had always loved her mother even though this was a feeling that had been 'kept buried inside' her for several years. Surinder feels optimistic about her future – she says she's stopped blaming herself for what happened and knows that she and her mother were both 'victims' but are now 'surviving and thriving'. Surinder feels confident that she and her mother will spend more time together and says that they each feel they've been given 'a second chance' to get to know each other as mother and daughter.

The Leaving Care Handbook

Conclusion

Feeling valued by people who are important in our lives makes a huge contribution to how happy we feel. Leaving care may bring new challenges, risks and rewards in terms of the relationships in our lives. People who know us well, including those we have lived with, may take the opportunity to remind us that we matter to them, and that they want us to keep in contact even though we might be moving on. Becoming more independent, and able to take more control over some aspects of our lives, may also mean that we want to re-connect with people from our past.

Building healthy relationships that are based on genuine concern and that really allow for 'give and take' is probably one of the most important life skills we can ever have. It is part of being human that we will sometimes get hurt by a person who is close to us. Sometimes this hurt may be accidental and unintended – for example, when a person forgets our birthday or perhaps moves a long distance away so that we will not be able to see them as frequently. Other people may realise that they are behaving in a way that is hurtful or upsetting to us but they still continue regardless of our feelings. The skill in making and keeping relationships that contribute to our happiness is to know that we are worth loving and caring about. It can be hard to value yourself when past experiences have knocked your confidence and perhaps led you to be rather quick to blame yourself – or perhaps in an effort to protect yourself you can rush to criticise others. Remember that 'getting the balance right' in any relationship demands:

- Honesty and commitment on both sides.
- Genuine liking and respect for each other.
- A belief that the relationship is important and that it is worth making some effort to overcome minor niggles and difficulties.
- 'Give and take' – knowing that this can vary so that there will be times when one of you might need to receive or take more from the relationship but other occasions when you are the main 'giver'.

Remember also, that however old we become, we can still expect to rely on established friendships at the same time as being interested in making new relationships. We should expect to carry on learning from new contacts and also from comfortable, long-lived, close relationships – so it's really worth paying attention to them whether they are old or new in our lives.

Resources

Biehal, N. (1999) Partnership and Leaving Care. In *Lost and Found: Making and Remaking Working Partnerships with Parents of Children in the Care System.* Aldershot: Arena.
Clayden, J. and Stein, M. (1996) Self-care Skills and Becoming Adult. In Jackson, S. and Kilroe, S. *Looking After Children: Good Parenting, Good Outcomes.* Department of Health: HMSO.
Howe, D. (1998) *Patterns of Adoption.* Blackwell.
Quinton, D., Pickles, A., Maughan, B. and Rutter, M. (1993) Partners, Peers and Pathways: Assortative Pairing and Continuities in Conduct Disorder. *Development and Psychopathology.* 5, 763–83.
Ward, H. (1995) (Ed.) *Looking After Children: Research into Practice.*

New website helps to reunite people brought up in care

People brought up in care are usually encouraged to put the past behind them when they become adults, and often lose touch with their childhood friends and carers, some of whom were like family to them. Many who try to trace fellow care home residents and foster families find their efforts thwarted by the Data Protection Act, says David Batty of The Guardian. He has spoken to

Family and Friends: Getting in Touch and Staying in Touch

Mary Clear, who grew up in care and struggled for five years to obtain her social services files only to find all information about third parties removed. As a result of her experience she helped set up a website called Careleavers Reunited (www.careleaversreunited.com). The website is run by the UK Careleavers Association and is based on the successful schools reunion website, Friends Reunited. Since going live in September, 141 care homes in Britain, Australia and New Zealand have been added to the site, and 73 care leavers have signed up. Jim Goddard, another of the website's managers, says members commonly want to compare their experiences, both good and bad, with those of their former peers. The next step for the site is to set up a reunions section, where members can talk about meeting up with one another.

Section Six: Practical and Other Skills

Practical Help

Ann Wheal

Helping young adults to cope with practical skills

Learning practical skills can be not just useful, but a confidence booster; it can prevent worrying and generally help the transition to adult life. Special kinds of practical help are dealt with in other parts of this book, such as in Chapter 9, which is about getting and keeping a job.

Young people develop and mature at different rates and may be very competent in some skill areas while being inexperienced in others. They are not expected to be fully competent in all areas; some skills can only be gained by experience.

If you are a leaving care worker, it may be a good idea for young people to complete an information sheet such as the one at the end of this chapter, *Preparation for Adult Life: Information Sheet* on page 120 so you know something about those who you are trying to help.

The material that follows may be used to run a regular programme, say on one evening a week for six weeks for a group of care leavers, to help them cope. Alternatively, it can be used as a checklist to ensure young people have as much knowledge and skills as possible to cope alone.

A few tips if you are planning a programme. The venue should be comfortable and accessible, so they can invite former care leavers if they wish. Ensure a telephone line is available. Idealy, there should be no more than six young people present, with relevant roles and responsibilities identified. Adequate refreshments and work materials should be to hand. Once you have planned the programme, consider how you are going to run it. Preparation must progress at a pace to suit the young people. Think about the following:

- Your introduction to group.
- Aims of group.
- Why the group has been formed.
- Group rules:
  - Switch mobile phones off.
  - Listen to others when they are talking.
  - Respect others.
  - Arrive on time.
  - Tell the organiser if you cannot make it to the group.
  - No friends allowed on the programme.
  - No smoking in the building.
  - Confidentiality.

Practical Help

What are the young people's definition of independence? What do we mean by preparation for adulthood?

Some thoughts and ideas:
- Use working agreements.
- Use icebreakers and games.
- Establish an agenda.
- Create rituals.
- Clarify appropriate language.
- Consult the group – use their feedback to influence content and delivery.
- Integrate school policies.
- Use safe methods, e.g. distancing techniques, avoid personal exposure.
- Use national campaigns, which are targeting young people, so you ask their opinions. National campaigns can be used as a springboard for discussion or to run projects and events.
- Use appropriate resources and displays.
- Use outside agencies as sources of help and advice.
- Provide information on outside links, services, and community groups.
- Work with groups in different ways, i.e. size, gender etc.
- Use a question or suggestion box.
- Remember to have a 'just in case' plan.
- Think about working effectively with young people.
- Be aware of what is going on in television soaps and the music scene and use these to generate conversations. Young people are likely to be talking about them anyway.
- Take opportunities to try to engage with young people about emotions and feelings.
- Encourage them to think about their hopes and dreams, role models, ideas for the future.

Making links

- Utilise opportunities to address health issues. If there are sporting activities use these as an opportunity to look at health issues e.g. hygiene, or testicular cancer.
- Have a poster board. Encourage young people to bring in articles and pictures that they find interesting or exciting. Talk about these pictures with them. Enlarging quotes for the poster board can generate discussion. Use the board to display leaflets and posters of other local services and information for young people and update it regularly.
- Use photo stories. Provide young people with cameras and ask them to take photos of hobbies, interests and pleasures. Use the photos as a basis for discussions – remember confidentiality issues change.
- Arrange visits for young people to local health services for example, or invite visitors to come and talk to young people about different topics and issues.
- At the end of the programme, young people could be given a certificate or sent a letter acknowledging completion of the programme.

The following sections are for use with the young people. There are also a series of checklists at the end of the chapter.

Time keeping

One thing that many care leavers have identified as causing problems is time-keeping. It is not something that is easily learned and some people are always going to be better at it than others. Simple things that may help are:

- Having two alarm clocks, with one by their bed and the other on the other side of the room.
- Having a watch with an alarm that can be used through the day.
- Understanding the importance that employers and college lecturers pay to good time-keeping.
- Working out how long it takes to get somewhere and then allowing a little extra time in case of delays.

There are cultural differences regarding time-keeping expectations. These need to be understood and acknowledged as does the fact that in the world of work, meetings and study, being on time is important.

Managing money

- What is your weekly income (earnings, allowances, benefit)?
- Do you save any money? How?
- What is the total amount you need to live on?
- Does this include rent, bills, food, personal hygiene, travel and clothes.
- What do you spend the rest on?
- Are you given any other cash by the adults, e.g. travel, leisure?
- Do you borrow money? How you do pay it back?
- Do you spend money on anything you wish that you didn't? If so, what? Would you like help to stop?
- Do you know where to go for help if you get into debt?

Paying bills

You will need money for gas, electricity and water rates. Work out how much you use and put money aside to pay the bill when it comes in: you can do this often, or at regular intervals, like every three months. Get someone to help you with this. There will also be a standing charge which you have to pay whether you use a lot or a little gas and electricity. Some utility companies provide information cards to enable people to read their gas, electric and water meters and work out what they have used and how much it will cost. The cards are very simple to read, thus, X amount of units at Y price=£XY.

They are also very good for checking the bills are correct.

You will also need money for:
- Rent – £X per week.
- Council tax – for 'keeping the community going'. Some local authorities pay your council tax if you are just leaving care.
- Insurance for your belongings in case of damage, or they are lost or stolen.
- TV licence – make this a priority.
- Food and living expenses.

If you are working you are responsible for all the bills, including rent. If you are on income support or housing benefit the council will pay your rent – **but** you are still responsible and it is up to you to fill out the form and chase the Housing Office. If rent is not paid you can be taken to court with possible eviction.

Care leavers need to know how to pay bills, and find out about direct debits and standing orders. Banks and building societies will help. Should bills be paid monthly, weekly or quarterly? Help the young person to decide what is best for them. They can always change later if they wish. Also, find out whether they will be charged for using the service.

Practical Help

What happens if things go wrong? A personal advisor, leaving care worker or a debt agency (get the number from a library or the citizens advice bureau) should be able to help.

> *As a care leaver myself, I don't feel I was warned about getting into debt with credit agencies. I was helped in terms of basic budgeting, but when you have not had much in terms of material possessions and are suddenly old enough for credit or store cards etc., it is easy to get into debt. I have found this is a common problem with other care leavers I have met and we all agree that 'spending' can be a source of comfort, the bills at the end of the month aren't!*

Will your leaving care allowance pay for all the things you think you need to live independently? How much do the following cost: cooker, washing machine, fridge, microwave, bed, bedding, settee, cutlery, television, chest of drawers?

Are there some places that are cheaper than others for these things?

Is it worth buying some things second hand?

Where would you buy carpets? How do you lay them? What's underfelt?

What do they cost?

What paint is needed to make a room look better? What else is needed to do the job?

Who can advise?

Where do you get the best value for money?

Before you read on, try the *Budgeting Exercise* at the end of the chapter, page 121.

Housing

Moving means changes. In different stages of your life you have to make a decision as to what step you want to take when choosing what's right for you, whether it's a rented bedsit, a flat with friends or on your own.

Some young people have highlighted advantages and disadvantages of having your own place:

Advantages

- A place of your own!!
- A lot of freedom.
- Chance to get to know yourself.
- Make new friends.
- Do things in your own time.

Disadvantages

- Feeling isolated and lonely, who will you turn to?
- You have to do everything yourself. That means, cooking, washing, laundry and possibly, worst of all, wake yourself up.
- Finances – manage your own money and pay bills.
- Experience difficulties on your own.

Hygiene

The message of the media tends to be that we are living in a germ-infested state and that we must use the latest product to protect ourselves and our family. *The Good Housekeeping Magazine* suggests that washing-up liquid and household bleach will in most cases offer similar protection at a fraction of the cost.

What is important is:
- The cloths used for wiping worktops are clean.
- The cloths don't need to be replaced but soaked overnight in washing-up liquid and a small amount of bleach or put in the washing machine.
- Kitchen floors don't need to be washed every day unless there are pets or young children crawling on the floor.
- Chopping boards only need to be thrown away if they are scored.
- Glass, melamine or wooden boards can be cleaned thoroughly using the same two products.
- Toilets can be kept sterile with bleach – but don't use this with other products as the two together may cause a chemical reaction that will remove the glaze from the pan.
- Fridges should be kept clean and wiped out in the same way.
- Food in fridges should be kept covered, especially cooked and uncooked meats that should also be stored separately.
- Bathroom and kitchen sinks can also be cleaned with these products as can cookers provided they are not allowed to get too dirty.

Warning: Care needs to be taken when using bleach as it can damage clothes, carpets and other goods.

Cooking, menus, diets

Our society expects adults to provide and eat suitable food. It is one of the basic rules by which we live. Any help we can give to empower young adults to be comfortable in this role will raise their self-esteem and benefit everyone.

> *Who can resist the tempting waft of freshly fried chips and burgers, or the intoxicating aroma of a succulent lamb biryani? OK, so it's about as healthy as being run over by a bus and probably makes my insides look like an explosion in a treacle factory, but that's entirely missing the point. Fast food is quick, cheap and convenient.'*

Self-confessed junk food addict

There are many experts only too ready to say what you should or should not eat as an adult or as a child, but food can give rise to tensions for many reasons other than its nutritious value. There may be concerns about time and cost etc. Advice about food needs to be carefully given and should not be too prescriptive. Here are some ideas:
- Suggest options that are reasonably within budget.
- Allow for diets, whether these are for medical or cultural reasons.
- Recipes should be simple enough to follow, backed by pictures and instructions.
- Ideas should allow for personal choice and for personal lifestyle.
- Suggest a broad range of options within the main food groups.

We are bombarded by media images, which suggest that we are less than perfect if we cannot rustle up a banquet for forty, in half an hour! There are many programmes on television about cooking which provide instruction in the exotic and unaffordable rather than the basic. These days people watch cooking programmes but are not motivated by them to try out the dishes – convenience foods do it all for us.

Whatever the arguments for and against, cooking a meal is a basic skill, which can lead to adult confidence and satisfaction when successfully accomplished. In order to foster skills in cooking, we need to help young adults to:

- Make suggestions for affordable menus.
- Show an interest in nutrition e.g. the benefits of fruit.
- Have information about the merits of different food groups, proteins, carbohydrates, vegetables.
- Provide a suitable forum in which ideas can be exchanged and recipes attempted together which are within budget, simple to remember, fun to eat and nutritious.
- Practice the same recipe again and again if you wish.
- Go to the supermarket together to select ingredients, or get a week's shopping within an agreed budget.
- Select recipes which can be given out in pictorial form so that those who are unable to read, or speak English, can join in.

What else will help?
- Encourage experimentation and diversity – try a new vegetable together.
- Ask members from different ethnic groups to hold tasting and cooking sessions.
- Compare home cooked and convenience foods for taste, price and nutrition.
- Enjoy a meal together in a restaurant as part of a group outing.
- Put the fun back into food – it may be a chore, but it **can** be enjoyable.
- Praise and respect all attempts to improve everyone's diet.

There is a huge amount of cookery and recipe books about. Jumble sales and second hand book shops are just two places where you can buy them very cheaply. Find simple how to cook books first and then if you wish, get some more complicated recipe books later.

Conclusion

When a young person leaves care they have to take on all sorts of responsibilities and learn many new skills just at a time when they should be out enjoying themselves.

> *I don't know why but I seem to enjoy the company of older people. All my friends seem to think about is what shoes or dress to wear on a Friday night. I've got so many other things to think about . . .*

Over 15 years ago, Steve, an 18-year-old care leaver said, 'I have nothing in common with people of my age. I'm 18 going on 40'.

Sadly, not very much has changed over the years. Care leavers still have to take on so much responsibility when they should be enjoying themselves. Clearly, what we all have to do is help care leavers to take their responsibilities seriously but at the same time find ways to encourage them to enjoy themselves and have fun.

Resources

Fostering Network/Greenwich Council/First Key (2003) *Preparation for Adult Life.* London: Fostering Network.
Mountain, A. (2004) *The Space Between: Bridging the Gap Between Workers and Young People.* Lyme Regis: Russell House Publishing.
Wheal, A. (2004) *Adolescence, Positive Approaches to Working with Young People,* Lyme Regis: Russell House Publishing.
Wheal, A. (2003) *Young People in Foster and Residential Care.* Lyme Regis: Russell House Publishing.
Wheal, A, and Emson, G. (2002) *The Family Support Handbook.* Lyme Regis: Russell House Publishing.

The Leaving Care Handbook

Preparation for adult life group: Information Sheet

Name ....

D.O.B ....

Address ....

....

....

Type of accommodation ....

Financial situation: Living allowance from leaving care team: JSA: Income support *(please circle)*. Are you studying

Are you a young mum?

What would like out of this programme?

What do you see as your strengths and weaknesses?

Practical Help

Budgeting exercise

Aim: to help carers and young people plan for the cost of living.

Imagine yourself living in a bedsit on benefits. You have £47 a week, the current level for an 18-year-old to cover all expenditure (except rent). Together with the young person, and using the following chart, draw up a plan of how this money could be allocated. Could *you* manage? How?

Managing on a shoestring	weekly	monthly	yearly
Rent			
Food			
Travel to work or training			
Travel for leisure			
Clothes			
Phone calls, stamps			
TV licence			
Water charges			
Electricity			
Gas			
Laundry			
Cleaning materials, general household goods			
Toiletries and make-up, meals out			
Alcohol			
Cigarettes, magazines, books			
Presents			
Entertainment (e.g. videos, DVDs, clubs, cinema)			
Loans/HP			
Other			
TOTAL			

The Leaving Care Handbook

Accommodation checklist

What type of flooring?	Wooden	Carpets
Advantages:	Does not stain No fleas! Easy to clean	Feels warm Looks nice
Disadvantages:	Can be cold Can be slippery Can mark more easily	Needs vacuuming weekly Scotchguard is expensive
What type of cooker?	Gas	Electric
Advantages:	Instant heat Faster to cook	Easier to connect Safer with on/off switch On wall, away from kids
Disadvantages:	More dangerous Needs expert fitting	Takes longer to heat/cool

NB Some estates do not give you any choice – most high rise blocks use electricity.

ⓘ *Moving In – Handy Tips!*

- Get a folder to keep all your paperwork in.
- Write down all your meter readings.
- Don't 'fiddle' with gas or electric appliances – call in the experts.
- Buy a fire alarm pack and extinguisher, make sure you know how to use it, and that you do use it!
- Buy rubber gloves.
- Buy a settee with washable covers, or a second set of covers.
- Check prices in certain shops for special offers.
- Buy small taster pots of paint to check out colour and to patch up marks later.
- Wash woodwork and let it dry before you paint.
- Use masking tape to put round windows to protect from paint and then remove it when paint is dry.
- Use gloss paint for doors and skirting boards (rub them down first using fine or medium sandpaper).
- Choose a brush that is the right size for the paintwork.
- Use matt or vinyl silk for walls (matt is not shiny at all).
- Use a roller for large areas and a brush for small areas and corners.
- Wash out roller and clean brushes after each use. The paint pot will have instructions.
- Get insurance – from council scheme or post office.
- Buy curtain material twice the width of the windows.

✔ *Questions when viewing a property*

- What is the exact rent?
- Is there a heating contribution that I have to pay each week?
- How do I pay the rent? Is there a Rent Book? Where is it? How often do I pay the rent? Where do I pay the rent?

Practical Help

- Is there help to complete the HB (housing benefit) form?
- Would I be better with a card or key to pay my bills? How can this be arranged?
- What state of décor is the place in? Do I get a decoration allowance? If so, how much and when do I get it?
- Do I need a gas or electric cooker? What size?
- Is there space for a fridge? Is there plumbing for a washing machine?
- Will I need carpets, or rugs?
- What size are the windows for fitting curtains?
- Do I have a shed, garden, parking space?
- What do I do with my rubbish?
- What furniture will I need immediately?
- How much cleaning needs to be done? What do I need to do it and where do I start?
- When do I get the key and who will help me to move in?

ⓘ *Housing safety tips*

- Never leave keys in the door – you may get locked into the room, flat, house.
- When visiting a new place, quickly look around and make a safety plan for exit if you think this might be necessary.
- Take someone with you if you have a doubt about safety.
- Make a decision about whether to enter someone's home or not; or whether to let them into your place – check their ID if you are not sure.
- Find out if anyone else is in the house if you visit alone.
- Read all safety procedures for the building you are using. If there aren't any, then devise some and get them approved.
- Use all safety locks provided on any premises – to prevent unwanted visitors entering as well as ensuring the safety of everyone and stopping children 'escaping'.
- If you have a child, make sure there is a safety bolt that you can use all the time, otherwise children soon learn to open front doors and may 'escape' to do some exploring without you knowing.

✓ *What do I need to have when I move in?*

- Cleaning materials – for toilet, sink, windows, paintwork.
- J-cloths.
- Toilet rolls.
- Light bulbs.
- Kettle/mugs/tea/coffee/milk.
- Tape measure.
- Sofa.
- Kitchen utensils.
- Pots and pans.
- Bed and bedding (one duvet, one pillow, two sets of sheets, pillowcases, duvet covers).
- Towels.
- Washing machine – optional, but may be cheaper in the long run.
- Fridge or fridge/freezer – optional.
- Cooker.
- Toaster.
- Iron/ironing board.
- Storage, e.g. wardrobes.
- First aid box.
- (A television, if you are desperate!)

The Leaving Care Handbook

✓ What do I need to do when I move in?

- Check the keys and give the spare one to someone you can trust.
- Tell the gas, electric and water company you have moved in so bills will be in your name – make sure you are not responsible for the previous tenant's arrears.
- Clean the bath, sink and, toilet.
- Wash the paintwork.
- Clean the windows (inside).
- Clean the floors.
- Paint or paper the rooms if needed.
- Put up curtains.
- Lay carpet/flooring.
- Buy furniture.
- Unpack your clothes.

ⓘ Other tips!

- Remember to apply for housing benefit if eligible and return the form the council sends you every six or twelve months. If your circumstances change, you need to reapply.
- If you complete a Community Care Grant Form, don't exaggerate the prices!
- Keep some of your Leaving Care Grant back in case you need money later.
- Decide if you want support.
- If you have any problems, tell someone – the earlier, the better!

✓ Other practical skills checklist

- Have you sewn on a button?
- Can you do other simple mending of clothes?
- Can you use a calculator? Have you got one?
- Can you weigh and measure? Length; weight; fluid?
- Can you do simple first aid? What?
- Can you mend a puncture on a bike?
- Do you need help with any of these? If so, do you know who will advise?

✓ Money checklist

- Can you add up a shopping price list?
- Have you made a budget for a week's shopping?
- Do you need help with any of these?
- Which of the following bills have you seen? Food, clothes, electric, gas, water rates, TV licence, council tax, telephone, and rent (as part of a written agreement).
- Do you understand all/any of them? If not, would you like some help?

✓ Food checklist

- Can you read and follow a recipe or follow instructions on packets?
- Where would you go for food shopping?
- How often do you go food shopping and where?
- Have you been food shopping on your own? Where? How often?
- Are you able to use a cooker safely? Do you know about gas or electricity?
- Can you help prepare or cook meals? Can you cook a hot meal for yourself?

- Do you know how to plan what you are going to eat so you get a balanced diet?
- Do you know how to use a fridge or freezer, e.g. how long food keeps; that you should keep certain food separate from others; to keep some things wrapped up or in boxes etc?
- Do you know about kitchen hygiene? How to wash up?

12

Social and Emotional Skills

Ann Wheal

Helping young adults to cope with personal skills

Many care leavers just don't seem to have fun. Having fun doesn't mean getting so drunk you can't remember what happened or to help forget what is going on in your life. Having fun means enjoying yourself, laughing, enjoying other people's company, having a good time. Hopefully, by learning about and working on some of the things in this chapter and understanding themselves better, care leavers may learn to leave their worries behind them and to **have fun**.

This chapter is written in response to requests by care leavers for specific help. Many of the topics discussed in this next section cannot be taught as such; more, they are topics for discussion, both individually and in groups. In this way young people can be helped to learn new skills and to make decisions about how they wish to behave in life. At the end of the chapter are some checklists for work with the young people.

It is always a dilemma to know how far one's own life experiences and cultural expectations should be imposed on young people. However, if you ask them, most will tell you they want to know how to behave or what to do in certain circumstances. As one young adult said, some weeks after her 18th birthday:

> *By the way, thanks for the present. My friend told me to thank you. I probably should have thanked you before but I didn't realise.*

Some social skills

Sharing and team working

> *Because I have never been parented properly I didn't know about sharing – I've always had to look after number one.*

Sharing is very hard to teach anyone who is already grown up as it is usually something you learn along life's way. However, sharing and team working go hand in hand. Joining in with things helps: a recreational or a regeneration project, playing football or hockey for a local team, playing in a band or doing voluntary work may all help. You have to learn to consider others, to share the information you find, to pass the ball in front of goal rather than always going for the goal yourself and ensuring that everyone gets their share of rotten jobs as well as the good ones.

Coping with reality

Coping with reality is also a very hard thing to learn. Whilst in care a young person may receive money for this, money for that, special allowances, free travel etc., and then when they leave care they are on their own to manage their finances.

They will know about their rights whilst in care, yet when they become employed their employment rights are considerably reduced. Similarly, they will have had someone to get them up in the morning and in all probability someone to wash their clothes and clean their accommodation. They will tell you they can't get up in the morning, so they don't get to work or college on time. For a very few young people this may be the case but for most they need to learn organisational skills so they can get their clothes ready the night before and buy food and cleaning products sooner rather than later. In other words, to plan ahead and to anticipate things.

Listening

Many care leavers are poor listeners. Somehow, the care system encourages them to give their views, to say what they think and to complain if things don't work out the way they should. There is nothing wrong with that, but too often they don't learn to listen to what others have to say, sometimes interrupting people in the middle of a sentence. Knowing when to keep quiet is an important skill that can be learned with practice. Interrupting someone or not listening can also give the wrong impression; being noisy and aggressive can be a sign of insecurity.

Social etiquette

At an inner-city multi-race college people from industry were invited to take part in a business game. Some students were serving tea and coffee for the guests and the other students were taking part in the game. It very soon became clear that some from both groups of students had not used a cup, saucer and spoon before. After the session some staff met with the student council where knowing the social norms about behaviour were discussed. The students overwhelmingly asked that everyone should have an opportunity to learn to eat using cutlery that has been set out in restaurant fashion; to drink from a cup using a saucer; to use a napkin; about whether to shake someone's hand or not; when to sit down or remain standing etc. They felt that everyone should have an opportunity to learn these things which would enable them to make choices about how they wished to behave in the future. Care leavers should have similar opportunities.

Communication

Being a good communicator is something most of us have to work at. Very few people are born with such skills. Care leavers are no different, but sometimes, due to their personal circumstances, they do not receive help and advice at an early age, so they often have some catching up to do in specific areas. Communication is all around us. It is the way we walk, the way we dress, the style of our hair, the music we like, the company we keep *and* the way we speak, both verbally and as the written word in e-mails and text messages.

Sometimes care leavers sound incredibly aggressive or seem extremely shy. They may not naturally be that way but they give the false impression because they lack self-confidence or the skills to express themselves in their intended way.

In care: to tell, or not?

A colleague who knew nothing about young people in care commented when she met some of them at a summer school that she couldn't understand why they kept telling her, and the rest of the peer group, that they were in care. Others deny to themselves they are or were in care and keep it a secret at all costs. Others try to not tell anyone when their circumstances change and they get away from their previous environment only to discover that the only way they can get appropriate services is to admit they are in care. Clearly all groups need help to decide who to tell, when to tell, what to tell and how to tell.

Self-confidence and self-esteem

'Confidence comes from achievement', and 'success breeds success' are two well-known sayings. If we can help young adults to achieve something in their lives, no matter how small, then this will help them up the rung of the confidence ladder. The achievements can be at a personal level: re-contacting an old friend or visiting an aged relative; learning a new sporting or artistic skill; getting and keeping a job; starting a new college course; or passing an exam. However, we all need encouragement, someone there to listen about our achievements and to offer congratulations when appropriate.

There are many pressures which result in some young people having feelings of low self-esteem. Many young people who have been in the care system still blame themselves for what happened years later as the following shows:

> *I went into care when I was nine years old. My dad had left me some months before. He couldn't stand my Mum's drinking. I remember feeling it was my fault Dad had left. I also thought, because everyone said I looked like my Mum, that I'd turn out like her.*

(Young person, aged 19)

This young person carried through into adulthood her belief that it was her fault her father had left. She thought everything else that happened was because of the father leaving. For a long time, whenever anyone moved to another area and said goodbye she believed the others were leaving because she did not like them.

Early decisions made with limited life experiences, can lead us to believe that we are:

- stupid
- evil
- worthless
- powerful
- smart
- clever

Experiences may reinforce these feelings and reinforce our early view of the world.

To change these beliefs a young person will need to be offered positive role models, offered alternatives, and be sensitively challenged on their current perceptions of reality.

As Anita Mountain says:

> *One way to deal with low self-worth is to use the technique of **positive reinforcement**. For example, if a young person tends to use illness to get attention but we know that they are very good at art we need to reinforce the legitimate ways of getting attention such as through their artwork. In this way the young person is enabled to move from defining themselves as ill, towards defining themselves as artistic and productive: and thus have a healthier foundation on which to base any subsequent self-assessment.*

(Mountain, 2004)

In order to reach one's potential, it is necessary to have a self-image with which we are happy and a level of self-esteem which makes us feel:

- valued
- worthy
- appreciated
- capable
- satisfied
- acceptable

Poor self-image may result from:
- Comparisons with media role models and with friends and family.
- Adverse comments from others.
- Perceived body faults which cannot be changed.
- Failed attempts to make changes.

Social and Emotional Skills

- Lack of emotional awareness of one's feelings and their effects.
- Lack of knowledge of one's strengths, limits and capabilities.
- Perceived attitudes of others.

In order to raise self-esteem we need to raise self-belief. We need to provide opportunities for young people to:

- Respect their feelings.
- Handle their feelings with care.
- Accept that they may make mistakes.
- Praise positive achievement.
- Resist comparisons with their peers.
- Listen to what they say.
- Explain their own feelings.
- Learn coping and surviving skills.
- Be praised for a skill or ability they already have.
- Be rewarded for tasks or achievements.
- Take responsibility for their lives long before they leave care.
- Learn to state and then work to achieve a goal.
- Share joyful experiences.
- Relax and enjoy being themselves.
- Be proud of themselves.
- Understand how their own thoughts can affect the way they feel about themselves.
- Examine the feelings which hold them back.
- Be motivated to change their lives.
- Learn skills which lead to a job or qualifications.
- Gain motivation and enthusiasm.

There is no easy solution to raising self-esteem and sometimes counselling is required in order to help change a mind-set which is giving rise to low self-esteem.

> *When self-esteem is high, they are likely to be confident, positive, sociable, kind to others and more willing to attempt new tasks. When it is low, children may be negative, withdrawn, socially insecure and can even be quite paranoid . . .*
>
> (Green, *Beyond Toddlerdom*)

Low self-esteem in young people is every bit a bar to progress as it is in adults. Young people are also susceptible to perceptions about their:

- body image compared with others
- academic abilities
- social success
- physical prowess

How they deal with these issues will largely depend on their temperament and their ability to bounce back after putdowns. Young people could draw up a list or chart on what they could do, say five years ago, now and what they hope to be able to do in five years time. They could then do a similar thing but make a list under 'I can', 'I can't', and 'I will'. This is useful for both individual and group work.

Some words for young people to think about and also to form part of discussions:

- ambition
- setting targets
- affirming
- aims, personal goals
- aspirations
- improving

- getting better
- developing
- encouragement
- positive versus negative
- constructive
- building up

Building self-confidence

Self-esteem and self-confidence go hand in hand. If we truly wish to prepare young people to feel comfortable in a variety of situations in their life where they might find themselves in the future then everyone has a responsibility to help them learn skills and behaviour patterns. At the end of the chapter are some things which may help them think about things differently and help them learn about themselves: *Life Plan*; *Feeling Down*; *Tips to Cheer Yourself Up*, etc., pages 144–5.

Coping strategies

Stress and pressure are part of modern living, but excess stress can lead to:
- Increased anxiety and irritability.
- Increased smoking or drinking – or both.
- Loss of interest and motivation.
- Reduced concentration.
- Poor performance levels.
- Increased anger and frustration.
- Inability to ask for help or delegate to others.

When stress builds up and is not dealt with it can lead to:
- physical illness
- depression
- loss of vocation
- low self-esteem
- extreme fatigue

Stress may result from:
- pressure of work
- lack of recognition
- low pay
- adverse environments or conditions
- lack of privacy
- lack of training or instruction
- bullying or harassment
- money worries
- loneliness

What can we do about it? Support systems act as an outlet for stress by supplying a forum for letting off steam.

Other ideas on how to solve problems:
- Find a listening ear.
- Mutual support – sometimes stress can be lessened by trying to help colleagues or other people deal with their own crises.
- An acknowledgement of feelings.
- Time out to cool off or relax for a few moments after stressful situations.

Everyone has to find and develop their own support systems. These may be family, friends or close work colleagues. If in work, some employers may offer a formal staff support scheme which may or may not be helpful.

We all experience stress to varying degrees. When it won't go away, we need to develop strategies to cope with it in order to lessen its detrimental effects. On the following pages, there are a variety of useful strategies to try. Some will work better for you than others, but all will be useful for someone. Go on, try them – just reading them might help too!

Social and Emotional Skills

Emergency coping strategies

1. **Humour:** Laugh it off outwardly or inwardly. See the funny side. Talk very seriously but wear a huge grin. Threaten to do something ridiculous, e.g. 'If you do that again, I'll pull your ears off'.
2. **Reason with yourself:** Tell yourself that this is not the life crisis you are making it out to be. In a week, month, year it will be a memory.
3. **Distancing:** Mentally step outside a circle, leaving the problem and the people inside the circle. Look at it from a distance and look at your participation in it.
4. **100 SRs:** Imagine you have only 100 stress responses left. If this were so, wouldn't you use them wisely? Is this person or situation worth using one up for? Say to yourself, 'You are not important enough in my life for anger and a rise in my blood pressure'.
5. **Mr Shiftit:** Move the problem to a later time. Suggest discussion at the end of the day or after the meeting. Be determined to calm down before that time and know what you are going to say.
6. **Calming:** Repeat softly to yourself, 'Calm down, calm down'. At the same time, make a conscious effort to relax your facial, shoulder and neck muscles. Count backwards from 10 to 1.
7. **Breathe it away:** Breathe in deeply and say, 'Peace in'. Breathe out deeply and say, 'Problem gone'. With **practice**, this can reduce tension in twenty seconds.
8. **Reason with others:** Someone who stays calm, calms others. Mentally stand above the situation and guide your behaviour as if using a puppet.
9. **Compartmentalise:** When a problem is worrying you, but you are unable to act immediately, mentally place the problem in a box or room, close the lid or door and walk away. Promise yourself that you will come back to it and **deal** with it when first able to do so.
10. **Worry session:** Develop a worry session. Store up the problems for a special worrying time that is allowed to last for a short specific time. All worries must be dealt with at this time only.
11. **Beam me up Scottie:** Saying this phrase to yourself often lightens your approach to a stupid or intolerable situation, and helps you to see the funny or pathetic side of your work.
12. **Thanks for small mercies:** Feel thankful that you do not behave like the person causing the problem. Reduce your anger to a sense of gratitude that you are not as irate as the offender.
13. **Karma:** A Hindu remedy is to try to accept that everything is 'Karma' – a little bit like 'That's Life' but deeper. It is more of an acceptance of life events **after** they have occurred. You cannot put the clock back and change the past, therefore you must accept that it has happened.
14. **Reverting:** Pulling faces and using silly noises can work wonders. Make sure there are no witnesses!
15. **Feign pain:** Appear to be deeply hurt and cut to the quick by a remark or by someone's behaviour. Play to a sense of compassion and honour.
16. **Imagery:** While the person is 'in action', imagine their face turning purple or a load of custard (or worse) dropping on them.
17. **Pause for thought:** Engage brain before putting mouth into action. A pause of only seconds can avert a crisis or an unpleasant scene.
18. **Perspective:** Ask yourself what the real priorities are in your life. *Are they these people or this place?* Your priorities are your own well-being and that of your loved ones. These problems are on the periphery of your life.

The Leaving Care Handbook

19. **Looking forward:** Bring your mind off your anger. Think of the nicer parts of your life. What are you going to do that evening, that weekend? Focus your mind on the **real** part of your life.
20. **Break the spell:** Look for reasons behind the other person's actions or words. Recognise when they are under stress or appreciate that they could be. Try being a tower of strength!
21. **Moaning deadline:** When at home, set a deadline (e.g. 7 pm) for moaning about work and the problems you are facing there. And make your partner stick to the deadline too.
22. **Be tough:** Be tough on yourself. Tell yourself to snap out of this anger or mood. There are so many people worse off than you. No-one forces you to do anything – it is your choice.
23. **Unlock:** Never get locked into disagreements. They have a tendency to spiral and draw you in. Better to stand away. Your opponent will think better of you when he or she has cooled off.
24. **Cutting off:** As you leave work or whatever you are doing (angry or annoyed) have your favourite music or an amusing tape to listen to on the way home. Set landmarks after which you promise yourself not to think about or dwell on the issues. If alone have time for a good scream or curse, after which say, 'That's it! No more! My real life now begins'.

Making friends and forming relationships

Some people find making friends easy, and others find it very hard. Some people call someone they have just met 'a friend'. Others use the term with more care.

A friend is someone you can trust, who you can talk to and want to spend time with.

It is often hard for care leavers to make new friends, as most 17-year-olds have very little else to think about other than clothes, parties and discos; whereas careleavers have to think about rent, bills, food, budgeting as well. Care leavers will also have had a wide variety of life experiences and may not be used to having a close relationship with anyone.

As a result of past experiences care leaver's sexual awareness may be heightened, or the reverse, and they may feel revulsion towards that person or anyone else who reminds them of that person. This often makes it more difficult for them to make or trust new friends. Similarly, they may have come from difficult backgrounds where they've moved around a lot and not had a chance to make 'best friends'. They may not, therefore, have gone through the usual process of making and keeping friends.

They may also be very lonely, so if someone from the opposite sex comes along and gives them some attention they may fall madly in love with them, sometimes to the exclusion of everyone and everything else. This person may also be much older than they are; a mother or father figure; a car owner; someone with plenty of money. Having not previously had a loving, caring, relationship with an adult may again make new and lasting relationships difficult.

One of the hardest lessons to learn about friendships is self-control – how not to lose your temper, to try to look at things from others' points of view, not just your own. If a relationship is worth having then it is worth maintaining; that sometimes you have to compromise, make allowances, or swallow your pride and say sorry – this goes for adults as well as young people.

Many care leavers are used to 'looking after No.1' and managing on their own. When they get into a close or loving relationship they often don't know how to share, not just practical things but information about themselves; they think they shouldn't bother someone, when in fact the person concerned would probably be upset and disappointed if they found out – naturally wishing to help the person they care about.

Care leavers need opportunities for discussing and talking about all sorts of things and listening to others' points of view, which will help them with their friendships.

The loneliness of living independently may be very hard to cope with for a young person who is used to having people around them all the time and someone to call on in time of need. Make sure they know of all the different points of contact available to help them.

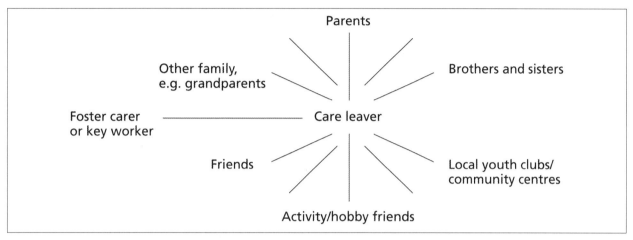

Figure 12.1 *Feeling lonely, who can help?*

Feeling lonely: who might help?

If a young person feels isolated or lonely they could contact or visit any of those shown below:

- Other people who have been looked after.
- Family and relatives.
- Samaritans.
- Carers.
- Other people who have been helpful in the past.
- Local after-care group.
- Ex-teachers.
- Local drop-in centres.
- Youth leader.
- Community groups.
- Church/temple/mosque members.
- Old school friend.
- Who else?
- (Other spaces can be filled in with any people who can give support).

There are lots of practical ways to help make the transition to young adulthood seem less daunting such as:

- Keep an up-to-date address book with names and contact details of people who are important.
- Swap addresses with friends.
- Let everyone know your new address if you move on.
- Give your address to someone who will know where you are and let other people know what it is. Someone may want to contact you.

Taking some positive action, such as any of the following, can help not just with loneliness and feelings of isolation, but it can also help to find and make new friends:
- Doing something to help others.
- Going jogging, swimming or doing some other physical activity.
- Taking up a new hobby or sport.
- Joining a club or society.
- Learning a new skill.
- Changing the layout of a room, spring cleaning it or even decorating it.
- Drawing a new support chart.

Decision-making

Ideas	effect on other people	judgements	what's best?
Observations	why did it happen?	the evidence	what might happen?
Freedom	if I do that then	what am I trying to achieve?	what are the alternative choices?

To make decisions, young people need to have opportunities to make decisions and to learn to think about the situation, take it steady, not rush, think about other ideas, weigh up the possibilities, think about what might happen, sift and organise the facts and information they have; if possible, experiment and then decide.

They also need support if the decision made turns out to be wrong; to understand that it may be better to have made a wrong decision than to not have made one at all. They will also need to learn from the experience and to be encouraged to try again. If they have been encouraged to make a decision it will increase their sense of 'ownership' of their life and thus increase their self-esteem at the same time.

If we really want to achieve success with young people then it is important that they should learn to be responsible for their own destiny. However, young people need adults to help them to develop the necessary skills, to be a role model, mediator, confidant and friend.

Critical thinking and decision-making

What's best	– predict
Choices	– decisions
Weighing up	– outcomes
Think about	– advantages
Perceptive	– disadvantages
Choosing	– what will happen
Looking behind	– confusing
Reflecting	– consequences
Taking responsibility	– image

Help young people to be in situations where each day they have to make decisions. For busy adults it is often easier to do tasks or decide themselves rather than spend time enabling children and young people to make their own decisions. Decision-making then is not an integral part of adolescents' lives so when they do have to make decisions this can be quite a shock and a difficult transition.

Social and Emotional Skills

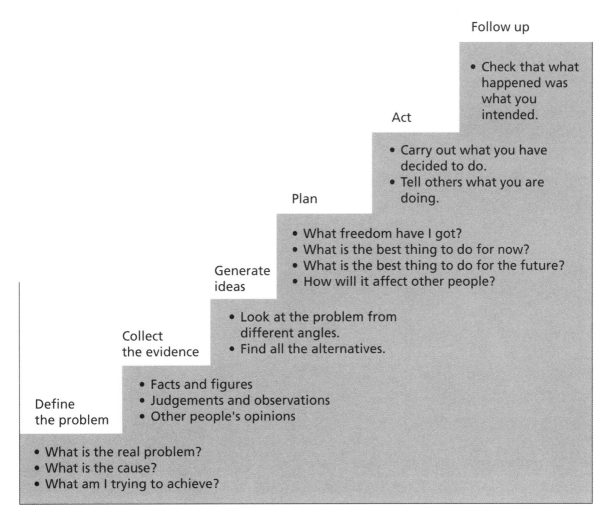

Figure 12.2 *Simple logical method*

Encourage carers to let them start with simple decisions at first, like choosing menus, helping choose holidays, outings, subjects at school, colour schemes, even if it is much easier for others to make the decisions themselves.

Here are two ways that could be used to help the decision-making process. You could work through them with the young people on a few minor issues at first. You could use them either with just one young person, or working in a group.

Decision-making methods

1. Simple logical method (Figure 12.2)

2. For and against (pros and cons) method (Figure 12.3, see next page)

Make a list of all the good points and all the bad points of making a decision, see table below for an example. It is surprising when you have done this how easy the decision will be. If you have more than one choice then you can compare the 'fors' and 'againsts'.

Choice	For	Against
Staying on at same school in 6th form		
Go to local college		
Going to college in next town		

Source: Young People in Foster and Residential Care. Wheal, A. (2003)

Figure 12.3 *For and against (pros and cons) method*

Negotiating Skills

Negotiating is not about having a fixed position on a subject and having a closed mind. It is about:
- Honesty.
- Thinking about where the negotiation should take place to ensure there are not undue influences or advantages in the choice of location.
- Getting the timing right.
- Being prepared.
- Defining your objectives before you start.
- Understanding the needs of the other person or group.
- Understanding the strengths and weaknesses of the other person or group.
- Being prepared to accommodate these needs unless you feel it will weaken your own bargaining position.
- Not being side tracked to include other issues.
- Not spending effort trying to prove yourself to others.
- Knowing what or how much you are willing to accept which may not be the ideal.
- Understanding that sometimes you have to accept less than you had hoped.
- Knowing when to stop if the negotiating is getting out of hand.
- Keeping calm.

Some tips:
- Think about what you want to negotiate – what you will accept or will not accept.
- Don't stick too rigidly to a fixed position, try to be flexible.
- Be honest.
- Plan some answers or responses that might crop up.
- Don't embark on negotiations with all the emphasis on your own needs – try to understand the needs of the other person, group or organisation.
- Be prepared to take these needs into consideration unless they weaken your own bargaining position.
- Don't be confrontational, 'don the velvet glove' rather than 'wield the iron fist'.
- Stay calm.
- Don't be awkward just to repay some previous hurt.
- Don't be cynical or sceptical – act from a position of strength.
- Don't expend effort trying to prove yourself as this may be to the detriment of the point at issue.
- If possible choose a venue where you feel comfortable or at least where you are on an equal footing with whoever you are negotiating with.
- Try to avoid making the negotiations personal – the subject may be personal to you but the other person may be doing their job the best they can.

Problem solving

What problems does the young person have? How deeply have they looked at the problem? Get them to try looking at the onion model of a problem.

Top layer.
The problem as presented. The problem expressed in 'tangible' way – costs, quality of life etc. The symptoms of the problem, not the causes – feeling useless or 'ain't it awful'.

Second layer.
Other people's contribution or blaming others. Blaming others and only seeing their contribution to the problem 'I am the victim'.

Third layer.
My own contribution *or* what can I do? What role am I playing in the problem? Am I helping the solution?
Am I hindering the solution?

❷ *The problem-solving checklist*

1. Identify problem – what exactly is going on?
2. Gather information – what do I know?
3. Analyse information – what are the root causes?
4. Determine acceptable outcomes – what do I want to achieve?
5. Generate solutions – what could I do?
6. Select the best solution – what is more likely to get me an acceptable outcome?
7. How do I go about doing it?
8. Do it, then test – have I solved the problem?
9. Can I improve on what I have done?

Culture, values, beliefs and religion

Culture

Everyone has their own culture. Culture has nothing to do with the colour of our skin. It is about the influences around us that make us the people we are.

Sometimes people move away from, or are born away from, the place of their heritage. It is important that they have the opportunity to learn about their own culture so they may make up their own mind about what influences they wish to affect their lives.

A neighbour of mine is from Scotland although he has not lived there for many, many years. He speaks with an extremely broad Scottish accent, mainly eats Scottish food and at every opportunity, wears his kilt. As someone who visits Scotland regularly to visit family and friends, I don't know anyone as 'Scottish' as John. You may know of similar examples from people of other countries.

It is natural that people who understand and love their own culture should want to share this with others. It is also natural that young people should want to develop their own culture based upon the life they wish to lead.

Tolerance is the key here. Tolerance is to respect not just other people's culture and heritage, but their beliefs and religion as well. Tolerance is to accept that, just because our own culture is special to us, it may not be special to others. Tolerance and the patience to learn, and understand, about other people's lives and influences. Tolerance in accepting this knowledge and way of life, whilst not necessarily agreeing with everything.

Values

Most people agree that it is important to have a set of values or beliefs to guide us through life. Our values and beliefs help us to decide what is right or wrong and how to behave in certain situations.

We get our set of values, the **dos and don'ts** of life, as we grow up. Some we get from the family we grow up with, some we get at school, some we learn at play and others we learn from friends and other people who influence us.

Some people get their set of values from religion. That is what religion is, a set of beliefs or values that influence a person's life and behaviour. Religion is personal to each individual.

There may be others who share these beliefs and values. There will certainly be others who do not do so. There will be others who have no religion at all but they will certainly have their own beliefs and values.

Beliefs and religion

People who have like-minded beliefs sometimes join together to form an organised 'established' religion. Some of these world religions are:

- Buddhism
- Chinese religions
- Christianity
- Hinduism
- Islam
- Judaism
- Sikhism

Religion means different things to all these groups of people. Within each religion, there is likely to be different sects with different beliefs and levels of commitment.

A religion needs continuity and rules to give it strength. It also needs to grow and change with the ideas and needs of a new generation and in an ever changing world. We all need to be understanding and respectful of each other's religions, customs, symbols and places of worship.

Racism

We need to be aware of the inherent and covert racism endemic in society, and the damaging effects it can have on us all. Such awareness should be part of social education for all young people. However, those of us working with them need to be particularly aware of, and change, our own prejudices to ensure that we offer the best service we possibly can.

We need to ensure that all young people have positive role models and images from all cultures. It is easy for white people to categorise all young black people together as one group and vice versa. Discussion can help everyone to become aware of, and come to terms with, their thoughts and feelings and that of others.

Sex, Getting Pregnant, and Being a Young Parent

It would be great if this part did not have to be written. Sadly, statistics tell us that young women leaving the care system are disproportionately more likely to be pregnant or already a parent than the general population. For further information see Chapter 15 on Health Needs.

A piece of research carried out in Southampton in about 2002 shows that care leavers have:
- Highest number of sexual partners.
- Lowest condom use in entire survey.
- Current abuse through prostitution.
- Lowest age of first sexual experience.
- Least access to sexual health education and information.
- First sexual information primarily gained from sexual partners.
- No access to information on lesbian, gay or bisexual identity.
- Least access to services, for fear of judgement and lack of confidentiality.

(Smith, undated)

Why can this be so?

Clearly:
- Staff need training to help young people with adolescence and all the associated pressures.
- Health services need policies and guidelines.
- The young people themselves need all the help we can give them to enable them to make informed choices about whether to have sex or not.

All young people should know:
- How their body is developing and maturing sexually.
- Some of the answers to typical teenage worries about sex.
- The health risks associated with sexual activity with multiple sexual partners.
- What the law is regarding sexual activity, e.g. age of consent.
- The mechanics of sexual activity: the different ways to have sex; getting pregnant; avoiding disease, etc.

The Leaving Care Handbook

- What the various methods of contraception are.
- How to get contraceptives and contraceptive advice.
- What 'safe sex' means – that there is no such thing as completely safe sex, only **safer** sex.
- How to withstand peer pressure about sexual activity.
- The risk, avoidance and treatment of sexually transmitted diseases.
- How to seek reassurance and physical contact outside sexual relationships.
- How value systems affect attitudes to sexual relationships.
- That sexuality is part of their identity.
- At their best, sexual relationships are an expression of love and commitment.
- Choosing not to have a sexual relationship does not make someone childish.
- Young people thinking about having sex need to know that they have the right to say NO.
- No-one should force another person to have sex. Everyone's body is their own and they should not be persuaded to do something sexual they do not like, feel unready for or that makes them feel unsafe.

If a young woman becomes pregnant they will need:
- Support, advice and guidance should they be thinking of terminating the pregnancy. If they so decide then they will also need support both at the time and for some time afterwards.
- Support and guidance in preparing for parenthood at a time when many young people are still developing their own maturity.
- Dealing with changing relationships with their partner or having to accept that they will be coping alone.
- Dealing with family conflict – intergenerational conflicts that are heightened by pregnancy and may lead to rejection by own parents or others.
- Unresolved feelings around past abuse and childhood trauma.

Longer term, they will need help with:
- Coping with the daily demands of a baby or toddler.
- Managing on welfare benefits.
- Difficulties in accessing educational and employment opportunities.
- Lack of adequate accommodation options with limited or no support.
- Fear of failing so that their own child comes into public care.

Many young women who are white have a relationship with a black young man. This can lead to problems about identity, e.g. denial that the baby is black and what that means, problems of violence and allegations of racism. These have implications for training, contact arrangements and placement planning and support.

What do local authorities need to provide?

- Financial arrangements for mother and baby placement, including source of funding for equipment.
- Definition of roles and responsibilities of everyone involved with the young parent.
- Development of services, to assist young people to make an informed choice about becoming parents or not.
- A way of meeting the practical and emotional needs of those who become parents but who need specific support for a period until they establish themselves more independently. Agencies need to recruit and prepare carers for this work and provide clear policies and guidance to both carers and young people because there are specific factors to be considered.

Social and Emotional Skills

Information and advice a pregnant young person might need

The following list includes some of the issues that will require further information. Support will be necessary for the young woman, and hopefully her partner, in finding the answers:

- The local authority's policy and practice on parenthood for someone in care.
- The roles of a midwife and a health visitor.
- Where local pre-natal classes are held.
- Health issues for expectant mothers.
- How a baby develops in the womb.
- What pre-natal testing involves.
- The pros and cons of breast and bottle feeding.
- Buying appropriate clothes and equipment for a new baby.
- What to expect when giving birth.
- How to register the birth.
- Information on available welfare benefits.
- Immunisation for a new baby.
- Where to get help and advice.
- The basics of caring for a baby.
- How a baby develops into a child.
- Recognising when a child is ill and the care that may be required.
- Preventing accidents in the home.

Information about most of these issues should be available in any family planning or health promotion centre.

Support and resources needed after the birth

- Young women who give up their babies for adoption need specialist support to help break the cycle.
- Accommodation – there needs to be a range of suitable options.
- Many of the young mothers need to be parented themselves.
- Help with loneliness or isolation.
- Child care.
- Roles and responsibilities of those working with mum and baby.
- Support network for young parents.

Food and babies

Babies are given much the best start in life by breast-feeding, but if this is not possible or desired by the mother, then advice should be given on:

- How much milk and how often. If reading is an issue, this advice should be in pictorial form.
- Hungry or crying babies may need to be offered an overall increase in milk throughout the day.
- Water instead of milk on some occasions.
- Water only at night in order to develop good habits.

The best people to advise on milk, weaning and diet for babies are:

- midwives
- health visitors
- GPs

Fathers

The male partner is equally responsible for a woman's pregnancy. He also has a responsibility to maintain the child until they are 18 years of age.

There is a need to find ways of engaging young fathers which demonstrates how the 'absent father syndrome' denies children, particularly male children, the role model of a good father, thus influencing how they themselves approach parenthood in their own adult lives. It is known that a poor parental attachment in childhood, especially amongst males, makes it harder for them to cope with the responsibilities of parenting and to attach to their own children.

There are many schemes to help young fathers to learn to be part of their child's life whether they stay with the mother or not. Participation should be actively encouraged. Fathers also have parental rights. They need to know what their rights are and how they can be implemented if they wish.

Many of the young parents will not have been properly parented themselves. They may not have any role models on which to base the standard of care for their baby. They will need all the help and support you can give them to enable their baby to thrive and grow into a happy and healthy child. They will also need support for their own personal development.

Health and sexuality

If we were to ask any young person what their major health concerns were, they might say anything from pregnancy and body image to visits to the doctor and internal examinations. Very often maintaining good health can be seen by young people as a problem, since so much emphasis is placed on the do's and don'ts such as drug misuse, eating disorders, preventing pregnancy and AIDS. Instilling some excitement and positive interest in our bodies might go some way to preventing such abuses as substance misuse. For more information on Health Needs see Chapter 15.

Sexuality

How many of us have been concerned about our looks? How much does that concern revolve around the images society wants us to have? As adolescents, we probably thought we were too tall or too small, had too many spots or too much body hair. In general we were 'too' something or not enough of something else to be acceptable, lovable and wanted.

Sexuality is not just about sex. It is about who we are: heterosexual; homosexual; male; female. Adolescence is a crucial time. As young people begin to experiment with different behaviours and boundaries, they need to be able to explore who they are as a whole person in a nonjudgmental atmosphere.

Lesbian, gay or bisexual young people

Growing up lesbian, gay or bisexual is a difficult time for anyone. Social services or other organisations may not always help with the issues and so the young person can feel even more rejected.

Homophobia expresses itself in many forms. Many young people are not believed if they say they are lesbian, gay or bisexual; or it is assumed to be a passing phase. It is important to try to ensure that all lesbian, gay and bisexual young people are able to live in accepting, supportive and caring ways.

Social and Emotional Skills

Aims should be:
- To improve attitudes within society towards lesbian and gay young people.
- To promote greater understanding of lesbian and gay young people wherever they live.
- To provide accepting, supportive and caring homes for lesbian and gay young people who would otherwise be homeless or in a hostile environment.

There are organisations throughout the UK who may be able to offer support, help and advice – search on the web under 'Lesbian, Gay and Bisexual Youth Organisations'.

Substance abuse

Many young people may not reveal their abuse of substances. Using drugs or alcohol may engender feelings of low self-worth, or these feelings may have prompted the use of substances. Drug abuse can be an escape from what is too often a harsh reality, or a part of their adolescent experimentation and exploration.

Abusing drugs, including alcohol, may be symptomatic of other difficulties. For instance, it is no use talking to a young person about love and caring whilst they are living in a house with holes in the roof and rats in the cellar.

Ways may need to be found to enable the young person to deal with their difficulties one at a time. Naturally, priorities will need to be made about which to tackle first. If the young person's use is at the level of addiction then it may not be appropriate for them to be in a group until the addiction is dealt with.

Frequently illegal drugs are cheaper than alcohol – the effects last longer and a greater high can be produced, although the end result may involve feelings of paranoia and depression, depending on the substance used.

Young people can use drugs to indirectly harm themselves without attempting direct suicide. There is no one reason why a person takes drugs.

Prescribed drugs also play a part: many a young person has been put on anti-depressants by their doctor without any counselling or support. However, today many GP surgeries are becoming more enlightened, and have counsellors attached to the surgery, so that patients can get the support they need.

We need to be alert to the dangers of becoming yet another person involved with a young person because of drugs. They may be getting attention from hospital social workers, doctors and health visitors, and may see us as another person who can join in this, albeit subconscious, game. Ways will need to be found not to collude with this.

How to help prevent drug, solvent and alcohol abuse:
- Talk to the young people about their views on drugs, drink, smoking and sniffing.
- Help them have new, interesting and challenging experiences.
- Get them to think about how they might refuse these drugs (they are all drugs) without losing their friends.
- Teach them to care for and value their health.
- Help them build up their self-esteem and respect for themselves.
- Treat them with respect.
- Take an interest in their opinions and worries.
- Check out any problems they may have.

- Suggest other activities and help them take part.
- Seek support from your local advisory centres.
- Be a good listener.

Conclusion

So much of our own lives is tied up in the way we feel about ourselves; the way we behave, the emotional and social support we have around us, and, to a certain extent, in the way we were parented.

Care leavers need all the help and support we can give them so they can develop emotionally and socially so they feel confident about themselves.

Resources

Fostering Network/Greenwich Council/First Key (2003) *Preparation for Adult Life.* London: Fostering Network.
Green, C. (2000) *Beyond Toddlerdom.* London: Random House Publishing.
Mountain, A. (2004) *The Space Between: Bridging the Gap Between Workers and Young People.* Lyme Regis: Russell House Publishing.
Smith, S. (undated) Southampton Primary Health Care Trust
Wheal, A. (2004) *Adolescence: Positive Approaches to Working with Young People.* Lyme Regis: Russell House Publishing.
Wheal, A. (2003), *Young People in Foster and Residential Care*, Lyme Regis: Russell House Publishing.
Wheal, A. and Emson, G. (2002) *The Family Support Handbook.* Lyme Regis: Russell House Publishing.
Young, A. (1996) *The Manager's Handbook: The Practical Guide to Successful Management.* London: Sphere Books.

ⓘ Feeling down? Tips to cheer yourself up

- Give yourself a treat – stroke a cat, watch the sunset, have a bath, draw a picture, read a good book, watch a favourite video.
- Remind yourself how nice you are – make a list entitled 'things I can do' and 'nice things I know about me'.
- Look after your body and your brain – go swimming, eat fruit, solve a puzzle, learn a song.
- Start a praise box – when someone says something nice about you, write it down on paper and put it in the box. Open it often to remind yourself how nice you are.
- Play the difference game – with a friend outline the ways you are different and tell each other the things you like about each other.

Feelings follow actions

Change your actions to change your feelings!

- Do something new.
- Indulge yourself.
- Take a walk.
- Call a friend – talk about it.
- Write down your feelings; keep a diary.
- Take some exercise.
- Have a massage.
- Read a funny book.

- See a funny film.
- Watch or do your favourite sport.
- Meditate.
- Have sex with someone who cares about you.
- Eat well; get plenty of rest.
- Get outdoors in the fresh air and sunshine.

What else works for you?

Life Plan

Step	Examples	Time frame
Diagnosis	Who are you? What is important to you? What are your attributes? What are your aspirations?	Past and present
Values	What is more/less important to you? What can you not live without?	
Personal mission/purpose	What do you have to offer? What do you believe in?	
Life goals	What do you want to do? What do you want to create? What do you want to experience? What do you want to be?	Long-term – may not be dateable
Resources	Strengths Talents Skills Experience Knowledge Relationships Finances	Medium-term – 6 months plus
Objectives	Career Family Financial Education/training Health/fitness Etc.	
Next steps	Speak to . . . Write to . . . Talk to . . . Decide on . . . Ask . . .	Short-term – now to 6 months
Review	What worked or did not work? What did you learn? How have you changed?	3–6–12 months

Reproduced by permission of Elsevier Science Ltd

✓ You and your social contacts

1. Do you attend, belong to, or take part in one or more of the following:
    (a) Church, temple, mosque, synagogue – name/tel.no:

    (b) Local Youth Club – name/tel.no:

    (c) Sports Club – name/tel.no:

    (d) Hobby/Activity – name/tel.no:

    (e) Outdoor Activity Trips – name/tel.no:

    (f) Duke of Edinburgh Award – what level and what activities? -name/tel.no:

    (g) Other – name/tel.no:

2. Is there any other outside event or place that you go to where you meet other people, e.g. a disco, the town centre? How often?

3. Do you know of any places where you can get a discount on leisure schemes in your area? If not, do you need help to find out? – name/tel.no:

4. Do you have friends of your own age locally? Do they visit you, or you them? – name/tel.no:

5. Do you have any older friends? – name/tel.no:

✓ You and your Nationality and Ethnicity

1. Do you know what your nationality is?

2. If you are not British, do you know if anything needs to be done to sort out your immigration, citizenship and nationality status?

3. Do you have all the documents needed for future dealings over passport, immigration etc.?

4. Do you know who can help?

5. Have you got an up-to-date passport?

6. Do you know who will be able to sign the form to support your application for a passport?

7. Do you know which ethnic group you come from?

If you come from a minority ethnic group do you need help to meet more people from the same ethnic background? Who can help?

✓ You and General Information and Rights

Where are these agencies and what are their telephone numbers?
- CAB
- Careers office
- Department of Social Security
- Doctors' surgery
- Employment service (job centre)
- Health clinic
- Housing offices
- Police station
- Samaritans
- Library

Social and Emotional Skills

Do you know what to do if stopped by the police or arrested?

Do you know you can get free legal advice? Would you like help?

Do you know how to get in touch with an appropriate adult? Would you like help?

Do you know where to find your birth certificate and national insurance number?

Who can help?

13

Involving Young People in Decisions That Affect Their Lives

Martin Hazlehurst

Introduction

> ... the participation of children, young people and their families in the planning and delivery of services and in decisions about their everyday lives. Particular attention should be given to the involvement of young people collectively and to enhancing their individual voices, for example through the development of individual advocacy services.
>
> The Government's Objectives for Children's Social Services, Objective 8, 1998

The major purpose of participation for young people in care and care leavers is that it helps to raise aspirations and creates opportunities so they have similar opportunities to their non-care peers. It also helps to reduce social isolation and the stigma of care by ensuring the service provided is appropriate to meet a young person's needs and that there is a significant improvement in the quality of care provided.

In recent years the question of why and how young people can be involved, influence the shape of their own individual support and care, and change the wider environment of the care system itself, has become a major issue for social services departments and other agencies working with looked after children and care leavers.

Young people have a right to be involved, and their involvement is essential if services are to appropriately reflect their needs. Participation is about raising aspirations, and creating opportunities so they have similar life chances as other young people. It is about reducing social isolation and the stigma of care.

In order to achieve effective participation there needs to be a genuine commitment to changes in attitudes and organisational culture as well as the use of methods that provide real opportunities and the resources to enable young people to become involved.

There is a growing body of practice and literature on involvement. This chapter will draw on some of this to provide practical advice on how to manage involvement at both a strategic and practical level.

User involvement and participation – some practical thoughts

In all areas of participation involving care leavers, and others, it is imperative that:
- The care leavers are suitably trained.
- The care leavers are provided with sufficient and relevant information.
- The information is appropriately produced to enable them to fully participate.
- Support should be provided to the care leavers.

It is *not* about:
- Using the same young people all the time.
- Inviting them to a conference and then having separate workshops for young people.
- Being tokenistic.

It *is* about:
- Inviting care leavers to participate in decisions made about them.
- Ensuring the young people's voices are heard and acted upon.
- Advising them of what they might expect and what is expected of them.
- Informing others as well as the young people about the aims and objectives so everyone knows what to expect and can prepare accordingly.
- Discussing issues of confidentiality with everyone.
- Having strategies in place should things go wrong.

Care leavers should be offered payment for time spent on any participation work, including payment for attending training. The rate should be a reasonable reward for the skills and responsibility involved. Expenses should also be paid and child care or other caring costs might also be re-imbursed if appropriate.

Different young people will be in different situations and there may be problems with payments that might affect benefit claims. The position should be discussed individually and discreetly, and appropriate decisions made. The law should not be broken regarding paying 'unofficial' cash and some young people may decide not to participate if they feel it will adversely affect their benefits; others may choose not to be paid. This is unfortunate but if the rate of pay is reasonable for the work involved then in most cases the young people will be able to gain both financially and developmentally from the experience.

Expenses may be paid in cash and should be paid on the day in question. In some cases an advance may be necessary although a good way is to buy, say, the train ticket and send it to the young person.

Before you start

The two activities that follow are to help you and your agency to think through what it is you are trying to achieve and whether you are prepared and ready for what this may entail.

1. The ladder of participation

The ladder of participation (Hart, 1992) has become a common tool for understanding the theoretical concepts of involvement. Its eight levels provide an incremental approach to achieving true involvement (see next page). That is not to say the top level should always be a short term goal.

Use it to clarify the aims of your involvement initiative and as a way of evaluating whether the outcomes met the initial aspirations.

Table 13.1 *The Ladder of Participation*

Rung on ladder	Example	Characteristics
Participation		
8th Rung Child or young person initiates, where decisions are shared by adults.	Some young people are worried about the level of bullying in a large residential home. They form a group and write to key adults to say they want to do something about the problem. As a result of their efforts a peer counselling and advocacy service is developed.	The young people identify the issue and work with adults as equal partners in a project.
7th Rung Child or young person initiates and directs.	A group of young people decide to raise money to attend a leaving care conference. They agree a strategy for raising the money, organise activities, collect the money and use it for the trip.	The idea and implementation of the idea comes from young people.
6th Rung Initiated by adults, decisions shared with children and young people.	Young people are involved in the recruitment of providers of supported lodgings.	Genuine partnership between managers and young people – young people fully involved in decision-making process because each party has equal say in decision.
5th Rung Child or young person consulted and informed.	A survey to find out young people's views about the opening hours of the leaving care service asked them to share their views. As a result a new policy is drafted and shown to them to check that their concerns have been addressed.	Project designed and run by adults but children and young people understand the process and their opinions are treated seriously.
4th Rung Assigned but informed.	Young people are invited to attend their review meetings and after everybody else has spoken they are given a slot to express their views.	Information obtained from young people but no effort made to explain how and if their views will affect decision making.
Non-participation		
3rd Rung Tokenism.	Young people are invited to open a conference with little preparation on the subject and no consultation with them about who they apparently 'represent'.	Young people are apparently given a voice but they have no choice about the subject, method of communication or how the event is organised.
2nd Rung Decoration.	A young person who is homeless is taken along to a council meeting with a leaving care team manager who is asking for additional resources.	Young person is asked to take part with no explanation of the issues or reason for involvement.
1st Rung Manipulation.	Young people are visited by a senior manager who asks them what they think about a recent decision to close their project.	Tokenistic exercise that does not allow a young person to influence or change the decision.

2. Twelve tough questions for the adults

1. What are we aiming to achieve?
2. Where have we got so far?
3. What will young people get out of it?
4. Are we prepared to resource it properly?
5. Why have we not done it before?
6. Are we prepared to involve young people from the start?
7. Are we being honest with the young people?
8. What are our expectations?
9. Are we prepared to give up some power?
10. Are we prepared to accept criticism?
11. Do we recognise this as a long term commitment?
12. Are we prepared to build in changes long term and not just have a one-off event?

(NYA, 2003)

Involvement or consultation

How does the ladder of participation operate in practice? The different levels represent a transition from consultation with young people to a degree of meaningful involvement. It may not always be appropriate, or possible, to aspire to the higher levels but managers should be aware of what they are seeking to achieve.

The next chart identifies some of the differences between consultation and involvement.

Consultation	Involvement
• Young people asked their views at the end of a process of development.	• Young people involved in development from the start.
• Questions for discussion decided by adults.	• Questions for discussion decided by young people.
• Agency is seeking information.	• Agency starts by giving information.
• Personal and skills development of young people not an aim.	• Personal and skills development of young people essential to the process.
• Meeting the needs of service providers alone.	• Meeting the needs of service providers and young people.
• Led by service providers.	• Led by young people.

Before you start – have you thought of?

- Do you have support from senior managers?
- Are all the parts of the agency who are involved in young people's lives on board?
- Do you know what you are trying to achieve?
- Has there been discussion about whether the involvement can be managed in house or whether you need to bring in someone independent of the agency to assist?
- Do you know your first objective or task?
- Do you know how you are going to contact young people?

- Have you worked out your sales pitch to young people, have you discussed this with those people you will rely on to encourage young people to get involved?
- Have you been given specific time to manage the process?
- Have you got the resources you need?
- Have you decided how young people will be given incentives or rewarded?
- Do you know how your work will end?
- Do you know how you will decide whether you have succeeded? How will you measure what change has resulted from your work?

What can go wrong?

You are all fired up and are going to change the world, or at least the way young people are listened to and involved. Somehow things do not work out as you had imagined and you are left dispirited and feeling isolated. You discover that your commitment and personality has not got the results you wanted.

Here are some of the most common problems and how they can be resolved.

Problem	Solution
You feel like you are working on your own.	Perhaps the organisation is paying lip service to involvement. You may need to start with work on a strategy that involves the whole organisation. It is not as exciting but the time spent will pay dividends.
Patchy support from your colleagues.	Perhaps you assumed that everyone was as committed as you and have the time to devote to it. Look back on how you sold your project to your colleagues. Are they sure about what you are trying to do and did you explain clearly how they could introduce the idea to young people.
Young people do not cooperate.	Did you make being involved sound attractive enough? Did you have an achievable goal as a starting point? Are you starting in the wrong place? Are the venue and travel arrangements wrong? Perhaps young people need something more active or fun.
Numbers and enthusiasm of young people drop off after a good start.	You have to keep your enthusiasm up. Make sure your tasks are manageable. Do not stop selling because things seem to be going well. Most young people will inevitably move on. Keep renewing the process and the young people involved.

Problem	Solution
You and young people are blocked when their ideas do not match those of your managers.	You need to remind people of the job you were given to do. Young people's ideas are rarely over-ambitious. If it is difficult for you to do this then it may be a case for bringing in someone from outside to help the process. Young people themselves are the best at challenging blockages. It is harder to say no to them.
Young people see through the limitations of what you are doing.	Be honest with them about how far the process can go at present. Work on managers to help them feel comfortable about giving away some of their power. Once again young people are best at doing this and someone from outside may not have the same problems you have of upsetting your bosses.
Poor timing.	A trick question. There is never a good time. It will always be – after this reorganisation, after this budgetary crisis. Has there ever been a time when organisations are not either restructuring or broke. Waiting for the perfect time means never.

Different methods of involvement

The answer to the often asked question, 'What is the best way to involve young people?' is that there is not a best way, or even a right way. How you go about it will depend on what you are trying to achieve, what is possible, what the time scales and resources available are and, of course, what it is the young people want to do.

Below are just some of the methods that have been used (NYA, 2003) together with the advantages and limitations they have been found to have:

One-off events or conferences

Strengths
- A good way to get started.
- High profile.
- Time limited.
- Develops young peoples' skills.
- Immediately useful information.

Limitations
- May only attract a few young people.
- Can be seen as an end in itself.
- Whose agenda is being addressed?
- Cost in time and money.
- Risk of going wrong.

There are a number of rules that should ensure a successful event:
- The event should be the part of a strategy of involvement not the involvement itself.
- Young people should be given control of the content of the agenda for the event without interference from staff.

- Young people's involvement should not end with the event.
- No effort should be made to limit the audience to particular groups of staff.
- The event should be held at a time and at a venue of young peoples' choice.

Advisory or reference groups

Strengths
- Ongoing and always available.
- Can have influence.
- Can be representative.
- Young people can take control.

Limitations
- Can become a clique.
- Constantly changing membership.
- Can be unrepresentative.
- Time consuming.

Research or consultations

These are not necessarily the same. Old fashioned academic research was done to rather than with young people. More recently, methods of involving young people in the design and implementation of research, some would say at the expense of accuracy and rigour – but, who cares!

Both, however, can have the same advantages and limitations.

Strengths
- Value for money.
- Useful Information.
- High credibility.
- Time limited.

Limitations
- Who owns it?
- Whose questions are being asked?
- What happens next?

There are a set of rules to ensure that your consultation can be both led by and involve young people:
- Young people should be involved in deciding the subject of the consultation or research question.
- Young people should be involved in the design of questionnaires and other media used to conduct the research.
- Young people should be involved in the analysis of data and in deciding conclusions, messages and recommendations.
- Research on its own will not improve the service young people receive. It should be followed by involvement in implementation and other initiatives arising out of the research. It should also be linked to national leaving care organisations and networks.

Newsletters and websites

These two areas are discussed together because both have the aim of communicating information to young people and getting feedback, and most of the advantages and limitations are the same.

Strengths
- Young people can be involved in writing and design.
- Can get information to and feedback from young people who are isolated.
- Can create high but realistic expectations.
- Visible to managers and policy makers.

Limitations
- Good quality requires skills and resources.
- Access difficulties, circulation, access to web, language and literacy.
- Expensive and time consuming to keep going.
- Limited number of young people prepared to put in the time.

Young people on committees or parallel committees

If young peopled are to be truly involved they need to be close to or round the table where the serious decisions are made. That is the theory.

There are two ways of doing this: either have young people on management committees, local authority scrutiny committees or similar: or establish parallel committees where young people can discuss issues and feed into decision-making processes. We will look at these separately.

Parallel committees

Strengths
- Young people able to influence.
- Real issues being discussed.
- Close to decision makers.
- Good experience for those involved.

Limitations
- Do young people really have any power?
- Likely to be exclusive.
- Which issues should young people have a say in?
- Do young people get all the information to give an informed view?

Reserved places on committees

Strengths
- A seat at the table.
- Challenges adult way of doing things.
- Access to information.
- Young people have access to all decisions not just ones adults decide they should have.

Limitations
- Requires high level of skill and commitment.
- Young people set up to be representative of all young people.
- Young people can become 'professionalised'.
- Requires change in how committee does its business.

Involving young people in selection and recruitment

Thankfully, it is now common for young people to be involved in the selection and recruitment of staff. This is not just an issue about involvement, but testing the candidate's ability to relate to and respect young people is crucial to assessing their capability for the job.

How young people are involved therefore needs to give them a meaningful role in selection and use a method that provides the information necessary for informed judgments to be made about the candidate's suitability for the post.

There are two commonly used methods of involving young people at the interview stage: having young people on formal interview panels: and having a separate young people's panel discussion group. Both have advantages and disadvantages.

Whichever method is used there are some initial questions to be answered and decisions made:
- Have young people been involved in or consulted on the job description and person specification?
- What weight will be given to the views of young people in the selection process? Who has the final say? Do young people know this?
- Have diversity and equality issues been taken into account in the recruitment of young people?
- Have young people been trained in selection and recruitment, including equal opportunity policy and practices?

- Will young people's views be recorded in a way that can be fed back to candidates?
- Have candidates been told about how young people will be involved in selection?
- Do the practical arrangements for the interviews make it possible for young people to be involved? Is the venue accessible and one that young people will feel comfortable in?
- How are young people being rewarded and paid for their involvement?

Young people on formal interview panels

Advantages
- Young people are an integral part of the decision-making process.
- Fits with traditional selection processes.
- Easily measurable.
- Good at testing whether candidates engage with young people on equal footing with adults.

Disadvantages
- A false environment that many young people are not comfortable with.
- Can only involve a small number of young people.
- Is not a good way of testing attitudes and values.
- Requires young people to have had formal training.

Young people's groups or panels

Advantages
- Can involve a larger number of young people.
- Good at testing attitudes to young people.
- A more informal setting therefore more attractive to young people.
- Able to assess ability to relate to young people.

Disadvantages
- Less easy to measure performance.
- Expensive in time and money.

Conclusion

Omri Shalom is a care leaver who has had a lot of experience of helping adults more effectively involve young people in the development of their leaving care services. Here are his 10 tips (Wheal, 2002):

1. Don't talk to young people as if they are kids; talk to them like you would talk to a friend.
2. Make the time to see young people. Don't restrict yourself to a limit, be flexible.
3. Hear what young people say, don't just listen.
4. Be prepared to act on things when a young person tells you of something that is wrong and should not be happening.
5. Remember each and every young person is an individual. Every young person will have different views.
6. Remember why you are involving young people in the first place.
7. Remember young people have expertise of the looked after care system.
8. Show young people you want to make a change.
9. Don't keep looking at your watch in front of young people.
10. Don't **consult** young people, **involve** them.

Then, most importantly, young people want high quality care which meets all their needs, including **being involved.**

Resources

CROA and DoH (2000) *Total Respect.* London: CROA.

Hart, R. (1992) *Children's Participation: From Tokenism to Citizenship*. Unicef.

NYA/LGA, (2003) *Hear by Right: Standards for the Active Involvement of Children and Young People*. NYA/LGA.

National Youth Agency for Department of Health (2003) *Involving Children and Young People: An Introduction*. NYA.

Wheal, A. (Ed.) (2002) *RHP Companion to Leaving Care.* Lyme Regis: Russell House Publishing.

Willow, C. (2003) *Participation in Practice: Children and Young People as Partners in Change.* Childrens Society.

Section Seven: Financial Support

14

Financial Matters

Ena Fry and Ann Wheal

The Children (Leaving Care) Act 2000 introduced responsibilities and financial arrangements by which local authorities undertake to prepare 'looked after' young people for adult life and support them through this transition. Social services departments assume primary maintenance role for the majority of 16 and 17-year-olds who qualify for services under the legislation. However, at 18 young people are seen as independent in their own right so their primary source of income should come from training, benefits or work just like any other young person. However, if they are in full-time education they may be supported up to the age of 24 years.

Good practice

Everyone leaving care should have:
- Written information on post-18 financial arrangements in respect of the individual young person which should be included in their pathway plan.
- Access to expert advice whether directly from the Personal Advisor (PA) or arranged by the PA to deal with specific queries.
- Updated information on financial changes that affect care leavers such as housing benefit, tax credits, welfare legislation, asylum legislation.
- Information on the 'leaving care' (setting up home) allowance.
- Information on Criminal Injury Compensation Board payments which will be disregarded post-18 only if a discretionary trust fund has already been set up.
- Information on the implications of setting up a trust fund for a young person.
- Information and access to complaints and representation procedures.

This means addressing the way budgets are configured, so 18-plus is viewed as a key milestone, not an end in supporting young people making the transition to adult life. This builds on the preparation and planning which starts at day one of a placement but which may become the targeted focus of work at 16 years.

The money a young person will receive will depend on their circumstances and also on whether they are eligible or relevant children – see Chapter 17 for clear legal definitions, but briefly this is as follows.

Statutory entitlements

Eligible 'looked after' young people from the age of 16 to the end of the school year eleven remain subject to current financial arrangements that are applicable to 'looked after' children.

Financial Matters

Other young people are **eligible** who remain 'looked after' in a social services or social work departments placement, are preparing for independence and who are involved in the transition. The incentives, allowances and financial framework should be in line with training allowance and benefit rates.

Clarity on what items the allowance is to cover and the proportion allocated to each item will help young people to develop their budgeting skills.

Relevant young people aged 16–17 who move into a semi-independent or independent placement would previously have been able to claim certain government benefits. They are no longer entitled to these benefits when they reach age 18 with a few exceptions.

Social services or social work departments have the primary income maintenance role for this category of young people. Departments must provide a minimum income standard to this group that covers their accommodation and maintenance costs. A minimum standard must cover:
- Housing costs.
- A personal allowance in line with benefit rates.

Additionally the guidance on the Act states that a number of items and areas should be considered a priority for funding. These include, but should not be restricted to:
- Travel costs, e.g., for education.
- Educational materials and special equipment.
- Other educational costs.
- Costs associated with special needs, such as a disability or pregnancy.
- Childcare costs.
- Clothing.
- Contact with family or other significant relationships.
- Cultural or religious needs.
- Counselling or therapeutic needs.
- Hobbies and holidays.

Information on these should be explained clearly to the young people themselves by their PA.

It is important to explore and develop procedures for young people who are working, providing incentives for low wage earners and a system of contributions for those earning over a given threshold. A sliding scale of incentives that is linked to young people's wages or, a system of bonuses should be made known to the young person.

The responsible authority does not have the primary income support role for **former relevant** young people. However, the local authority does have a duty, rather than a power, to provide assistance in kind or cash in respect of former relevant children.

These duties include:
- Providing general assistance.
- Providing assistance with expenses associated with employment.
- Providing assistance with expenses associated with education and training.
- Providing vacation accommodation (or the funds to secure it) to care leavers in higher education or on a residential further education course that requires them to live away from home as agreed in the Pathway Plan.

Additionally, young people who do not meet the Children (Leaving Care) Act 2000 eligibility criteria, but have been 'looked after' for a period on or after their 16th birthday are termed **qualifying children and young people.** This group are entitled to the general powers and duties associated with Section 24 of the Children Act 1989 and:
- Assistance with education and training up to age 24.
- Vacation accommodation if attending higher education or residential further education courses.

Money

Each young person will have a different set of needs and different capacity to manage a budget. This means that in each case the responsible authority will have to agree with the young person a personal support package and how it is to be managed. The details of this will be recorded in their Pathway Plan.

Who is responsible for maintenance payments?
Under the existing arrangements local authorities have the primary income maintenance role for both eligible and relevant children. The local authority's duty to maintain relevant children is established under section 23B (8) (a) of the Children Act as amended.

Exceptions to the duty to maintain
This duty will not apply to relevant children once they have returned home for a period of 6 months or more. In addition, children who are 'looked after' on a series of short-term placements (less than 4 weeks) will not be defined as eligible children, even where the total period looked after is more than 13 weeks. Ongoing responsibilities under Section 24 of the Children Act, as amended, will remain.

Disqualification from benefits
Under Clause 6 of the Children Leaving Care Act, eligible and relevant children are not entitled to government benefits. Lone parents and disabled children continue to be eligible for benefits due to them because of their disability or parental status. They will not, however, be eligible for housing benefit. Independent advice from a welfare rights specialist such as CAB should be sought to assist in potential claims for benefits.

Those defined as disabled and therefore able to claim benefits include someone who:
- Is entitled to statutory sick pay.
- Is incapable of work because of incapacity.
- Has appealed against a decision that they are not incapable of work.
- Is registered as blind.
- Is in work but because of a physical or mental incapacity their hours or earnings are 75 per cent or less than that of a person without that disability in the same job.

Young people who are disabled and young parents may be entitled to any of the following:
- Disability benefits (DLA, Incapacity benefit).
- Housing and Council Tax Benefit.
- Sure Start maternity payments.
- Working Tax Credit.
- Child Tax Credit.
- Education maintenance allowances.

- Dependant's additions to NI and means-tested benefits access funds.
- Care to Learn Funds (for young parents).
- Local bursaries.
- Certain charitable funding.

The process of assessment should be streamlined as far as practicable.

Asylum seekers

There is often considerable confusion about what will happen to unaccompanied asylum seekers when they reach 18, partly reflective of the legislative changes that are frequently introduced. It is essential that young people are prepared for changes in support and finance at 18 and that professionals are clear on how to help young people access necessary funding and support. Each young person will have an assessment of need and a pathway plan that will address post-18 arrangements.

Briefly the following arrangements apply after the age of 18:
- If the young person has previously been supported under Section 17 of Children Act 1989 then financial support will normally transfer to National Asylum and Support Services (NASS) at 18.
- If the young person has been supported under Section 20 of Children Act 1989 then they are entitled to services under the Children (Leaving Care) Act 2000, so the local authority is responsible for identifying and managing suitable accommodation, with NASS being financially responsible for the cost of the accommodation, utilities, subsistence and education costs.
- Young people who have been refused leave to remain, or were subject to exceptional leave to remain (ELR) until 18, but have not been granted further leave to remain. Those not entitled to any long term/continuing support are subject to removal. However, until a removal date has been fixed they are still entitled to support.

Assessment of need

The multi-agency assessment of need, which forms the basis of the Pathway Plan, has a particular emphasis on those areas that require intervention to support the young person until 21 years or older. The assessment follows the dimensions of *The Framework for the Assessment of Children in Need and their Families* (DoH, 2000).

A flexible and creative approach which actively engages with young people themselves helps to ensure that the eventual plan is realistic and likely to be met. Practical assistance, including travel or subsistence costs, should be provided to help young people attend meetings and ensure the process is young-person friendly. Information should be presented to young people in a way that is suitable and meets any special needs they may have.

The views and wishes of the young person should be central to the decision on who to involve. Others to involve should include:
- Parents or anyone with parental responsibility.
- Carers.
- A representative from school or college.
- An independent visitor.
- GP.
- The Personal Advisor.
- Anyone else whom the responsible authority or the young person considers relevant.

A copy of the written Needs Assessment Statement should be given to the young person and all those consulted during the assessment process (with the consent of the young person involved) which should take place around a young person's 16th birthday.

Rate of allowance

For most 16 and 17-year-old care leavers this would normally be the higher rate of personal allowance plus any premiums due to any special circumstances.

Claims for additional special funding for such things as visits to hospital should be processed by the Personal Advisor as part of the 6-monthly assessment and pathway planning process.

Access to financial support

Payment should be through a bank account, wherever possible, with arrangements to pay young people in cash, possibly through an out-of-hours service should this be required.

Decisions on which elements of the financial assistance will be paid directly to the young person and which will be managed on their behalf should take account of the individual needs and abilities of the young person. Decisions should take full account of the views of the young person and be set out in the Pathway Plan together with details of any leaving care grant to be paid.

Worries

In some instances the responsible authority may have concerns that financial support, over and above what is being provided to cover accommodation and maintenance costs, is not being used for the agreed purposes. In these circumstances the Plan may need to be revised or specific funding withheld. It is important to note that any sanctions applied should not reduce the package of support to less than the accommodation and maintenance allowances (equivalent to the appropriate Income Support or Job Seeker's Allowance, and Housing Benefit rates).

Emergency Assistance

Short-term emergency assistance should be provided as necessary. For young people who have moved from another authority, contact will have to be made with the originating authority and agreement reached, together with the young person, on how support should best be provided.

Disputes

Disputes in relation to financial matters must be dealt with by means of the 14-day informal resolution stage before the full complaints procedure may be invoked. The responsible authority should ensure that the young person has access to an independent advocate. Clearly in relation to a dispute in this area it will be important to ensure that the advocate is a specialist in both child-care and welfare-rights law.

Local discretion and transparency

Many local authorities operate within limited resources and competing demands which they may not always be able to meet in full. It is important that the criteria are clearly set out to ensure young people are aware of the authority's responsibilities in this area. The authority should produce a written schedule of the items they would normally expect to provide funds for and how other sources of income are to be treated.

Financial Matters

Minimum standards of entitlement

The Guidance states that the focus on the individual needs of young people in relation to particular areas unrestricted by DSS rules on accommodation options should ensure that the value of the package 'should generally be well above the level which would have been supplied through the benefits system'.

Waiting for a first benefit claim to be processed, which in some parts of the country can take 4–5 weeks at least, can leave a young person having to claim crisis loans and other emergency payments. Some social services departments (SSDs), Housing Benefits departments and Job Centres Plus have developed a detailed protocol and procedure that allows young people to submit a claim for benefit four weeks before their 18th birthday. Part of the protocol enables Personal Advisors and benefits staff to discuss the progress of the claim after the young people have given signed consent for this. SSD will financially support the young person until their first payments are received, usually within three weeks.

From their 18th to their 19th birthday, a young person who is on a full-time non-advanced education course of at least 12 hours per week can get income support if they are 'estranged' from their parents or people acting as their parents. Entitlement stops as soon as the person reaches 19.

A student of 18 plus can undertake a part-time course of education for 16 hours or less of guided learning each week and claim benefit. However, they have to say that they are willing to give up the course should a job be offered to them, which often detracts from educational performance. Many colleges now provide courses of just under 16 hours of guided learning each week; these may enable young people to study and work part-time. If young people earn a low income they may be eligible for full housing benefit.

Special payments

Criminal Injuries Compensation Board payment

The Children Leaving Care Act 2000 states that CICB should not be taken into account when considering payments to young people by SSD's However, CICB payments could affect a young person's entitlement to state benefits, unless the money is put into appropriate forms of trust.

Birthdays, religious festivals, and Christmas grant

SSDs may have a discretionary fund available to enable young people to receive a small grant for their birthday, religious festivals or at Christmas.

Conclusion

Accommodation and Finance are the two most fundamental causes of worry for care leavers. The financial situation for each care leaver may be different and also changing. For peace of mind, what must be clear is:
- How much they will get.
- When they will get it.
- How it will be paid.
- What support will be there in case of difficulties.

Questions and answers: young people's survival guide to money

What is the setting up home grant (sometimes known as leaving care grant)?
A setting up home allowance is a one-off payment to help with the cost of setting up home. It covers the cost of such things as furniture, cooking equipment, crockery, cutlery and bed linen.

How do I know what my leaving care allowance is, how do I get it and when is it paid?
It will partly depend on your circumstances, age, and also status, e.g., whether you are eligible or relevant (see below). It is important that you know what your leaving care status is as it may affect how much money you get.

All information regarding money should be written down clearly and in a manner that you can understand. It should be written into your pathway plan and reviewed every 6 months. Everything should be agreed with you and you should have been given a copy of the plan.

How will it be paid to me?
It could be given to you in cash by your PA, or sent direct to your bank or building society, or as a cheque.

What if I don't have a bank account?
Go along to several different bank or building societies and find out which offers you the best deal and suits your needs best. You can get their leaflets to read and then ask to see their personal advisor who will help you open an account. You will only need a small amount of money to open an account. Keep an eye out for special deals on offer such as free banking – it is easy to change your account to get the best value for money.

Once you have an account you can arrange for your bills to be paid through the bank if you know you have money coming in regularly. In this way you won't have to worry about paying them yourself. If you have budgeted well you will know that any money left on a certain date is yours to spend. You may use either direct debits or standing orders. Banks and building societies will explain the differences and tell you what is best for you.

Managing and budgeting – how do I make money go round?
There is a budgeting exercise in Chapter 11, but before you leave care you should have had lots of help to budget, e.g., being given money to shop for certain meals and being given the equivalent of income support to try to manage on it for a week. You should do budgets 'for real' each week or month when you leave care. If you have access to a computer you can do your budget on a spreadsheet.

What happens if I go overdrawn?
Don't go over-drawn (taking out more from your account than you have in it) as it will cost you a lot of money in interest and charges. It may also mean that the bank or building society will close your account. This may make it difficult for you to open another account as references may be required.

What if I do run into difficulties?
Speak to your PA – they have a responsibility to help you. CAB may also be able to help and there are also debt counsellors. Don't worry too much if you get into difficulties at first – even the brightest, most intelligent people sometimes can't manage money. **But** it is important that you tell someone sooner rather than later when you are really into debt.

Financial Matters

There is also available from your local authority a small sum of money to help you out in the short term but you will need to listen to your PA and others to look at what caused the crisis and how it can be avoided in the future.

It is a good idea to save some money if you possibly can, no matter how small. It will help you out in emergencies or you can use it to treat yourself if you are feeling down or to buy something that you really need.

Keeping money at home is not really a good idea as it may be stolen and it is easy to spend the money if it is readily available.

What is the difference between gross pay and take home pay?
Gross pay is the amount of money that you earn, e.g., £4.50 an hour or say £100 per week. Take home pay, often called net pay, is the amount you have left after tax and national insurance has been taken off. Take home pay is the amount you have to live on.

I am going to study at college. Do I get any extra money?
Some local authorities will give a small additional incentive payment to encourage you to study and achieve your qualifications. Travel may also be paid and books and equipment should be covered. If you are studying at a residential FE college you should receive similar allowances to students studying at university – see below.

I am hoping to go to university. What financial help will I get?
- Financial support available during term time for university students.
- Support available during the Christmas, Easter and summer vacations.
- Support available to foster carers if they are able to offer their previously fostered young people the opportunity to return to them during vacations.
- Support to enable young people to apply for:
    University access funds.
    Student loans.
    Tuition fee exemption.

Ideally you should agree the amount you will be paid, when and how it will be paid, before you start your course, plus any additional specific items you will need such as particular clothing, books, IT equipment etc.

I am disabled. I am a young parent. I am an asylum seeker. Am I entitled to the same money as others?
Disabled young people are entitled to certain benefits which may replace their leaving care allowance or it may be in addition to the allowance. Young parents are also provided with additional sources of funding to help them care for their child. Asylum seekers will never be left without receiving any financial assistance but the sources of funding may change as their circumstances change.

As far as finances are concerned:

> *A pathway plan should state how much money a care leaver is entitled to; when it will be paid and the payment method, e.g. cash, by cheque, or into a bank or a building society.*

> *A personal advisor must ensure the correct amount of money is paid; that it is paid on time by the agreed method and to organise changes if appropriate. A PA should also give advice on managing money.*

The Leaving Care Handbook

A local authority is responsible for providing the finances and ensuring that systems are in place so the money is paid as stated in the pathway plan.

A care leaver should have an opportunity to discuss their pathway plan and to be given a copy in writing by the PA.

Leaving care planning should start from the day the young person enters the care system. They need practice in: budgeting; managing money; shopping; comparing the cost of different goods; value for money; and what to do if they get into debt (see Practical Help Chapter 11). These should be reinforced during the preparation for adult life work.

Resources

DoH (2000) *The Framework for the Assessment of Children in Need and their Families*. HMSO.

Fostering Network (2003) *Preparation for Adult Life.* London: Fostering Network Greenwich Council, First Key.

Short, J. (2002) Financial Arrangements for Care Leavers: Developing a Service. In Wheal, A. (Ed.) *The RHP Companion to Leaving Care.* Lyme Regis: Russell House Publishing.

Section Eight: Health Needs – How Are They Best Met

Health and Healthy Lifestyles

Jane Scott

We are all guilty of taking health for granted until we lose it. We all begin diets, which stop because the right food wasn't available, or we begin attending the gym, but are too tired to go after work. The healthy choices must be part of the fabric of our everyday life. It should not be something 'extra' or 'special' that we have to do, but something that becomes second nature, that happens automatically, without even considering it.

(Dunnett, 2005)

Introduction

Working to Healthy Care standards will have a positive effect in how we have prepared the young people for leaving care. The standards (Healthy Care Programme Handbook. National Children's Bureau, 2004) say young people:

- Should experience a genuinely caring, consistent, stable and secure relationship with at least one committed, trained, experienced and supported carer.
- Should live in an environment that promotes health and well-being within the wider community.
- Are given opportunities to develop the personal social and life skills to care for their health and well-being now and in the future.
- Should receive excellent quality health care, assessments, treatment and support.

This chapter sets out then to provide information on:

- The roles and responsibilities of health care professionals.
- How they might be accessed when required.
- Healthy eating strategies.
- Physical exercise.
- Sexual health and infectious diseases.
- Sexual orientation – gay issues.
- Plus it offers health record sheets.

Some roles and responsibilities in health

The Children Act 1998 says there is a duty to:

> To advise, assist and befriend children who are looked after, with a view to promoting their welfare when they cease to be looked after.

(S24 (1))

Under the Children (Leaving Care) Act, Regulation: 4(a), the responsible authority must:
> ... undertake an assessment of young people's health and development as part of the needs assessment, within three months of the young person becoming eligible or relevant. This should be a holistic assessment and should follow the guidance issued by the Department of Health in 2001 'Promoting the Health of Looked after Children'.

No young person should be allowed to leave care unless they have access to a doctor, dentist and an optician.

When a young person is in care and needs to access the health service, it is often their carer who makes the arrangements for them. Therefore, for many young people, when they leave care, it may be the first time they will have to access the health service as an independent user. Health services often present themselves to users as a complicated network of agencies and some young people will need support initially to find their way through the system.

Many areas in the country will now have specialist health workers for looked after young people. Their job is to assist young people in accessing their own health information. Much of the information may be available via the social worker, foster carer or parents and young people may only need to be signposted to the appropriate services.

Health services should be aware of the Pathway Plans and should be encouraged to take ownership by completing the relevant health information that the young person may require. Health services should make this information readily available, and in so doing assist social care and health workers to fulfil their role as corporate parents, thus ensuring that young people are prepared for independence.

Having ownership of your health history is a vital part of who you are; therefore we need to make this information more easily accessible to this group of young people.

Confidentiality is an issue for most young people and we should remember that information they share with us must remain confidential, unless that information is putting them or other young persons at risk, e.g. child protection issues raised.

How to access doctors, dentists and opticians

Young people need to be advised about obtaining the services of all these kinds of health professionals, and of how NHS Direct operates. When supporting young people leaving care, you can work through the Information Sheet at the end of the chapter, *Doctors, Dentists and Opticians*. All young people should also be given the telephone number for NHS Direct.

NHS Direct

This is a 24/7 service that gives advice and help in an emergency. Your care worker will give you the telephone contact number. Write it here: . . .

In addition to helping in an emergency, NHS Direct can give you a list of local GPs, dentists and opticians who you can approach for services. If you have difficulty getting services, NHS Direct can help you.

Doctors

Doctors (general practitioners or GPs) are the main source of direct health delivery. It is possible to access many health services via referrals, or recommendations, from GPs. One of the first tasks you will need to undertake when becoming independent is to register with a GP.

Health and Healthy Lifestyles

When looking for a GP, think about the following:
- Find a practice in your locality.
- If more than one practice is available, speak to friends or neighbours; which practice are they with and why?
- Ask for a copy of the practice leaflet. Find out if they have both male and female GPs, if this is important to you.
- Look at the services the practice has to offer; are they services you wish to access now or might wish for in the future?
- Is the practice, or its doctors, open for registration for new patients? If not, you might need to contact NHS Direct, see above, to help you find one that is.
- Can you get there easily – is public transport available?

If you find a practice in your area that meets all, or most of your requirements you will then need to ask to join the list, in the first instance by approaching the reception staff, either by telephoning or calling at the practice. They should be able to tell you if they are taking new patients at the present time. They will then send you an application form to complete and send to your local Health Authority. The address will be on the form provided. The reception staff at the practice may ask for the address you will be living at, as many practices will only register patients within allocated postal code areas. It may be useful therefore to have with you on first approach your new address and the postcode.

The following information is usually required:
- Current address.
- Previous address.
- NHS number if known.
- Full name.
- Date of birth.
- Previous GP.

If you have your current NHS medical card you can approach the surgery direct with your card. If the surgery will take you onto their books they will sign the form for you at the time and they will send it on to the local Health Authority. You may then access treatment and services immediately. A new medical card will be sent to you in the post showing the name and details of your new GP.

Many services, e.g. hospitals, opticians, can be accessed by a referral from your doctor. Should you need to see a consultant at the local hospital, for example, then your GP will be your first point of contact. They will write to the hospital on your behalf requesting an appointment with them. The GP will also be able to assess how urgent the request is and how quickly you will need to be seen. Hospitals and GPs have close communication links and the hospital will always send a letter to your own GP when they have seen you, and delivered, or offered you any services. They may require your GP to follow up initial services or treatments and therefore it is vital that you keep your GP informed of any changes in circumstance, e.g. changes of name or address.

Examples of services offered or accessed via your GP:
- Well man or woman clinics.
- Antenatal services (midwifery, health visitors).
- Asthma or diabetes clinics.
- Chiropody.
- Sexual health sessions or family planning services.
- Mental health services.
- Counselling services.
- Minor operations at the practice.
- Pharmacy services.
- Baby clinics and immunisation service.
- Smoking cessation clinics.
- Addiction services including alcohol.

If you approach the local GPs in your area and are unable to register as a patient with them, you should contact NHS Direct. NHS Direct will give you the contact number relating to the local Primary Care Trust in which you are resident. You will then be able to contact the PCT and they will allocate you a local GP.

Dental services

Many areas in the country at the present time have few or no NHS dentists who are registering new NHS patients. Therefore, if you are registered with a dentist in the town or city where you live, remain with that dentist (even if some miles away) until you find a local dental practice that is willing to take new NHS patients.

If you don't have a dentist and need emergency treatment then contact NHS Direct who will give you the name and address of the 'on duty' dentist. It will then be your responsibility to make and keep the emergency appointment. This registration will only last for the duration of treatment and will not then make that practice responsible for any future work needed.

To find a dental practice that is accepting new patients for registration for NHS treatment, try using the Local Dental Practices search on www.nhs.uk. To identify whether a practice is accepting patients, make sure you check the treatment policies for that practice. If practices are not accepting patients, the policy will be shown in red. If they are accepting patients, the policies will be shown in green.

Alternatively, you can use the www.nhs.uk Dental Searches to locate a dentist that is registering NHS patients.

If this is not suitable, your local Primary Care Trust (PCT) or NHS Direct, on 0845 4647, can provide you with details of other dentists accepting NHS patients.

Most dentists will carry out NHS work. This will mean that the dental patient will pay only the rates stated by the NHS for a particular treatment or course of treatment.

You are entitled to free dental treatment:
1. Up to the age of 18 (19 years if in full-time education).
2. If you are pregnant and for 1 year after the baby is born.
3. If you are on income support or on income-based job seekers allowance.
4. If you are on family tax credit you *may* be entitled to free dental treatment.
5. If you are a full-time college or university student.

Note: If you are in groups 3, 4 and 5 above you will need to apply for an Exemption Certificate when you receive benefit or from your dentist. You will complete a form each time you attend a NHS dentist which will ask relevant questions of you, and you will be informed of what charges you will need to pay.

Note: Private dental costs are substantially more than NHS costs. It is therefore imperative that you establish with your dentist that you wish to remain an NHS patient.

Eyesight and opticians

Young people should have an eyesight test at least once a year. It is not necessary to use the same optician for each appointment for a routine vision screening. You can shop around and find an optician you are happy with. Should you require glasses the optician will provide you with the prescription for the appropriate lenses. You will then be free to buy your glasses at any optician taking the prescription with you.

You are entitled to a free NHS sight test:

1. Up to the age of 18 (19 years if in full-time education).
2. If you are pregnant and for one year after the baby is born.
3. If you are on income support or on income-based job seekers allowance.
4. If you are on family tax credit you *may* be entitled to free eye treatment.
5. If you are a full-time college or university student.

Note: If you are in groups 3, 4 and 5 listed above you will need to apply for an Exemption Certificate when you receive benefit or from your optician.

Healthy eating strategies: prevention is better than cure

Healthy eating

If we are setting plans and making adequate preparation for care, and leaving care, we should be achieving those standards for our young people. The National Obesity Strategy particularly looks at issues such as school meals. We should be looking at the standards of food and its content (fat etc.) that young people are being offered in their care settings. They should also be given advice, help and guidance on the food they eat when they leave care.

Good examples are breakfast and Sunday lunch clubs for care leavers; life skills courses, with food, bathing and washing facilities all under one roof at a one stop shop.

Good nutrition is fundamental to growth and development. Young people who are preparing to leave care often feel they have stopped growing in height and it is no longer relevant for them to consider growth and nutrition. Not so. We need to use the time wisely prior to young people leaving care by offering them many and varied programmes on cooking simple nutritious meals on a budget.

Eating well for looked after children and young people

Some basic advice on healthy eating should be given to all young people who are moving to independent living.

There are a variety of guidelines, books and leaflets available giving nutritional and practical guidelines for food provided for children and young people. Based on current dietary recommendations, the guidelines (The Healthy Care Standards, see Page 1 of this chapter) are intended for use by all those involved in the care of looked after children and young people. They contain a wealth of practical advice on ways of encouraging healthy eating among looked after children and young people (The Caroline Walker Trust, see Resources).

Key messages from the manual

Breakfast is a very important meal. Always try to allow yourself time to eat breakfast. Get up 30 mins earlier! Cereals are an excellent source of fibre, vitamins and minerals. If you eat breakfast you are much less likely to snack on high fat, high sugar snacks later in the day.

Eat the recommended five portions of fruit and vegetables per day. This need not be too expensive. Remember – baked beans, for instance, will count in the five per day – as will a handfull of raisins.

Aim for a balance in your diet. You should aim to include the five food groups in your daily intake. The groups will give a balanced diet if the correct portion of each group is understood.

Bread and other cereals and potatoes can be eaten in larger amounts. However, try to choose wholegrain bread, and cereals, e.g. brown rice, wholemeal pasta. Potatoes should not be eaten fried, try to have them baked or boiled.

Milk and dairy foods. Eat or drink moderate amounts of these. Choose lower fat versions.

Foods with fat and foods with sugar. Eat only small amounts of these; don't eat foods containing sugar too often.

Meat and fish and alternatives (proteins). Eat moderate amounts of these. Choose lower fat versions.

Drink water. Fizzy drinks should be avoided as much a possible as they can be harmful to teeth. Diet drinks can also be harmful to our teeth as they may erode the tooth enamel. Milk, milkshakes and fruit smoothies are good alternatives.

Snacks. It is important that snacks as well as meals are varied. Young people will often choose to snack on crisps, biscuits and chocolate as they are instantly available and require no preparation. Try to have alternatives in your food cupboard. Some suggestions for alternative snacks are:
- Any type of bread, white or brown, crumpets, teacakes, malt loaf, and bagels, pitta bread, cheese scones, etc.
- Plain biscuits such as rich tea, breadsticks, crisp bread, Melba toast.
- Home-made popcorn, home-made oven-baked potato crisps.
- Raw vegetables, such as carrots or celery served with dips made from fromage frais and soft cheese or salsa dip, as these are low in fat.
- Breakfast cereals.
- Vegetarians need to look at their diet to ensure all the necessary vitamins and minerals are being included in the diet in required amounts.

Information is available in the Caroline Walker Book. However, you can obtain more information from the Vegetarian Society, see end of chapter.

Food

Safety and hygiene

Before they leave care young people should learn about basic food hygiene, for example:
- Always wash hands prior to food preparation.
- Always wash hands after using the toilet or using a handkerchief.
- How to reheat food safely.
- How to recognise whether food is safe to eat.
- Preparing raw and cooked food separately.
- Understand how to store, prepare and cook food safely.
- Keep equipment and surfaces clean.
- Do not smoke where food is being prepared.
- Make sure cuts and sores are covered with waterproof dressings.
- Keep food covered.
- Cool leftover food quickly and refrigerate.

Health and Healthy Lifestyles

- Do not allow pets to walk on food preparation surfaces.
- Follow the use-by-dates on food, this includes fresh, dried or canned foods.
- Keep cooking and eating utensils clean.

Cooking on a budget

Young people should be encouraged to practice cooking on a budget. This needs to be over a long period, not a one-off meal or even just for a week. One month is recommended as a minimum period. There are many booklets and books available to give help in this direction.

It will be very tempting for them to think of other ways of using their disposable income when they leave care so it is vital for them to work out the minimum amount of money they will need to eat properly.

Young people should have the opportunity to understand the prices in different food outlets e.g. the fruit market, the local baker, the prices at the corner shop. The costs of cooking should be born in mind; making the best use of the oven, for instance, when cooking a meal. Can they cook more than one dish at a time, e.g. chicken roasting and a rice pudding on another shelf?

Useful items to keep in store cupboard

- Breakfast cereals.
- Pasta.
- Cooking oil.
- Flour.
- Milk powder.
- Canned or jacket soups.
- Tomato puree.
- Dried potato.
- Rice.
- Condiments, salt and pepper.
- Canned fruit.
- Jam, honey.
- Marmite, stock cubes.
- Variety of canned food.
- Beans, sweetcorn, tomato, carrots, peas.
- Tinned tuna.

Young people leaving care should be able to:
- Make a simple stir-fry.
- Prepare potatoes, or other starchy food by boiling, baking or microwaving.
- Cook rice, pasta or noodles in the right quantities.
- Boil scramble or fry eggs.
- Prepare and cook vegetables.
- Grill, oven-bake or fry foods such as sausage, fish fingers or bacon.
- Make a simple dish of something on toast.
- Make a simple pasta sauce.

When visiting young people, who have left a care environment, find out:
- What they ate the day before.
- Who they ate with.
- What foods they have in the cupboard or fridge.
- Whether they have gained or lost weight.

These are all the issues that we would address with our own children who leave home. None of us will have managed to 'get it right first time' so we need to give them space to make their own mistakes but be safe in the knowledge that we are interested in how they are coping and will be there to offer support, guidance and help when needed.

Physical exercise

Many young people today enjoy physical activity. We need to ensure those moving to independence are able to continue with activities in their new area. As carers, or young peoples' support workers, we should try to have an overview of the area the young person wishes to move to, and be able to point out the main leisure facilities, pools, football clubs etc. that they may wish to access. If the local authority has a leisure card scheme, we need to ensure our young people have a card and understand how they can use it.

For those young people who are not interested in joining a club or organised activity programme, we need to develop an understanding with them on how important a healthy lifestyle is for them.

Research has shown us that physical activity, exercise and sport have an important role in:
- Stimulating appetite.
- Preventing obesity.
- Enhancing physical, mental and social well-being.

People who have been active when young have better physical and mental health in later life.

Try to establish what exercise the young person does. For instance, many young people will walk rather than pay a bus fare, or will choose to save the money by walking yet they do not consider this to be a form of exercise. Dancing is an excellent form of exercise and some young people will go out two or three nights per week and spend many hours dancing.

Swimming, cycling, or even using a dance mat in the home can give them the exercise they need especially if done two or three times per week. Boys tend to be better at keeping up with activities such as sport or simply meeting mates on bikes or skates or attending the local gym. Girls tend to let go of school-based sports when they leave school. Perhaps if we accompanied them to the local gym until they felt comfortable in using the facilities themselves it would encourage the girls to continue with the activity. We need to set examples for our young people to follow.

Joining a Salsa Club and having lessons would be a great way to meet new people and get exercise. Let's take time to know and understand the young people we work with and try to impress upon them the benefits of a healthy lifestyle.

Sexual health

Young people leaving care should have the opportunity to discuss their sexual health in a setting they find comfortable and with a person they are able to trust, and who is able to offer accurate up-to-date information. This may be:

- Their personal advisor.
- Their foster carer.
- A specialist nurse.
- Staff at the local sexual health clinic.

Sexual health services are free, and available to all people in many different settings The people delivering information to young people should be aware of local services, time, days and frequency etc.

Some young people may choose to access services away from their local area and therefore information on regional services should be available to them. We need to ensure they are making informed choices about where, when and who they access services from.

Where do we access sexual health information services?

Health and Healthy Lifestyles

- Yellow pages.
- Local family planning sessions.
- General practitioner.
- Sexual health outreach services.
- Young peoples' one-stop shops.
- Hospitals.
- GUM clinics (genito-urinary medicine centres).
- Leaflets.
- Connexions staff.
- School nurses and teachers.
- Health visitors.
- Social workers.
- Help lines.
- Brook Advisory clinics.

Pregnancy

Some of our young people will be parents or will be pregnant. Health visitors attached to the GP surgery will be able to offer regular advice and support and will ensure that the young people, their babies and children, are accessing any extra support they are entitled to, e.g. Sure Start programmes or courses available in Healthy Living Centres.

All local authorities should have equal opportunity policies that will ensure all young people from a variety of backgrounds are able to access the same levels of services.

Contraception

Did you know that there are at least 10 methods of contraception available at present? Family planning clinics, doctors' surgeries and health centres give advice and guidance as to which method is best for an individual and on how to use the particular form of contraception. If contraception is used to prevent pregnancy, people are:

- Free to make choices in their lives.
- Free to enjoy sex without the worry of unwanted pregnancies.
- Able to go where and when they please.
- Able to live with whom they wish.
- Able to have children when *they* and *their* partner want and are ready.
- Given time to learn about relationships.
- In a position to decide with whom they would like to have a child.
- Able to say yes or no to sex with confidence and freedom.

Condom use

Using a condom is an effective form of birth control if applied carefully, ensuring it does not split. Using a condom is also an effective way of preventing the spread of disease from infected semen. When having anal sex, a strong condom should **always** be used.

Note! Using contraception is beneficial in most cases. However, there may be circumstances when this may not be the case. For example:

- Girls or women with learning difficulties may have their rights infringed if they are not given choices.
- Non-articulate families are sometimes not offered a full choice of contraception and so may receive contraception that may have side-effects.

Information packs

Young people tell us that it would be useful to have a pack available to them containing written and pictorial information on contraception methods. There are many user friendly leaflets for young people available from your local Health Promotion Departments. These can be accessed from the Primary Health Trust area that you reside in. This Department will be able to give young people and their carers and parents the times and venues of local clinics, courses or facilities available to them. Information given could then be studied at a time convenient to the young person and follow-up appointments sought if necessary to discuss any issues raised.

Basic information could be provided on:
- Condoms.
- Oral contraception (the pill).
- Emergency contraception.
- Hormonal implants.
- Injections.
- Barrier methods (cap).
- Intra-uterine devices (the coil).

Sexually transmitted infections

Information on sexually transmitted infections should also be available to all young people. If the issues are dealt with in a factual, sensitive way, then the young person will have much to gain from this opportunity to explore any myths and misunderstandings they may have. They will then be equipped with the knowledge to seek guidance or advice in the future. Knowledge based on fact may often empower young people to have greater control of their relationships and help them to make informed choices that are right for them.

Some infections to discuss

Chlamydia

Cause:	Bacteria
Symptoms:	Most women and some men don't have any symptoms. If you do it may not happen for a long time. Symptoms may include:
	• discharge
	• heavy periods
	• low abdominal pain
	• pain on passing urine
Effect on health:	If untreated in women it can spread to the womb and fallopian tubes leading to pain, blockages and infertility (inability to have a child).
Diagnosis:	Swab from area that may be affected. Sometimes a urine sample.
Treatment:	Antibiotics for about a week.
Other information:	Transmitted by:
	• Unprotected penetrative sex.
	• Unprotected oral sex.
	• Can be transferred by the fingers from the genitals to the eyes.
	• Can be passed from the mother to baby during birth.

Gonorrhoea

Cause:	Bacteria.
Symptoms:	Most women and some men don't have any symptoms. If you do it may not happen for a long time. Symptoms may include:
	• Discharge, may be green or white and smelly.
	• Heavy periods.
	• Low abdominal pain.
	• Pain on passing urine.

Health and Healthy Lifestyles

Effect on health: If untreated in women it can spread to the womb and fallopian tubes leading to pain, blockages and infertility (inability to have a child).
Diagnosis: Swab from area that may be affected. Sometimes a urine sample.
Treatment: Antibiotics for about a week.
Other information: Transmitted by:
- Unprotected penetrative sex.
- Unprotected oral sex.
- Can be transferred by the fingers from one genital area to another.
- Can be transferred by the fingers from the genitals to the eyes.
- Can be passed from the mother to baby during birth.

Genital warts
Cause: Virus.
Symptoms: Growth or warts in genital area.
Effect on health: Very unsightly.
Diagnosis: Diagnosed visually.
Treatment: Ointment, freezing.
Other information: Transmitted by:
- Skin to skin contact.
- Can take a long time to develop.
- Treatment can take months.
- Warts reoccur.

Genital herpes
Cause: Virus.
Symptoms: Small painful blisters in the genital area that heal in a week or two. May also be tingling or itching. Burning sensation when passing urine; or feeling like you have flu.
Effect on health: Very painful.
Diagnosis: Visually diagnosed. A swab may be taken.
Treatment: Cream and tablets available. There is no known cure.
Other information: Transmitted by:
- Direct contact including kissing.
- Unprotected oral sex.
- Unprotected penetrative sex.
- Can be passed from mother to baby during birth (but very rare).
- May cause miscarriage in early pregnancy or early labour in late pregnancy.
- Frequency and severity of attacks tend to get less.

HIV
Cause: Virus (Human Immunodeficiency Virus).
Symptoms: Usually none for a number of years. Body's defence system is damaged so it cannot fight off certain infections and diseases.
Effect on health: Develops over years leading to AIDS (Acquired Immune Deficiency Syndrome) when serious infections are occurring.
Diagnosis: Blood test taken about three months after possible infection.
Treatment: Treatments available to try to slow down the progression of HIV.

Other information: Transmitted by:
- Unprotected penetrative sex.
- Infected needles, syringes of drug users.
- Can be passed from mother to baby during pregnancy.
- By receiving infected blood or blood products.

Sexual orientation

It is important that young people have access to services that recognise and support the needs of lesbian, gay and bisexual (LGB) young people. These services vary nationally and we need to ensure that workers have regularly updated knowledge of services in their area.

Questions commonly asked by LGB young people.

If I am gay am I normal?
Yes, being lesbian or gay means you fancy people of the same sex as yourself, being bisexual means that you may fancy people who are the same or the opposite sex; this may change from time to time. Who you are as a person doesn't change.

Why am I gay (LGB)?
There is no definite answer; it's just the way you are.

Who can I talk to?
There are projects set up for LGB people all over the UK. To get the contact details for groups in your local area, ring directory enquiries (118180, for example) and ask for Lesbian, Gay and Bisexual Projects and tell them your area. The workers at the projects will be able to offer you confidential support on many issues.

Coming out

Telling people about your sexuality can be a difficult time for you. It is up to you when the time is right but you may wish to consider:

- Are your parents or carers 'gay-friendly' or open-minded? This is often a difficult judgement: is there a close family member or worker who you could discuss this with first? Could it be your social worker or support worker?
- How well do you know your carers and workers? Once you have told them it will be difficult to take back, so try to ensure you have someone who understands and supports you to help you at times you may find difficult? If you are moving into a semi-independent living scheme or supported lodgings is there going to be a source of support for you? Your social worker or placement officers should have already identified providers where the sexuality of young people will not be an issue. You can check this out with your social worker prior to meeting your new provider.

Remember, think about your decision on when to come out. It is OK to come out – and it is OK not to. Just do it when the time is right for you, and you feel supported.

Conclusion

With so many other pressures on their lives, care leavers often do not see health as an important issue. If only they knew! If they feel good about themselves, they will be more confident. If they knew about how to go about getting help in different circumstances, they would get better more quickly and so would not have to take too much time off work or from their studies etc.

Health and Healthy Lifestyles

Being healthy really is important. We have to give them all the support, help and advice we can so they can be healthy and stay healthy.

Resources

National contacts information

FFLAG Helpline 01454 852 418
Child line 0800 11 11
Terrance Higgins Trust (THT) 0845 12 21
16–25 Counselling 0207 835 1495
The Vegetarian Society, Parkdale, Dunham Road, Altrincham, Cheshire, WA14 4QG. 0161 928 0793.

www.tht.org.uk
www.avert.org
www.fflag.org.uk
www.queeryouth.org.uk

www.ndh.org.uk
www.teenagepregnancyunit.gov.uk
www.ash.org.uk
www.childline.org.uk

Suggested reading and references

Annual Report from Local Teenage Pregnancy Co-Coordinators in Local Areas.
Department of Health (2000) *Children (Leaving Care) Act 2000.* DoH.
Department of Health (2002) *When Leaving Home is also Leaving Care.* DoH.
Dunnett, K. (2005) In Wheal, A. (Ed.) *RHP Companion to Foster Care.* Lyme Regis: Russell House Publishing.
Getting it Right. Good Practice in Leaving Care Resource Pack.
Resource for Teenage Pregnancy Co-Coordinators. Deena Haydon, Principal Officer Research and Development, Barnados.
Social Care and Health. *Local Development Plans*.
Teenage Pregnancy Unit. *Guidance for Field and Social workers and Foster Carers on Providing Information and Referring Young People to Contraceptive Services*.
The Caroline Walker Trust. *Improving Public Health through Good Food.* www.cwt.org.uk
Toolkit. *Practical Strategies for Sexual Health Promotion*. Jo Adams Sheffield Centre for HIV and Sexual Health.

The Leaving Care Handbook

Health record sheet 1

Name ....

Name and address of **doctor** ....   Blood group ....

....   Allergies ....

....   Necessary medication ....

Telephone number ....

Date	Treatment

Date	Type of Injection

Health record sheet 2

Name and address of **dentist** ....   Telephone number ....

....

....

Date	Treatment

Name and address of **optician** ....   Telephone number ....

....

....

Date	Treatment/Advice

16

Mental Health of Care Leavers

Cynthia Fletcher

Introduction

Every young person has a right to expect that their emotional needs will be met as they grow into a mature adult. These needs are:

- Basic physical care.
- Affection.
- Security.
- Stimulation of innate potential.
- Guidance and control.
- Responsibility.
- Independence.

This chapter is in five parts:
1. A definition of mental health.
2. The National Service Framework.
3. The role of the Child and Adolescent Mental Health Service (CAMHS).
4. Anticipating and managing difficult behaviours.
5. How care leaver workers can help.

Many of the ideas contained in the chapter can be used in group work, e.g. for training care workers, or facilitating groups of young people, or in one-to-one coaching and counselling of young people.

The material in this chapter, which has been seen and checked by young people who have spent time in care and have experienced self-acknowledged mental health problems in their teenage years, is based upon:
- Work done with a number of groups of leaving care workers.
- Work with some residential carers.
- Some work done in the community to build on earlier experience gained when the author was supporting residential and foster carers and leaving care workers.

1. A definition of mental health

There are a number of issues that concern people who work with children who have been or who are in the care system, all of which relate to the young people's emotional health and well-being, in effect, their mental health.

If, on a training seminar or in a group discussion, you ask participants to list what comes to mind when thinking about the term 'mental health', you will usually get a list of mental illnesses, illustrating the fact that, in this country, 'mental health' is interpreted as 'mental illness'. There is a view in society that mental illness is something to hide and to be ashamed of and therefore it is little mentioned except in tabloid headlines when mistakes have been made. This stigma attached to mental health prevents young people and their carers seeking appropriate help until small problems become crises.

We are an illiterate country as far as emotional literacy goes. It is important to change people's focus onto 'good mental health' rather than 'mental illness'. We need to promote the importance of good mental health in young people. We also need to stress that by early intervention there is more chance of success in avoiding mental illness. Helping young people become emotionally literate is a key task for all carers and professionals who work with young people.

Before trying to understand why some young people are more vulnerable and why some young people have more challenging behaviour than others, it is important to be clear about child development, the stages children and young people go through as they grow up. The teenage years or adolescence can be a particularly difficult time for vulnerable young people. It is also worth remembering that many young people who have been in care go on to lead successful lives, but for some young people their care experience combined with the experiences before they entered the looked after system continue to impact on their lives into adulthood and in particular on their mental health.

The teenage years

The teenage years are one of the most challenging times for all young people when they are trying to discover who they are, where they belong and what they will do in the future. This is particularly hard for young people who have been in care and possibly had a number of carers, surnames, addresses, schools, groups of friends etc. Cultural differences also play a role here and often complicate the identity issues for young people who have been in care, especially if their carers have not been a cultural or religious match for the young person. Frequently asked questions for all teenagers are:

- Who am I?
- Where do I belong?
- What am I going to do?
- Why me?

For young people who are in care or who have spent time in care this is a particularly vulnerable time as the disruptions in their life caused by their placements in care impact very heavily on their choices for the future. How do you know where you belong if you have had multiple placements (it is always worth reminding yourself of how many placements young people have had) and many other life changes? How do you know who you are? How can you learn about and discover yourself, when you are in a continual state of angst, always fearful that others control your life and can make changes to it at their whim? No wonder the risk-taking actions of this group go off both ends of the scale.

Risk taking is part of the 'normal range' of teenage behaviour; when young people try to attempt to answer the questions about themselves and become more independent. The maturation process demands that the young person seeks independence and self-actualisation. So refusing to accept help and support is a natural reaction from a teenager. Learning to accept help when you need it is a lesson all teenagers and some adults have to realise at some point but the majority (many of whom will have had supportive family environments) manage to do so without taking life-threatening risks. Young people who have been in care and who may have suffered multiple trauma may feel impelled to take great risks at this age or to self-harm.

It is very hard to watch your own children making mistakes but learning from your mistakes is an essential part of growing up. The difficulties of doing this when you are working with a young person professionally and sometimes having to watch them taking such huge, and often life-threatening risks, is impossible to handle alone, and supervision for everyone working with these young people is essential. Supervision is not a luxury, it is a right and is essential if the carers and workers are to maintain their own mental health. Carers and workers should ensure that they request this supervision regularly if they are not being offered it.

In some young people the emotional turmoil is so great it has become internalised by them as stress, and has become part of their natural state of being. Even when they are relaxed they don't feel really alive. Perhaps this is one of the reasons why they self-harm; and understanding the reasons why, will help carers and workers cope better with the behaviours. Continuation of repeated self-destructive behaviour patterns long after help is available and has been taken up, baffles and frustrates the young people and their carers and workers alike.

When stress becomes illness

Sometimes, despite interventions and support, a point is reached when it is essential for a person to receive treatment in order to prevent them from harming themselves or others. If the person is unwilling or unable to agree to the treatment – often involving secure hospitalisation – then the person has to be 'sectioned' which means that at least three qualified people need to agree to this action. This is a legal requirement. The person cannot then leave the place where they are taken, usually a mental hospital, until the section is rescinded or expires. A first section is usually for about 28 days.

2. The National Service Framework

Standard 9

All children and young people, from birth to their eighteenth birthday, who have mental health problems and disorders, should have access to timely, integrated, high-quality, multi-disciplinary mental health services to ensure effective assessment, treatment and support, for them and their families.

The National Service Framework for Children, Young People and Maternity Services, Standard 9 (DES/DoH, 2004) (NSF) establishes clear standards for promoting the health and well-being of children and young people and for providing high quality services which meet their needs. Standard 9 is The Mental Health and Psychological Well Being of Children and Young People.

The framework sets out an agenda for change in the Child and Adolescent Mental Health Services (CAMHS) where by 2006 comprehensive CAMHS services must be provided for all young people and also, importantly, the 16-18 year age band who traditionally have not been offered a service unless they are severely mentally ill. The NSF will mean:
- An improvement in the mental health of all children and young people.
- Multi-agency services, working in partnership, to promote the mental health of all children and young people, provide early intervention and also meet the needs of children and young people with established or complex problems.
- All children, young people and their families will have access to mental health care based upon the best available evidence and provided by staff with an appropriate range of skills and competencies.

*The NSF Targets (*A Comprehensive CAMHS by 2006, DES/DoH, 2004*) are:*
- Clarity about how users' needs are met.
- Clear pathways for accessing CAMHS.
- Collaborative arrangements between agencies and voluntary providers.

- Multi-agency partnerships to plan, commission and deliver comprehensive CAMHS.
- Evidence-based practice and a CAMHS which evaluates the outcomes of its work with young people and families.
- A range of services to meet the needs of all young people who have mental health problems including black and ethnic minorities, those in the youth justice system, those in the looked after system and aftercare, those with disabilities, and those with complex behavioural problems.
- Provision of 24 hour cover.
- All tiers have a CAMHS service including appropriate inpatient, outreach and inreach services.
- Workforce and training issues need to be planned if the new workforce is to be achieved.
- Organisation and protocols particularly with adult mental health.
- Mental health promotion and prevention of mental illness form part of each CAMHS strategy.

Unfortunately there are constraints to this:
- CAMHS teams are often very small, so growth at the rate needed is going to be very challenging.
- There are insufficient trained and skilled staff to accommodate this growth.
- 'Cures' for all these conditions do not exist, but interventions and management is possible with multi-agency support. The evidence base for intervention is quite limited at present but will grow over time

It is necessary to pioneer new and innovative treatments that will clearly need to involve psycho-social multi-agency packages of care in the community, and sometimes in residential settings, very few of which exist at present. Also, it involves the co-operation of *adult* and *child* mental health services, working together which in most areas is not well developed. There are a few projects which demonstrate how effective 'wrapping' support services around the young person and carer can be, for example, the Rosta Project in Liverpool (and treatment foster care projects elsewhere). Voluntary groups offering counselling and drop-in facilities for young people can be helpful especially when this work is supported by local CAMHS teams offering supervision and consultation to the volunteer counsellors.

3. The role of the Child and Adolescent Mental Heath Service (CAMHS)

Psychiatry and psychology and other CAMHS professions have advanced in terms of dealing with the more severe mental illness. Usually, an initial assessment will take place and then an intervention offered if appropriate. In some cases medication is used with young people.

The talk therapies have been shown to be useful if the young person can engage, but if the therapy is clinic-based, or if the therapist has 'psych' in front of their title, often the young person will not turn up or engage. Consequently, the most damaged and the most vulnerable have not always been able to access a service, and although research into *what works* is now growing there is not a large body of evidence of what the effective treatments are.

The Children and Adolescent Mental Health Services (CAMHS) embodies various professions:
- Psychiatrists – both child and adolescent, who prescribe for patients and can access in-patient facilities.
- Clinical child psychologists.
- Family therapists.
- Psychotherapists.
- Cognitive behavioural therapists.
- Play therapists.

- Music therapists.
- Movement therapists.
- Drama therapists.
- Social workers.
- Nurses – community psychiatric nurses, registered mental health nurses, CAMHS trained nurses.
- CAMHS counsellors.
- Occupational therapists.
- Primary mental health workers.
- Adolescent mental health workers.
- Educational psychologists.
- Specialist teachers.

Mental illness

This is an attempt to list the disorders and conditions with which CAMHS may be involved. Note: Previously, not all CAMHS have been involved with all of these, but the NSF will over a ten-year period seek to equalise access to the range of therapies and skills needed for these conditions.

- Disturbances of conduct.
- Disturbances of attention.
- Anxiety disorders.
- Depressive disorders.
- Psychotic disorders.
- Eating disorders.
- Deliberate self-harm.
- Substance abuse.
- Pervasive developmental disorders: Tourette's Syndrome.
- Coping with physical symptoms with no known cause.
- Coping with painful procedures.
- Coping with chronic physical illness and disease.

The range of interventions and therapies offered include:
- Behaviour therapies.
- Creative therapies, e.g. art, drama, dance, music.
- Cognitive behavioural techniques.
- Multi-modal therapies.
- Narrative therapy.
- Parent training.
- Physical treatments (use of prescription drugs).
- Psychodynamic therapies.
- Psycho-social approaches.
- Systemic family therapies.

This is not intended to be either a complete list nor does it attempt to explain what each of these mean. CAMHS do not routinely offer all these therapies, but with the advent of the NSF and the growth of the evidence base of the effectiveness of each of these, there should be equity of provision for all young people wherever they live within ten years.

Knowing when to refer a young person to another, appropriate, mental health professional is a difficult decision and it would be helpful for leaving care workers to build up a good working relationship with CAMHS and other adult mental health services so that they can work together. It is important to receive training in understanding *when* to refer and *how* to refer, and for CAMHS staff to understand the work of the leaving care team, as this will help to ensure the right decisions are made about referral. It will also help with supporting young people on medication and those receiving therapy.

Those who turn inwards with their problems can be those young people who have problems accepting they have difficulties (they just tell themselves they are a bit down) and because their behaviour isn't 'psychotic', accessing a service of any kind can be difficult. This group often have very low self-esteem. Those whose behaviour is violent towards others or objects, at the far end of the scale, can be labelled as having conduct disorder, borderline personality disorder or being

The Leaving Care Handbook

'psychotic' and can often seem to be the most frightening to deal with. It has traditionally been very difficult to access a mental health service for this group, but Early Intervention Services for Psychosis are being developed now and mental health services for 16 to 18-year-olds have to be provided as part of the NSF Standard 9. The provision of services will improve as we train an expanding workforce.

4. Anticipating and managing difficult behaviours

It is worth remembering that *all behaviour* has meaning for the person involved and often it is a case of trying to work out with the young person what is *behind* the presenting behaviours. Noticing when the difficult behaviours occur, and, at an appropriate moment, reflecting this back to the young person, with support to work it through, will help them begin to see the patterns and avoid making the same mistake next time the situation presents itself. The difficult behaviours will often be the result of stress.

Pro-active measures

Prevention is better than cure so if possible try to identify the causes of challenging behaviour in advance, and avoid the things that trigger the challenging behaviours. First list the unwelcome behaviours that are to be dealt with. One way of doing this is to draw or imagine an iceberg with some of the iceberg above the water but most of it below the water (see Figure 16.1). List the unwelcome behaviours above the water, keeping 'acting-out' behaviours to one side and 'acting-in self-harm' and 'suicide' to the other side. Then, reflect on the feelings that lurk below the water and what the behaviours might really be saying about the young person's needs.

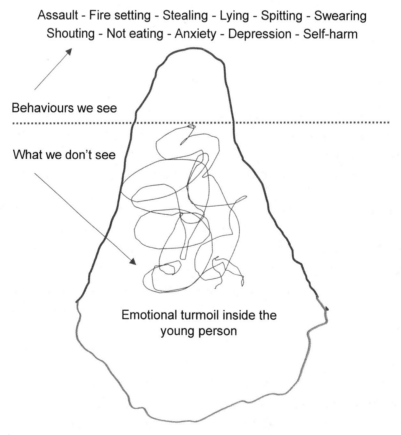

Figure 16.1 *Behaviours*

Mental Health of Care Leavers

This exercise can be done alone as a thought-clearing activity or it can be done within a group. If the climate is right, then it can be done with the young person as a one-to-one exercise. Hopefully, in this way, the young person will begin to recognise – and anticipate – potential outbursts and hence be in a position to manage them if they have the will to do so.

Post-crisis review: reactive measures

A similar approach to that above is still valid 'post-crisis'. By listing the behaviours and identifying the 'triggers', lessons can be learned for the future, by asking what might have averted this, e.g. behaviour or anger management. Try to get the young person to:
- Reflect on what triggered the crisis.
- Review what actually happened and see this from other people's perspectives.
- Learn what triggers them.
- Work out what to do to prevent it happening again.

Reinforce this new behaviour through practising (talking it through, and then role playing it) and then when a young person uses this strategy, noticing and praising them.

When a young person has been brought up in a household where the reaction to stress is to get drunk, or shout, or be violent, they have never experienced an adult example of other, better, ways of coping with stress. Simply modelling this in your own behaviour provides an example for them to copy.

Coping mechanisms

Discussing with the young person how *you* cope with stresses may also help but always work out beforehand what you are willing to share. Get the young person to try to visualise a volcano (see Figure 16.2) with all the 'bad feelings' and turmoil on the inside and then add the sorts of

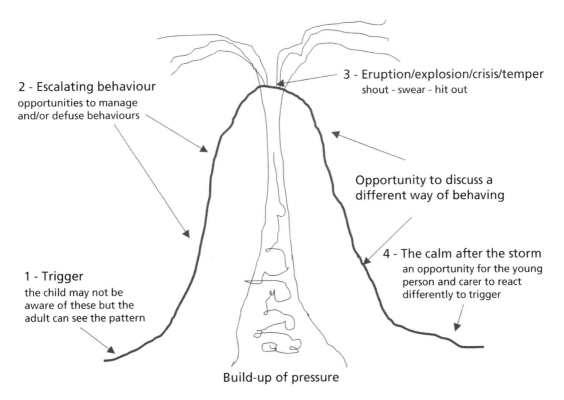

Figure 16.2 *Eruptions are a chance for change*

behaviours which erupt from the top and pour down the slopes as the stress becomes unbearable. Then get the young person to suggest a list of the coping mechanisms they use when they get angry.

Remember that these young people have very low stress thresholds brought about by the trauma they have suffered so are more likely to exceed their stress tolerance easily. The young people themselves are as bewildered by what they do as you are. They want to feel safe, but this is an unsafe feeling. Just by you being a consistent factor in their life of turmoil is recuperative for them.

Experienced case workers can almost predict the sort of behaviour that will be the reaction to certain types of abuse.

Make a list of your own coping mechanisms – or generate a list with your colleagues at work. You could discuss this list with young people; and you could also ask them to make their own list.

Guided fantasy

To help you really understand the feelings of young people who have been in care, imagine a scenario:

> *You have a row with your best friend – you know you are right but before you can finish the argument they rush off home. You are at home for the weekend alone without resolving any of the issues. It is very unfair that you have been left high and dry with these feelings. You try to settle down in front of the TV but you can't get the thought out of your head. What do you do, think, and so on.*

Close your eyes and try to think how they would feel, and to go to extremes if that is what you felt. Then write these down. Look at the list of coping mechanisms you wrote before and note that even with these, you failed to cope with this stress.

How then can we expect young people without coping mechanisms to cope with the stresses of teenage life, the choices, temptations, etc.

Remember when you did it, it was an exercise. It may be one you could do with a group of young people or one-to-one?

The fizzy drink bottle theory of behaviour

A useful way of explaining what happens when we lose our temper is the coke bottle theory, see Figure 16.3. The anger or temper in a young person can be thought of as the fizz in a bottle of fizzy drink that has been shaken. To prevent the fizz (temper) exploding all over the place the cap must be undone very slowly and gently.

Another way to prevent fizzy drink from being fizzy is to add a lump of sugar, which is like being supportive and tolerant with the young person. Being supportive and caring (sugar) to young people who have suffered trauma or are losing their tempers (fizzy drink) helps them to calm down. Even when they don't seem able to accept your support it is helpful for them to know someone can relate to them or care about them even if it is your job to do so.

It is a small minority who take up so much time and with whom the work often seems much less effective. Young people in this situation have been described by leaving care workers as, 'a bottomless pit draining workers around them emotionally whilst working their way through every piece of available accommodation at a rapid rate'. What professionals constantly need to remind

Mental Health of Care Leavers

Figure 16.3 *The coke can theory of behaviour*

themselves is that the early experiences have made the young person very vulnerable to stress and more likely to lack coping mechanisms.

Getting sufficient attention and emotional support

For all of us, but for young people especially, it is important to feel loved and have emotional needs met. These are called positive strokes, bits of attention that make us feel good – e.g. if someone says 'you look nice today', or 'that was good'. These positive strokes give us a 'feel good factor' inside, usually like a warm glow in our chests. People must have these positive strokes when they are young if they are to grow emotionally, understand other's needs and have real friendships.

People are like beakers or pots when it comes to strokes. Some of us are small pots, and don't need much attention. They are easily reassured by positive comments or appropriate touching. However, some of us are big beakers and need a lot of attention to feel cared about, see Figure 16.4.

Think about which pot are you? For some young people who are acting out a reaction to their personal history of abuse, neglect and/or unresolved grief it is sometimes almost impossible to accept positive strokes and so they do not feel 'full' or satisfied or complete.

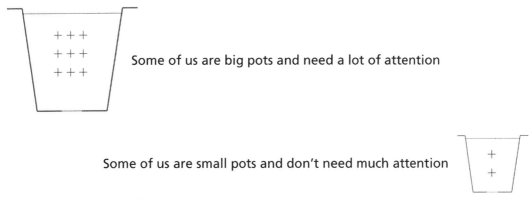

Figure 16.4 *Big and little pots*

The Leaving Care Handbook

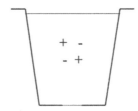

Figure 16.5 *Negative strokes*

This is because they have only really experienced negative attention. They have got used to feeling full on negative strokes (verbal abuse, or physical abuse, or emotional abuse) see Figure 16.5. But the feeling of being full doesn't last very long and so more negative behaviours are needed to generate more and more negative reactions to keep the young person feeling satisfied. So a negative pattern of behaviour is set up, and a habit forms which is difficult to break. But this habit has formed because of the circumstances in which the young person has been raised. The young person has little control over these very basic urges and instincts to feel satisfied. These young people are often referred to as 'manipulative'. In effect, *they* are manipulated by their basic instincts to seek satisfaction in having sufficient attention to survive.

Some young people have to work very hard to get their emotional needs met, see Figure 16.6. They end up behaving badly in order to get the attention, the negative strokes that they need. These young people get into a habit of behaving in this way that is hard to change. Some young people get different messages from carers at different times; these young people are very confused and find it very difficult to trust adults at all.

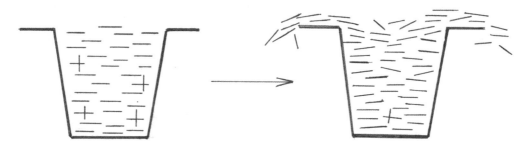

Figure 16.6 *Behaving badly*

Some young people, through repeated trauma, develop an inability to stay feeling emotionally full and it is as if they have a 'hole' in the bottom of their beaker. They need to keep getting attention in order to keep feeling full. Unfortunately, they are often used to negative strokes, which give them feelings of being emotionally very full, but this soon goes away and they are empty again.

Some children have suffered so many traumas that they are unable to receive positive (and sometimes even negative) strokes and it is as if they have a lid over the top of the pot which makes the strokes bounce away, see Figure 16.7. These young people need very special care, with love and support over a long period of time in order to be able to accept positive strokes (love) again, and trust adults.

Young people in the 'looked after' system carry rucksacks which weigh them down and prevent them from taking the life chances they are given, see Figure 16.8. Each failed placement is another brick in the rucksack of unresolved grief and loss. (NB: We need to be very clear here what we

Mental Health of Care Leavers

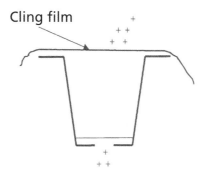

Figure 16.7 *Pots with lids*

Figure 16.8 *Weighed down by baggage*

mean by 'failed'. In this context, failed means that the placement has failed the young person, not that the young person has failed.)

One idea is to ask the young people or their carers to imagine a person carrying a huge rucksack weighed down by bricks, each with an address, and a carer, and a teacher on it. Ask each participant to think about one young person who had more than one placement in care, and to keep thinking about this young person for the next few minutes.

Each 'failed' placement results in another brick in their personal rucksack to be carried around with them. The rucksack takes up so much emotional currency in managing the pain from it, they have very little intellectual energy left for learning of any sort. This is very unfortunate, as all the important 'education', the external examinations such as GCSEs and 'A' Levels on which future success depends, takes place during these years. Lack of exam passes compounds the problems of those who have histories of abuse, neglect and multiple placements during their early school years, when concentration and learning proved impossible in the emotional turmoil. These young people fall broadly into two categories: those who 'act out', such as becoming aggressive, and those who 'act in, such as becoming withdrawn or non-communicative. Which of these a person may be depends on their genetic make up, the extent and type of trauma they have suffered, and the effect of both of these within the environment in which they were raised by their carers.

For a very few young people this means that they may develop a mental illness. This diagnosis often has the effect of frightening carers and workers. With the help and support of the CAMHS professional most young people can be managed in the community. Very rarely, a young person is so mentally unwell they might need intensive support from an in-patient unit but the CAMHS professional and other people such as a young person's personal advisor can monitor the young person's progress and advise them.

Resilience to trauma

It is worth remembering that the majority of young people survive and are helped by the care system, and go on to lead 'normal' lives. Even those who have suffered badly from their experiences, and then have a chaotic and turbulent adolescence with mental health problems, survive to become members of society, often choosing the caring professions themselves, expressing a wish to give something back to the system. Resilience is affected by:
- The severity and scale of the abuse or neglect.
- The genetic inheritance of the young person.
- The environment or multiple environment situation in which the young person has been raised.

Sometimes it's a combination of all three.

Some Resilience factors:

In the child:
- Secure early relationships.
- Being female.
- Higher intelligence.
- Easy temperament when an infant.
- Positive attitude, problem-solving approach.
- Good communication skills.
- Planner, belief in control.
- Sense of humour.
- Religious faith.
- Capacity to reflect.

In the family:
- At least one good parent–child relationship.
- Being shown affection.
- Clear, firm, consistent discipline.
- Support for education.
- Supportive long term relationship with an absence of severe discord.

In the community:
- Wider supportive network.
- Good housing.
- High standard of living.
- High-morale school with positive policies for behaviour, attitudes and anti-bullying.
- Schools with strong academic and non-academic opportunities.
- Range of positive sport and leisure activities.

(Northwest Children's Taskforce)

Reciprocity, or carer to child bonding

Some of the root causes of the difficult behaviours sometimes seen in care leavers are attachment issues. Human babies need to form the majority of the pathways between their brain cells during their early life. This is why the environment in which a child is raised, and the behaviours of their carers, are so important. Human babies are programmed to evoke 'love giving' from their carers,

Mental Health of Care Leavers

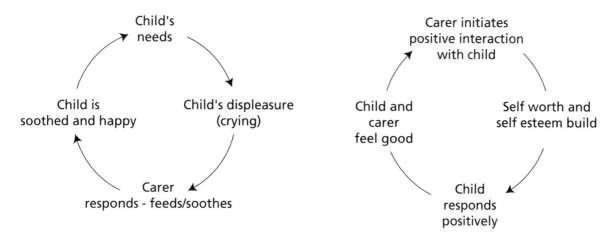

Figure 16.9 *Reciprocity or carer to child bonding*

and respond by becoming calm, rewarding the carer with a smile, or going to sleep when their needs have been met. This reciprocal relationship forms the basis for love and empathy for the rest of a person's life.

Reciprocity happens when a baby is distressed because it needs feeding, changing, comforting, or attention – and the carer provides what is needed, and the child is soothed. It is the basis of the child beginning to understand when its needs are met, and to learn how to be sensitive to the needs of others and to empathise.

By this process, attachment happens, from child to carer, and bonding occurs, from carer to child. This is the basis of the child understanding their own and other people's feelings.

Early months and years are the critical period for this to happen, and it is at this time that the brain pathways are forming in this area. It is possible to form these pathways at another time and another age, as the brain retains some plasticity, even in adulthood, but it becomes progressively harder as the child grows older. If you are raised in an environment where there is always violence and aggression, those pathways may become more ingrained than if you are raised in an under-stimulated environment, e.g. with a depressed or drug abusing carer. Then, your interaction pathways have low stimulation and the interaction pathways may not develop fully. If you are raised in a chaotic environment, your brain pathways form in a chaotic way and you may find it difficult to interpret the world.

If something goes wrong with this attachment process the child, and later the adult, can find it very difficult to form and keep relationships. For them putting trust in others is very difficult. They become reliant on themselves and find it almost impossible to believe anyone else can help or love them. It often also affects their self-esteem and self-confidence, factors important for success at school and work.

Some children have serious attachment difficulties stemming, perhaps, from the behaviours of their first carers or parents. The difficulty is made much worse by multiple placements where they learn not to trust adults, carers, or others and above all the 'system', which takes control of their lives and leaves them with the feeling of being out of control. This is very frightening for them. All children and young people need to have boundaries so that they feel safe. This is especially the case for children and young people who have had disrupted lives.

It is very difficult to provide this safe environment for the most damaged young people who are often the most challenging to the system. These, unfortunately, are the ones more prone to the huge risk-tasking behaviours that we witness.

These difficulties in coping can manifest themselves in substance misuse and drug and alcohol abuse, and sexually promiscuous behaviour. The young person is in continuous emotional pain but often does not recognise this as understable given their history. Even if they do accept that this is not their fault they still are sometimes driven to 'numb the pain' using alcohol, illegal drugs, etc.

How people deal with trauma

When we suffer trauma often we are able to share our problem with our friends and family and sometimes, if we need extra support, with a counsellor or therapist. We gradually leak out the trauma until we can forget it and pull it down into our long-term memories, where it won't trouble us any longer, or at least not until we are under very great stress or trauma again. Young people in care and leaving care do not always have these supportive networks and need to use their social worker or personal advisor or after care worker in this way (see Figure 16.10).

Figure 16.10 *Leaky sack*

Sometimes, however, the trauma is so great that we cannot even think about beginning to do this. The fear of letting it all out may be too great. Or, because we didn't have the chance to leak out the trauma soon after it happened, the trauma becomes hidden within our minds but still continues to affect what we do and think and dream. It continues to generally interfere with our lives even though we may be unaware of what is happening. The only way you can support someone in such a situation is to continue to give what support you can, and try to interpret their behaviours with this in mind. Unconditional positive regard (the nearest to love that carers can be expected to give) is the best thing you can offer in addition to the practical support of your service.

Trauma theory suggests that most of us recover from trauma by talking it through (leaking) with the support of our friends and family. Care leavers often lack the very people who could help them recover from the abuses (trauma) they have suffered. They can't leak it out and so they continually are affected by the fact that they can't process the memories down into long-term memory; and so the trauma continues to impact on the young person's life, dreams, ability to learn and

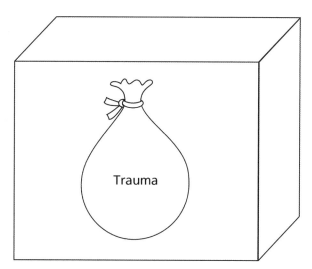

Figure 16.11 *Concrete box*

relationships – using up valuable brain power to suppress them. No wonder the traumatic memories occasionally pop out in the form of 'bizarre' behaviours and temper tantrums.

There is some anecdotal evidence that illegal drug use can prompt the onset of psychosis, such as illusions, delusions, hallucinations, confusions, etc., but this is still to be shown by research. But it can cause problems accessing a service if there is a drug problem combined with mental health issues (dual diagnosis). All professionals need to agree who will manage the case, and how they can support the young person together.

In some young people the pain of the abuse is so great that, in order to survive it, the child creates another person to whom the abuse happens, the alter-ego(s). Although contentious scientifically as an idea, this does explain the confusion we sometimes see in multiple-abuse victims. In others, their reaction to the pain is to withdraw into themselves and they become depressed and are difficult to motivate. They stop washing and caring about themselves, and in extreme cases, find it impossible to do anything other than carry out functions necessary for life. Social interaction becomes too hard for them and the body shuts down the higher functions first, such as mental arithmetic and logical thought, and leaves the basic bodily functions keeping the young person alive.

How people make decisions

Teenage years are when some of the most important decisions are taken about our future lives. As we have demonstrated, it is also a challenging time for young people who have been in care. They may have low self-esteem and low self-confidence, when it is the opposite that is needed in order to take advantage of all the opportunities for young people at this age and stage. Unfortunately, if young people are still working through the effects of trauma they will find taking decisions very hard, and if they are being angry for some or most of the time they will not be able to make rational decisions. At our most stressed we are at our most stupid whether we act out or act in.

Again, providing a consistent point of reference for them is a very valuable role and although you may not see the benefits in the time you work with the young person, it is often these same relationships which enable the young person to eventually turn their lives around.

The Leaving Care Handbook

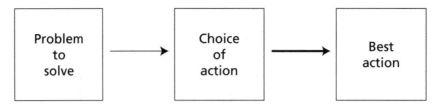

When we have to find a solution to a problem we weigh up the alternatives and choose the best option. We think intelligently.

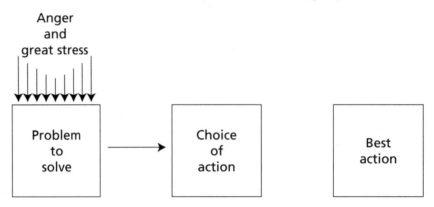

At our angriest we are at our stupidest; we find it impossible to think clearly and make intelligent decisions.

Figure 16.12 *Decision making*

Remember how difficult it is to give up a habit such as smoking. Well, changing behaviour patterns, which can be even more destructive, is equally challenging: even if the benefits seem immediately obvious to you, they will represent a huge challenge, which is very frightening for a young person with low self-esteem and shaky self-confidence.

How care leaver workers can help

Since the 1970s, society has encouraged us to believe that the 'experts' have the answers; and so expert professions have grown up to 'mend' or heal' illnesses. At the same time, new professions have grown up around Child and Adolescent Mental Health, mainly in the 'talk therapies', which work predominately with young people who are articulate and co-operate and turn up to appointments in clinics. The very vulnerable young people, such as those who were still or had been in care, those in the youth justice system, and those with learning disabilities, or from black and ethnic minorities, sometimes could not benefit from a CAMHS service.

What you can do is work with the young people by discussing some of their emotions:
- What makes them happy?
- What makes them angry?
- What makes them sad?

Note: there are some coping strategies in Chapter 12 (Social and Emotional Skills) that also might help them.

Some people control their tempers to such an extent that they don't realise what makes them angry, and in this way they store up immense amounts of stress which is bad for their own mental health.

Think about a toy from childhood that you have lost. Picture the toy and then reflect on your feelings. Provided you have not suffered the death of someone close to you recently think about how it feels when someone close dies. Remember that feeling of intense emotional angst which follows the initial shock or numbing reaction. There is a need to search for the loved one and yet a feeling of huge loss.

Many of these young people carry these feelings around all the time and some are constantly 'aroused' in this way which makes normal life almost impossible. In others it results in a deadening of feeling in order to survive. The normal bodily functioning shuts down bit by bit, as the pressure to keep the feelings under control mounts, and the feelings continue to rise. One way to numb this pain is to get drunk, use drugs or other substances which take them 'out of their own mind'; it is easy to see why this becomes an addiction in many and why having found a way to take the pain away they find it very difficult to stop and thus get caught in a vicious spiral of crime to feed the drug habit etc. Unfortunately because they have often learnt not to trust adults they continue in this cycle; and support from a worker is insufficient to break it, unless it goes on over a long time, and is of sufficient quality to form a relationship.

A variety of therapeutic skills are needed, including behavioural, cognitive, interpersonal/ psychodynamic, pharmacological and systemic skills. (Taken from the National Service Framework for Children, Young People and Maternity Services, Standard 9, 2004 – Developing Tier 3 Services.)

Therapies include:
- Creative therapies such as art, drama, dance and music therapies.
- Psychotherapy.
- Family therapy.
- Cognitive behavioural therapy
- Occupational therapy.

No magic wand

CAMHS can help young people with mental ill health but where there are significant complex problems CAMHS may be only one part of the support package.

What we know is that significant people in the lives of these young people (the carers and leaving care workers and friends) are the ones who can make a difference. That is not to say that young people with pronounced or severe mental illness should not access a service, they should: that service will be able to offer diagnosis and management of the case, alongside the continued support of the worker, who will need to work with that young person when they return from any in-patient service, if that has been necessary.

This points up the necessity of training in mental health awareness and support for workers, firstly so that they understand:
- When to ask for support.
- What a diagnosis may mean in terms of caring for and supporting that young person.
- The need for leaving care services to have strong relationships with both adult and child and adolescent mental health services so that they can work together to provide the support packages needed for the individual, from diagnosis to treatment or placement alternatives.

If the young person can continue to live safely in the community (safe for them and safe for others) the mental health professional will need to rely on workers and carers to carry out the treatment plan; to support the young person to live in the community whether it be school, college or work; and to help the young person recognise their progress towards full mental health.

Is it good enough for my child?

The motto to bear in mind all the time is to do what you would do for a child of your own, and if the service isn't good enough, seek out support until it does measure up to what you will accept for yourself and your family. You now have the NSF Standard 9 to refer to.

These young people may need re-parenting which is a much more difficult and longer task than parenting. This is where the work of leaving care service fits in. The parenting role needs to extend beyond the teens and well into the twenties for some young people. As the age at which our own children leave home extends so we become more aware of the problems of surviving in this world for all young people. For this most disadvantaged group they are probably almost insurmountable.

Being able to be there for a young person no matter what they do and helping them pick up the pieces, learn from the experience and try again is the main role. If it is possible to do this in a non-judgemental way this will help a great deal. What these young people have not had, and which is the right of every child, is unconditional love. We cannot expect carers or leaving care workers to offer this but we can expect them to offer unconditional positive regard. It is this which allows you to continue to help a young person time after time after time even though they continue to get things wrong or are unable to make good choices to help themselves. By understanding why they fail to learn different ways of behaving, you can more easily support them.

Regular and quality supervision for the carers and workers is essential. Support from mental health professionals is also essential where there is mental ill-health or where the young person is clearly mentally unwell, although they might not have a mental illness as such.

Conclusion

The NSF Standard 9 has set clear targets for the mental health services in terms of ensuring access to services for all children and young people who need them.

The advice remains the same, challenge any service (however scarce) which the young people are offered, until it reflects the fair and equitable service it should be. Do not be afraid to encourage the young person to ask for another opinion – not all professionals agree nor are they always right; however, they can be very re-assuring with a difficult case, both to the young person and the worker, and they do hold the key to prescription and to in-patient beds should that be necessary. If a young person is given prescription drugs be sure to seek advice as to how to support the management of this.

It is important to remember that you work most of the time with care leavers some of whom are not sufficiently resilient to withstand their negative life experiences and who are unable to take advantage of the opportunities they have been offered. They need all the help you can give them.

Always remember that carers and leaving care workers are doing a valuable job. It may not always seem like that when a young person finds it difficult to accept your support. However, over time, the effects of your work will become clearer to the young person, and hopefully, yourself.

Resources

Bowlby, J. (1988) *A Secure Base: Parent/Child Attachment and Healthy Human Development*. New York: Basic Books.
Briere, J.N. (1992) *Child Abuse Trauma: Theory and Treatment of Lasting Effect*. Sage.

DES/DoH (2004) *The National Service Framework for Children, Young People and Maternity Services.* London: HMSO.

Evans, N. (1984) *Taking the Lid Off* (video from Central TV documentary 1984) available from Community Unit Central Independent Television plc Broad Street Birmingham B1 2JP.

Fahlberg, V.I. (1996) *A Child's Journey through Placement.* BAAF.

Howe, D. (2000) Attachment, Chapter 12: *Reader Framework for the Assessment of Children in Need and their Families.* DoH 2000 or www.open.gov.uk/doh/quality.htm

Maslow, A. (1970) *Motivation and Personality.* 2nd edn., Harper and Row.

Northwest Children's Taskforce (2003) *Meeting the Mental Health Needs of Children and Young People: A Guide for Commissioners.* Northwest Children's Taskforce.

Norwood, G. and Maslow, A. (1996) *Hierarchy of Needs*, http://www.connect.net/georgen/maslow.htm, June, 1996.

Perry, B. (1993) Neurodevelopment and the Neurophysiology of Trauma: Conceptual Considerations for Clinical Work with Maltreated Children. *The APSAC Advisor.* 6: 1-12.

Perry, et al. (1995) Childhood Trauma, The Neurobiology of Adaption and 'Use Dependent' Development of the Brain: How States Become 'Traits'. *Infant Mental Health Journal.* 16: 4, 271-91.

Van der Kolk (1987) *Psychological Trauma.* American Psychiatric Press.

Wolpert, M., Fuggle, P., Cottrell, D., Fonagy, P., Phillips, J., Pilling, S., Stein, S. and Target, M. (2002) *Drawing on the Evidence: Advice for Mental Health Professionals working with Children and Adolescents.* The British Psychological Society.

Section Nine: Legal Matters

The Law and Your Rights

Amanda Allard and Jane Sufian

Introduction

The Children (Leaving Care) Act is the piece of legislation with most central importance to care leavers since it sets out what they are entitled to in terms of help and support from their local authority. However, being a care leaver isn't all that a young person leaving care is. In addition to setting out the key tenets of the Children (Leaving Care) Act, this chapter therefore attempts to pull together key information on those areas of the law which regularly impact on young people's lives and are not covered in detail elsewhere in this book.

Where this chapter applies

In general, this chapter describes the law as it exists in England only.

The Children (Leaving Care) Act 2000 applies to England and Wales, although the Welsh Assembly issued regulations and guidance under the Act that differ in some details from England's. For the Welsh Guidance and Regulations, see end of chapter.

The legislative frameworks for leaving care in Scotland and Northern Ireland have similar aims and impose similar duties and responsibilities as in England and Wales.

The only section of the Children (Leaving Care) Act 2000 that applied to Scotland was the section that deals with access to social security benefits. However, Scotland amended the leaving care provisions of its Children (Scotland) Act 1995 in 2001 in the Regulation of Care (Scotland) Act, and issued new leaving care guidance and regulations and a Pathways framework, effective 1st April 2004. Overall, rights and duties in respect of care leavers in Scotland and England are now very similar. For Scottish Regulations and Guidance, see end of chapter.

In Northern Ireland, the Children (Leaving Care) Act (Northern Ireland) 2002 received Royal Assent in November 2002. It amends the leaving care provisions of the Children (Northern Ireland) Order 1995. Before the Act can be brought into operation, however, supporting regulations and guidance must be put in place to give effect to the legislation. Draft regulations and guidance have been issued for consultation with a view to final regulations and guidance coming into force in April 2005. For Northern Ireland Draft Regulations and Guidance, see end of chapter.

Age-related rights

For many, but not all purposes, 18 is the age at which a person becomes an adult and can make decisions and do things without the consent of another person. For example, a care order comes to an end when the looked after young person turns 18, unless the order was discharged by a court at an earlier date.

The Children (Leaving Care) Act 2000 and its associated Guidance and Regulations

The Children (Leaving Care) Act ('the Act'), and its associated guidance and regulations for England, came into force on 1 October 2001. The Act amended the leaving care provisions of the Children Act 1989 ('the 1989 Act'), and it also changed the financial-support arrangements for many 16 and 17-year-olds who leave care on or after their 16th birthday.

Purpose and aims of the Act

The purpose of the Act is to improve the life chances of young people living in and leaving care. The main aims of the Act are:
- To delay young people's discharge from care until they are prepared and ready to leave.
- To improve the assessment, preparation and planning for leaving care.
- To provide better personal support for young people after leaving care.
- To improve the financial arrangements for care leavers.

How are these purposes to be achieved?

Under the 1989 Act, local authorities had some duties to help young people leaving care, but mostly they did not have to do so. Under the new law, more duties have been imposed on local authorities, so they now **must** provide the following services:
- Appoint a Personal Advisor (PA). The PA must carry out functions spelled out in the regulations (Reg. 12), such as providing advice and support to the young person; participating in the pathway planning and reviewing process; and co-ordinating the provision of services, including financial support.
- To assess and meet needs.
- To prepare a Pathway Plan based on the assessment, saying how the young person's needs will be met, including who will do what and by when (Schedule 1 of the Regulations says that the plan has to cover: personal support; accommodation; education, training and employment; family and social relationships; independent living skills; financial support; health; and contingency plans).
- To review the Pathway Plan at a minimum of every six months.
- To provide assistance to achieve the goals agreed in the Pathway Plan.
- To provide support and accommodation.
- To provide financial support.
- To keep in touch.
- To provide assistance with education, training and employment.
- To provide vacation accommodation during full-time higher and further residential education.
- To provide support for young people aged 18 and over.
- To provide a representation and complaints procedure.

Who is entitled to the new leaving care services?

The Act does not apply to all young people leaving care. The Act created three new categories of young people. The Act requires each local authority to provide services only to the young people who fall into one of these categories, although local authorities still have the power to help other young people. The categories are:

- Eligible children.
- Relevant children.
- Former relevant children.

The general definitions of these categories are:

Eligible children are 16 or 17 years old and still looked after. They must have been looked after for a total of at least 13 weeks after reaching the age of 14.

Relevant children are 16 or 17 years old and are no longer in care. They must have been looked after for a total of at least 13 weeks after reaching the age of 14, including at least one day when they were 16 or 17 years old.

Former relevant children are 18 to 21 years old (or older, if still receiving services listed in their Pathway Plan). They must have been either an eligible or a relevant child before they became 18.

However, as you might expect, there are some exceptions. The Act, and the regulations that are associated with the Act, have created some groups within the categories who, although they meet the general definition, will not be considered eligible, relevant or formerly relevant and will not be entitled to the new services.

For example, one important exception is: young people who are looked after for no more than four weeks at a time, in what is commonly referred to as 'respite care'. Even if they were looked after in respite care for a total of 13 weeks, they will not be covered by the Act. It is necessary to check the Act and the regulations to be sure you fall into one of the categories and are not excluded by one of the exceptions. The Children (Leaving Care) Act Guidance has a useful table at pages 8 and 9. (Available at: http://www.dfes.gov.uk/qualityprotects/pdfs/regs2000.pdf)

Who is not entitled to the new leaving care services?

Young people who leave care on or after their 16th birthday and who do not fit into any of these three categories, are not entitled to the new leaving care services. This includes young people who left care before 1 October 2001, when the Act came into force. This category of young people is called: **persons qualifying for advice and assistance**.

Local authorities continue to have the same powers and duties toward them under the 1989 Act as before, plus a couple of new duties added by the new Act.

Which local authority is responsible for providing leaving care services?

The local authority that is looking after an eligible child or who last looked after a relevant or former relevant child is the local authority responsible for providing them with services. If the young person is living in the area of a different local authority, their responsible authority can request the other authority to assist them in providing services to the young person. There is a National Protocol (England) on inter-authority arrangements for care leavers outside of their responsible authority (LASSL (2004) 20), which is designed to be a model for local authorities to use in making such arrangements. Scotland and Wales have agreed similar protocols.

For young people who were accommodated by someone other than a local authority or were privately fostered, the responsible authority is the one where the care leaver is living.

The Law and Your Rights

What leaving care services are young people entitled to?

Eligible children

- All the provisions of the looked after system, such as a care plan.
- A personal advisor.
- Needs assessment.
- Pathway Plan and review.

Relevant children

- A personal advisor.
- Needs assessment.
- Pathway Plan and review.
- Maintenance, support and accommodation: **This is a major change brought about by the new Act.** Except for lone parents and young disabled people, 16 and 17-year-old care leavers are no longer entitled to income support, housing benefit or job-seekers allowance. Lone parents and young disabled people are no longer entitled to housing benefit.
- Assistance to reach goals, such as educational ones, based on the needs assessment and as agreed and set out in the Pathway Plan.
- Access to the representations procedure.
- Responsible authority must keep in touch.

Former relevant children

- A personal advisor.
- Pathway Plan and review.
- Assistance with employment, education and training.
- General assistance.
- Vacation accommodation for higher education or residential further education.
- Access to the representation procedure.
- Responsible authority must keep in touch.

Persons qualifying for advice and assistance

- Same as before under section 24 of the 1989 Act.
- In addition, for those young people who were **looked after by a local authority**, the relevant authority:
  – Must keep in touch.
  – Must provide vacation accommodation.
  – May assist with education and training up to the **age of 24**.

Criminal Injuries Compensation awards and other money

Sometimes a *relevant child* has received money from the Criminal Injuries Compensation Authority for injuries the young person suffered as the result of a crime – such as child abuse.

The Guidance to the Children (Leaving Care) Act says that their local authority, which has a duty to support *relevant children* financially, can **not** take that compensation money into account in deciding how much money the young person needs (Guidance: Ch. 9, para. 4).

In addition, the local authority is expected to arrange for the young person to receive sound financial advice about what to do with the money. This is particularly important because when the young person becomes 18 years old, if they apply for income support benefits, savings over £3,000 *will* affect their claim.

The local authority *will* take into account any other money that *relevant children* may have, such as through inheritance or working. The local authority should follow the Department of Work and Pensions' income support regulations, Income Support (IS) (General) Regulations 1987. Under those regulations, savings over £3,000 will be taken into account in deciding how much money the young person needs.

Sleepovers for looked after children

Children in care, living in both residential accommodation and in foster care, should as far as possible be granted the same permission to take part in normal and appropriate peer activities as would reasonably be granted by the parents of their peers. Decisions on overnight stays should in most circumstances be delegated to foster carers and residential care staff. The arrangements for such decisions should be written into the placement plan or foster placement agreement.

Only where there are exceptional reasons should the permission of the responsible authority be required or restrictions placed on overnight stays. There is no statutory duty for Criminal Records Bureau checks to be carried out on adults in a private household where a child may stay overnight. Such checks should not normally be sought as a precondition of an overnight stay.

The Government recently issued Guidance on the delegation of decisions on 'overnight stays' for looked after children, see LAC (2004)4, which applies in England.

Access to Files

The Data Protection Act 1998 (DPA) provides a right of access to personal information about you held by public authorities and private bodies. It also requires those holding personal data about you to explain why they are holding that data and to tell you to whom else the data may be disclosed.

To obtain access you should write to the person holding the information (the Data Controller) saying that you are applying under Section 7 of the Data Protection Act 1998 for access to any personal data about yourself. If you are not sure who to write to check with the Data Protection Register, as under the DPA organisations have to provide contact details on their Data Protection Register entry.

The Data Controller should normally give you access to any data held within 40 days of receiving your request.

You can apply for access to your files at any age as long as you are old enough to understand the nature of your request.

For most records your rights are limited to access to information held on you in structured files, i.e. files that bear your name or some other identifying feature, such as your address. However, with health, social work, housing and school records you have the right to see any record held on paper. So, for instance, if a letter about you has been filed in a general correspondence file rather than in your own file you would still have the right to see it.

With social work records, information can be withheld from you if the Data Controller feels that access would be likely to cause serious harm to you, or any other person's, physical or mental health.

The Data Controller does not have to reveal to you which exemption they are relying upon to justify withholding information from you. If you feel that the Data Controller may be unjustly withholding information from you then you can ask the Information Commissioner to look into the matter for you. The Information Commissioner can provide you with further information to enforce your rights or he can consider your complaint and make an assessment. If he believes your rights have been breached he may issue an enforcement notice to the Data Controller. Failure to comply with that enforcement notice is a criminal offence.

The Information Commissioner's Office has a help line number should you wish to discuss your case or make an appeal, and a website should you require further information. Helpline: 01625 545 745. Website: www.informationcommissioner.gov.uk

Being a parent, parental responsibility and entitlements

As a father you are not automatically recognised as having parental rights, duties and responsibilities (parental responsibility). If a child's parents are married at the time of his birth they automatically share parental responsibility. If not, then it belongs to the mother alone.

However, if an unmarried father jointly registers the birth with the mother this gives them both parental responsibility. Unmarried fathers whose children were born before this change in the law (December 2003) can still get parental responsibility in some situations. If you have a good relationship with the mother of your child then this is relatively easy and can be done by a legal agreement which is completed by both parties and then officially registered. If you want to be recognised as having parental responsibility and the mother of your child does not agree then you can ask the court to give it to you. The court's decision will be based on: how much commitment you show towards your child; and how attached you and the child are to each other; and also, on your reasons for wanting parental responsibility. The courts do usually grant parental responsibility to fathers who wish to be involved in their children's lives.

Where both parents have parental responsibility then major decisions about their child should be made jointly.

Once a father has parental responsibility he can only lose it if a court order ends it on the basis that he is a danger to the welfare of his child. This only happens in extreme cases. The parental responsibility of both parents is ended if an adoption order is made.

Child maintenance

Child maintenance is paid for children who live away from one or both of their parents. It is an amount of money paid regularly for the child by the parent who doesn't live with the child.

The Child Support Agency calculates and collects child maintenance for parents and children who normally live in this country. It can also arrange child maintenance for some non-resident parents who live abroad.

The Child Support Agency uses child support law to decide if someone has to pay child maintenance and to work out the right amount. Only non-resident parents can be required to pay child maintenance through the Child Support Agency. Child maintenance will in most cases be based on a percentage of the non-resident parent's net income. This will be between 15 per cent and 25 per cent according to how many children maintenance is due for.

In some cases, such as during a long stay in hospital, a non-resident parent may not have to pay child maintenance. In these circumstances, persons with care who are not in work may be able to get extra Income Support to help with the costs of bringing up the children.

Non-resident parents who have a very low income or who receive certain benefits may only have to pay a flat rate of child maintenance. The flat rate does not change with income or number of children.

Responsibility for paying maintenance is not dependent on parental responsibility but on where the children are living and the income of the mother and father. You can be responsible for paying maintenance even if you do not have parental responsibility.

Responsibility for paying maintenance continues while Child Benefit is being paid to the parent the child lives with and the child is:
- Aged under 16; or
- Aged 16 to 19 and in full-time non-advanced education.

The definition of full-time education is 12 hours or more a week of study on a course up to and including A-level standard.

Parental rights

The UN Convention states that parents have a right to family life. However, if there is a conflict between these rights and the welfare of the child then the court will make decisions (such as residence, contact or care orders) based on the welfare of the child.

However, a local authority does have to justify any interference in your family life. They have to be able to show that it is necessary for the protection of health or morals or for the protection of the rights and freedoms of others. They also have to make sure that any interference is necessary and *proportionate.* Even if they can show this the local authority may be acting in breach of your parental rights under Article 8 if they have not properly considered or promoted *rehabilitation* of the family – so, for instance, if they have not provided you with support, or if they have not ensured you have contact with your child.

If the local authority wishes to end your parental rights or to end contact between you and your child they must show that this is in your child's best interests.

Maternity rights

All pregnant employees (whether or not you have a permanent contract) have essentially three rights:
- To be paid time off for antenatal leave, i.e. midwife or doctor's appointments.
- 26 weeks ordinary maternity leave.
- Not to be dismissed on account of pregnancy.

In addition if you have been employed with the same company for 26 weeks by the time you are 15 weeks away from giving birth, you are entitled to statutory maternity pay for 26 weeks (Statutory Maternity Pay is 90 per cent of your earnings for the first 6 weeks of absence and £100 per week after that). If you do not qualify for Statutory Maternity Pay you may qualify for Maternity Allowance. Again this can be paid for up to 26 weeks. The level of Maternity Allowance depends on how much you usually earn.

Employees who have been employed by the same employer for at least 26 weeks by the time they are 15 weeks away from their baby's due date are entitled to an additional period of unpaid Maternity Leave. This starts immediately after the 26 weeks and lasts for a further 26 weeks.

In order to be entitled to Maternity Leave you must give your employer 28 days notice before the start of your maternity leave.

Paternity rights

Fathers can take up to 2 weeks Paternity Leave, paid at a rate of up to £100 per week.

Parental leave

All employees who have been employed by the same employer for a year or more have the right to take parental leave in order to care for a child. Each parent has the right to take up to 13 weeks leave for the purpose of caring for each child until the child's fifth birthday. A maximum of four weeks parental leave can be taken in any one year and the leave can only be taken in blocks of one weeks duration. The leave is unpaid unless the employer says otherwise.

Time off to care for dependents

All employees have the right to take a reasonable amount of time off to deal with family emergencies. This time off would not be paid unless the employer agrees otherwise. This covers a variety of situation but means that if you have children and your normal arrangements break down, for instance your child minder is ill, or your child is ill and cannot go to the childminder's or to school, then you can take time off to care for your child.

Despite these rights, discrimination, particularly against pregnant women, is widespread. Every year thousands of women are sacked or threatened with dismissal just because they are pregnant. The Equal Opportunities Commission gets more complaints about this than any other area of discrimination. Employers who discriminate against pregnant women are breaking the law and if you are sacked for this reason your employer could be made to pay you compensation.

The police

Stop and search

The police have the power to stop and search you or your vehicle for stolen or prohibited items or knives which may be seized. However, this power can only be exercised if they have reasonable grounds for suspecting that they will find stolen or prohibited items or knives. In other words, the officer must have a concrete reason for the search and cannot search you simply because you have a previous conviction, or you are a member of a group (such as football fans) who the officer believes are often guilty of carrying the item he wants to search you for.

The police also have the power to stop your vehicle if they think it may be unroadworthy or stolen.

In the course of a search the police cannot force you to remove any clothing in public other than an outer coat, jacket or gloves. They can request that you do so, but you can refuse. You are 'in public' even if the street is empty. They do have the power to do a more thorough search, for instance ask you to remove your hat or shoes or to strip search you, if they provide somewhere private such as a police van. But it must be near to where you were stopped. They cannot do an intimate search which involves exposing intimate parts of the body in a police van and any such searches must be carried out by a police officer of your sex unless you request otherwise.

Searching your home

The police have the power to enter and search your home in a number of circumstances. They can do so if you give them permission, but you must give your permission in writing and before you consent they should tell you the reason for the search and that anything they find may be taken and used in evidence.

They can also enter and search your home without your permission: if they have a search warrant; or without a search warrant, in order to search for drugs, or firearms, or to deal with or prevent a breach of the peace, to arrest someone or to recapture someone who has escaped from lawful custody. If you have been arrested then again the police can search your premises, without a warrant, for evidence of the offence for which they have arrested you, or for evidence of a similar offence. If you have been arrested, the police have the power not only to search your own home but also to enter and search any other premises you were in, at the time of, or just before your arrest.

Arrest

The police can arrest you with or without a warrant. If you are arrested you should be told why at the time. If you are not arrested but agree to go to a police station to be questioned, you can leave at any time. If you resist arrest then the police are entitled to use reasonable force to arrest you. But only force which is absolutely necessary is permitted.

On arrest, and before you are interviewed, you should be cautioned, which means that you are told of your rights and also that you do not have to say anything at all if you wish.

If you are arrested and held at a police station you have a right to consult a solicitor, in private and free of charge at any time. A duty solicitor scheme is in operation at every police station in England and Wales, so that free telephone advice or a free visit from a solicitor is available.

If you are detained at a police station you have the right to let one friend or relative know of your whereabouts as soon as possible. If you can't get in touch with that person, you can try two others, and after that it is at the discretion of the police as to whether they let you try and contact any others.

An accurate record should be made each time you are interviewed. The police normally tape or video record interviews but if notes are made then you have a right to see the interview record and should only sign it if it records exactly what you have said.

Although you can remain silent when questioned, at the court hearing, the charge against you may *draw negative conclusions* from your silence.

After arrest you can be detained without being charged for up to 24 hours. This period can be extended by 12 hours on the authority of a police officer of the rank of superintendent or above. If the police want to detain you for any longer than that then they must apply to a magistrate. The magistrate can authorise your detention for a further 36 hours. At the end of that time the police can apply for a further extension of 36 hours. The total maximum period of detention without charge is 96 hours. The only exception to this is for those people suspected of terrorism who can be detained for up to seven days without charge.

If you are younger than 17 then you should not be placed in a police cell, unless no other secure accommodation or supervision is available. You should never be placed in a police cell with another adult.

The Law and Your Rights

Once you have been charged with an offence you should be released unless:
- The police don't know or think you may be lying about your name and address.
- You were arrested for an imprisonable offence and the police think detention is necessary to prevent you committing further offences.
- The police think you will not turn up for your court appearance.

If you have been involved in any incident with the police or have witnessed an incident then you should try to make and keep full notes as soon as possible after the event. The reason for this is that if you make notes at the time or immediately after then you have the right to refer to those notes in court to help refresh your memory. If you are detained at a police station the police must supply you with writing materials if you ask for them.

Drugs

The Misuse of Drugs Act 1971 places drugs into three categories – Class A, B, and C. Drugs which fall into one of these three categories are known as controlled substances. Class A drugs are considered to be the most harmful.

It is an offence to:
- Possess a controlled substance.
- Possess a controlled substance with intent to supply it.
- Unlawfully supply a controlled drug (even if you don't ask for money for it).
- Allow your home to be used for the purpose of drug taking.

The Medicines Act 1968 regulates drugs used for medicinal purposes. Possession without a prescription of prescription-only medicines is a serious offence.

Someone who is found guilty of committing crimes in order to fund a drug habit can be tested for drug use and made to undergo treatment for their habit.

Amphetamines

Doctors can legally prescribe amphetamines, but possession of amphetamines without a prescription is an offence. Amphetamines are a Class B drug. Maximum penalties are:
- Possession – five years imprisonment.
- Supply – 14 years imprisonment.

If amphetamines are prepared for injection they become a Class A drug and the maximum penalties increase accordingly:
- Possession – seven years imprisonment.
- Supply – life imprisonment.

Amyl nitrite

It is illegal to sell amyl nitrites if they are to be inhaled as they would then be classed as a medicine; but the law does allow them to be sold legally as room deodorisers.

Anabolic steroids

These can be prescribed by a doctor. Possession without a prescription is an offence. Anabolic steroids are a Class C drug.

Maximum penalties are:
- Possession without prescription – two years imprisonment and/or a fine.
- Supply – five years imprisonment and/or a fine, even if you gave them away rather than selling them.

Cannabis

This is a Class C drug. It is illegal to grow, possess or supply cannabis or to allow your home to be used for growing or smoking cannabis.

Maximum penalties are:
- Possession – two years imprisonment.
- Supply – 14 years imprisonment.

However, for young people under 18 a first offence of cannabis possession will lead to arrest and a formal warning or reprimand. A warning is being told that if you do it again you will be in more serious trouble, while a reprimand is a serious 'telling off'. Further offences will lead to a final warning or charge. For adults found in possession the most likely outcome is a warning and confiscation of the drug, unless there are aggravating factors such as smoking in a public place or repeat offending, in which case arrest and prosecution may follow.

Cocaine

This is a Class A drug. Maximum penalties are:
- Possession – seven years imprisonment and/or a fine.
- Supply or intent to supply – life imprisonment.

Cocaine is classed as one of the hardest drugs because of its addictive qualities and therefore the most severe penalties can be expected.

Crack

This is a Class A drug.

Maximum penalties are:
- Possession – seven years imprisonment plus a fine.
- Supply – life imprisonment.

Again, because of its addictive qualities, the most severe penalties can be expected.

Ecstasy

This is a Class A drug.

Maximum penalties are:
- Possession – seven years imprisonment plus a fine.
- Supply or intent to supply – life imprisonment.

GHB (gammahydroxybutyrate)

At the moment possession of GHB is not illegal, but manufacture and supply is. There is growing concern about its use as a 'date rape' drug. It is expected that GHB will soon become a Class C drug. If this happens possession would lead to a maximum penalty of two years imprisonment but it is more likely that the drug would be confiscated and a warning given.

Heroin

This is a Class A drug.

Maximum penalties are:
- Possession – seven years imprisonment.
- Supply – life imprisonment.

Ketamine

This is a prescription-only drug, possession is not illegal, but supply is and penalties can be severe.

LSD

This is a Class A drug.

Maximum penalties are:
- Possession – seven years imprisonment.
- Supply – life imprisonment plus a fine.

Magic mushrooms

These are not in themselves a controlled substance, but they do contain psilocin and psilocybin which are controlled as Class A drugs.

In the past the courts have decided that possession of magic mushrooms is not the same as possession of a Class A drug because they are a naturally-occurring substance. However, where mushrooms have been prepared by drying them or making them into a powder they are no longer in their natural state and so can be viewed as a product or preparation of a Class A drug.

Tranquillisers

These are a prescription-only drug, but also a Class C, Schedule 4 drug, which makes it illegal to supply them but not illegal to possess them. However, Temazepam and Flunitrazepam (Rohypnol) are full Class C drugs so both possession and supply are illegal and carry a maximum sentence of two years imprisonment for possession or five years for supply or intent to supply.

Debt

Some kinds of debt have more serious consequences than others, so if you owe money you should get advice on which debts to deal with first.

Council Tax

If you haven't paid or are behind with your Council Tax payments the council can apply for a liability order from the Magistrates Court. If the court grants them a liability order then they can:
- Use bailiffs to get money from you by taking things of value that you own; or
- Take money from your wages or benefits.

You may be able to reduce what you owe, for instance if you were entitled to Council Tax Benefit but hadn't claimed it, you can have your claim backdated for a maximum of 52 weeks.

Hire purchase

You cannot enter into a hire purchase agreement until you're 18. If you buy goods such as a car or furniture under hire purchase you don't own them until you have made the final payment. Until then they belong to the creditor (person you owe the money to). If you miss payments before you've paid a third of the total money (this amount will be on the front of your agreement) which you owe, the creditor can 'snatch back' the item but only if it is in a public place. So, they could snatch back your car but not come into your home and take furniture.

Once you have paid more than a third of what you owe the creditor must start court action to either get their goods back or get you to pay for them. A date will then be set for the court to decide whether or not you must return the item or if they trust you to make up the payments. You can ask for a time order under which the court can reduce the payments to a level you can afford.

The court can also make a suspended order which means your creditor will only get the goods back if you miss future payments.

If you want to avoid court action you can write to your creditor and arrange to end your contract and return the goods. You will then have to pay half of what you originally owed (again this will be on the front of your hire purchase agreement) and the cost of repairing any damage to the goods.

Gas, electricity and phone bills

Gas, electricity and phone companies can all disconnect the service if you haven't paid your bills without taking you to court. But they should write to you and tell you that this is what they are planning to do. They should also allow you to repay the money you owe over at least a year, if that is all that you can afford instead of either disconnecting you or fitting you with a pre-payment meter. The problem with pre-payment meters is that you get charged more for the gas and electricity you use and you can end up without fuel if you run out of payment cards.

If you owe money and are receiving a benefit such as Income Based Jobseekers Allowance, you can ask to go onto the Fuel Direct scheme. This will enable you to have a weekly payment taken straight from your benefit to pay off your debt (for more details about Fuel Direct, contact energywatch). If you come up with an amount that you can afford to pay and the company won't accept your offer then you should seek advice from someone like the Citizens Advice Bureau or get in touch with the gas and electricity consumer body (energywatch – www.energywatch.org.uk) or the phone company watchdog (Ofcom – www.ofcom.org.uk).

If you are living in a house and the bill isn't in your name this does not necessarily mean that the energy company won't chase you for the debt. Companies can demand payment from people living in households whose names do not appear on the bill under the grounds of joint and several responsibility i.e. you had benefit from and knew about the supply. However, in several recent court cases the courts have refused to allow energy companies to pursue this kind of debt. So, if you are being pursued for non-payment of a bill which was not in your name then it is definitely worthwhile seeking expert advice.

Water bills

It is illegal for the water company to disconnect you for missing payments. The only way they can force you to pay is by getting a 'money-only' county court claim.

Loans and credit problems

Unless you own your own home and have taken out a loan which is secured on your home (i.e. you could lose your home if you don't pay) then if you have several debts any loans ('regulated' credit agreements) are probably not a priority. This is because you can get a time order from the courts under which the court can reduce the interest that is adding up on the money that you owe and reduce the instalment payments to a level you can afford. As long as you continue to pay what you've agreed on time your creditors cannot use methods like bailiffs (see below) to get your belongings.

If you do get a time order then the missed payments will still be listed on your credit reference file, so you may have trouble getting credit in the future. If you are thinking of getting a time order then make sure you first take advice, because depending on how the case comes to court, you rather than the creditor, may have to pay the court fee of £120.

If you don't apply for a time order (or the court won't give you one) the creditor's main legal option to get the money is through a money only claim in the county court. The creditor will ask the court to send a claim form to you. You can then either defend the claim, or admit the claim. If you admit the claim you should come up with a payment plan based on what you realistically think you can afford. If the creditor accepts this offer it will be recorded by the court and you will have to stick to it. But if they don't accept it then the court will decide what you should pay. If you ignore the claim form the court will make a decision on how much you should pay anyway but you will not have had any say.

Once payments are decided upon, the creditor will usually stop adding interest to what you owe. However, if you miss a payment set as a result of the money only claim, your creditor then has the right to use bailiffs or other measures to get the money from you. This is obviously very serious. The only circumstance in which you wouldn't have to pay is if for some reason you never received the claim form because you had moved or were away. If this is the case you should get expert advice as soon as possible. If a creditor succeeds in a money only claim you will have a county court judgement (CCJ) registered against you. This will go on your credit file and affect your credit rating which will make it more difficult for you to get credit in the future.

If you are really struggling to make the payments set then you can ask the court to break it down into smaller instalments. This is called varying the judgement. If you really can't repay the debt because you have no money or you are having a genuine crisis then the court may be able to suspend the judgement so that you don't have to pay for a period of time. You will still owe the money and have to pay it but you will get a break from payments.

If you are in a situation where you owe lots of different creditors money and are struggling to pay them then there are a number of things you can do:

- **Administration orders** (AO) – If you have at least one CCJ against you but owe less than £5,000 you can apply for an AO. This means that you make one monthly payment to the court and they then decide how it should be split amongst your creditors. Once this happens a creditor can't take any further action against you and can't add any interest to your debt. AOs can include Council Tax; gas, electricity, phone and water bills; and fines.
- **Individual voluntary arrangement** (IVA) – This is a legally binding agreement between you and your creditors drawn up by a qualified insolvency practitioner (someone who specialises in debt and bankruptcy). The agreement means that your creditors don't take action against you and write off some of your debt in return for you paying an agreed sum. This isn't a cheap option however since you will still have to repay a lot of the debt and will also have other costs like the practitioner's fees.
- **Bankruptcy** – This releases you from your debts after 2–3 years, but you will have to make reasonable payments towards your debts for the first 2–3 years if you can afford to do so. Although it may seem like it, bankruptcy isn't an easy option. It will bar you from certain types of jobs and may cause you problems if you are self-employed. Bankruptcy does not release you from all debts; even if you are made bankrupt you are still responsible for paying any magistrates fines, maintenance for a partner or child and some forms of student loans. Bankruptcy isn't free. You have to pay a lump sum of £250 to make yourself bankrupt, even if you are on benefits.

Bailiffs

Bailiffs work by threatening to take your possessions to persuade you to pay what you owe, or taking and selling things you own to repay your debt. Bailiffs are not allowed to force their way into your home. But, if you do let them in and they take walking possession of some of your belongings (make a note of things they will take in the future if you don't pay), this means that if you miss future payments they can then force their way into your home and take those items. So, remember, if you never let them in the house in the first place they have no right to force their way in. They can, however, take things from outside your house such as your car. Usually, bailiffs can't take away basic household items such as your bed, but they can take things that *you* may think of as basic necessities, such as your television.

Debt collectors

Debt collectors are not the same as bailiffs and cannot take any direct action against you. They can only ask you to pay. If you are being physically threatened, then contact the police.

Harassment to pay

It is a criminal offence for a creditor to harass you to repay a debt. Harassment includes:
- Pretending to be a court official.
- Sending letters which look like court letters.
- Telling other people such as your neighbours or your employer about your debt to try and force you to pay.

If you think you are being harassed then keep a record of what has happened and talk to the Trading Standards Officer at your local council about it. Also, if your creditor takes you to court, and if they have been harassing you, then the court may reduce the court costs you have to pay.

Prison

You can only be sent to prison for three types of debt:
- Unpaid fines from the Magistrates' Court.
- Unpaid Council Tax.
- Unpaid maintenance to your husband, wife or children.

You can only be sent to prison if the magistrate believes that you are not paying because you don't want to, not because you can't afford to. For further help, see end of chapter.

Health care

Some of this information is covered in the Health and Mental Health chapters (15 and 16). However, it is retained here for reinforcement.

Dental treatment

You are entitled to dental treatment under the NHS. However, this doesn't mean that it is always easy to find a dentist willing to treat you. Some dentists do not accept any NHS patients and others have decided not to take on any more. All health authorities have to maintain lists of dentists in their area who do NHS work. NHS direct (Tel: 08454647) can provide you with details of local dentists accepting NHS patients, or you can go onto the British Dental Association's website (www.bda-findadentist.org.uk).

In some areas there are also Dental Access Centres. Anyone who is not currently registered with an NHS dentist can get treatment from one of these centres. Once you have found a dentist who will agree to treat you under the NHS you become one of their registered patients. Registration lasts for 15 months and is renewed each time you see your dentist. So if you have a check up at least every 15 months then your registration will continue, as long as both you and dentist want it to. Your registration lapses if you get treatment, other than emergency treatment, from another dentist. Your dentist is required to give you a treatment plan and estimate of any charges you would have to pay before they give you any treatment. They should also provide you with emergency cover while you are a patient.

A dentist can remove you from their list but they should usually give you three months notice. If your behaviour has been in any way threatening or violent then the dentist could remove you from their list immediately.

You are entitled to free (or mostly free) NHS dental care if you are:
- Under 18 (i.e. up to your 18th birthday).
- Under 19 and in full-time education.
- Pregnant, or the mother of a child under one year.
- Receiving Income Support, Working Families' Tax Credit, Income-based Job-Seekers Allowance or Disabled Person's Tax Credit (or your partner is).
- An NHS in or out-patient (if the treatment is carried out at the hospital).
- Over 19, in full-time education and have an HC2 certificate (available from the Benefits Agency or DSS office).

If you don't fall into any of the above categories but are on a low income you may still be able to get help with costs even if you can't get completely free treatment. Further details are given in leaflet HC11, *Are You Entitled to Help with Health Costs*, available from Benefits Agency offices and post offices and the Department of Health website (www.doh.gov.uk/nhscharges/hc11.htm). If you do have to pay, then NHS leaflet HC12 contains a list of current NHS dental charges.

A dentist can charge you if you miss an appointment without giving notice.

General practitioners (GPs)

Every UK citizen has a right to be registered with a local GP and visits to the surgery are free. Health authorities are obliged to help patients find a GP. If you don't have a GP they should find you one within two days. If you want to change doctors they should send you details on how to change along with a list of local doctors, again within two working days. You can find your health authority in the telephone book under H.

Except in an emergency, you do need to be registered with a GP before you receive treatment, so it is important to get registered. Health authorities are obliged to provide comprehensive information about local GP practices. They compile lists which give details such as the doctor's sex, qualifications, how long they have been qualified, and surgery opening hours. These lists are available by contacting the health authority; they will also be held in your local library and can be found at www.nhs.uk or by phoning NHS direct 08454647.

In order to register with a GP you need to take your medical card along to the practice you have chosen. If you have lost it you can contact your health authority for a new one. The GP you have chosen is not obliged to take you on as a patient, but is unlikely to refuse unless they have no vacancies on their list. If you want to change your doctor you simply go through the same procedure as when you initially register. You can change GP without giving a reason although your new GP may ask why you wanted to change, if it isn't obvious (e.g. house move).

A GP can remove you from their list without telling you why. If they do then you will receive a letter from the health authority telling you that this has happened and advising you to find another GP. Your former GP has to treat you for 8 days from receipt of this letter or until you register with another doctor – whichever occurs first. The most common reasons for GPs to remove patients from their list are violence, rudeness, relationship breakdown, abuse of services and non-attendance.

According to the NHS plan, from 2004 everybody should be able to see a GP within 48 hours.

There is no automatic entitlement to a home visit from your doctor. GPs are only required to do home visits if the condition of the patient 'so requires', for instance, if your state of health means that that you cannot get to the surgery.

Your GP does have to provide you with a 24 hour service. Your GP must ensure that medical services are available to you when the surgery is closed. Often several doctors' surgeries will work together to provide an out-of-hours service. If you need to see a doctor out of surgery hours and phone up the practice there will usually be an answerphone message giving an out-of-hours contact number. When you ring that number a nurse or doctor will answer your call and decide, on the basis of what you say about your condition, whether you need to see a doctor.

If you are away from home for a short period of time, less than three months for instance, or you get ill on holiday or staying with a friend, then you can ask a GP local to where you are staying to accept you as a temporary resident. You remain registered with the GP where you live but can be treated by the temporary GP.

There are also NHS walk-in centres throughout England. They give you fast access to health advice and treatment. They are open seven days a week from early in the morning until last thing in the evening. They offer:
- Treatment for minor illnesses and injuries.
- Assessment by an experienced NHS nurse.
- Advice on how to stay healthy.
- Information on out-of-hours GP and dental services.
- Information on local pharmacy services.
- Information on other local health services.

The NHS website will help you find your nearest walk in centre – www.nhs.uk

Mental health

The thought of being put in hospital without your consent is very frightening. But there are very strict rules governing when and how people can be sectioned under the Mental Health Act.

Under the Mental Health Act if you have a mental disorder you can be detained (usually in a hospital) and given treatment without your permission. But the decision is usually made by two doctors and a third person and they must all agree that it is necessary for you to be detained. One of the doctors should know a great deal about mental disorders and the other should know you (if

The Law and Your Rights

possible); often the second doctor would be your GP. The third person would normally be an approved social worker (ASW) who is a social worker who again knows a great deal about and has experience of dealing with people with mental disorders. The two doctors and the ASW must assess you to see whether or not you should be detained. They must give you the chance to have your own say about what you think you need and what would help you manage your mental health problems. After the assessment the two doctors and the ASW must each make their own decision about whether or not you should be detained and you will only be detained if they all agree.

Admission for assessment

You could be detained in hospital if the doctors and ASW think you need a period of assessment in hospital either because your mental disorder is very severe or because it is in the interests of your own or other people's safety. You might be detained for this reason if this is the first occasion on which you have come into contact with psychiatric services. Detention for the purposes of assessment lasts for 28 days and cannot be renewed. If your doctors want you to stay in hospital for longer they would have to do another assessment to see whether or not you should be detained for 'admission for treatment'.

Admission for assessment in cases of emergency

If one doctor thinks you need to be detained urgently and there is not time for a second doctor to see you, you could be detained in hospital on the recommendation of one doctor for up to 72 hours. If during that time a second doctor sees you and agrees with the assessment that the first doctor has made then this detention would become a 28 day detention, as above.

Admission for treatment

The rules on being detained for treatment are stricter than those covering assessment. You can only be detained for treatment if:
- Your mental disorder is very severe or is of a nature which means the treatment you need has to be given to you in hospital.
- You need treatment for your own health or safety or to protect other people and this treatment can only be given if you are detained.
- You have a specific form of mental disorder.

You can be detained in hospital for up to six months to begin with but this can be renewed for six months and then annually for as long as your doctor thinks you need to stay in hospital.

If you agree to go to hospital and get the treatment the doctors think you need you can be admitted on an informal basis which means you can leave any time you like. However, if you say you want to leave and a doctor thinks you need to stay they can stop you leaving for up to 72 hours during which time they could go through the steps necessary to detain you against your will. A qualified nurse can detain you in hospital for up to six hours if they think you need to stay in hospital.

If you are detained in hospital rather than agreeing to go in then you can only leave with the permission of the doctor in charge of your treatment. You may also be given treatment without your permission. They cannot treat you without your consent if you have been admitted for assessment in an emergency. Even though they may have the power to treat you without your consent doctors should always ask you if you want a certain treatment. You should be told:

- What the treatment is.
- Why they are saying you should have it.
- Any possible side effects.
- How it will help you.
- Any alternatives.
- What could happen if you don't have the treatment.

If you are being detained under the Mental Health Act and want to be discharged from hospital and your doctor thinks you should stay, then you can apply to have your case reviewed by a mental health tribunal at any time. The tribunal is an independent panel made up of a lawyer, a doctor and a lay person (e.g. a social worker). The tribunal can discharge you from hospital immediately or on a date in the future. If you are being detained for assessment then you should apply to a mental health review tribunal within 14 days of being detained. The hearing should be held within 7 days of receipt of your request. Staff on your hospital ward can help you apply for a mental health review tribunal hearing. They can also tell you how to find solicitors who can help you and represent you at the hearing. You would not have to pay the solicitors fees yourself.

If you are detained in hospital your friends and family can visit you. Although the hospital or a doctor can stop visits for your own health or safety they must have a very good reason to do so. If you are stopped from having visits then this decision should be recorded and made available to the Mental Health Act Commission. The Commission visits hospitals where people are being detained and checks that their detention is lawful and that they are being cared for properly. The Commission can look at any complaints you may have about your care, treatment or detention, but you should usually have gone through the hospital's internal complaints procedure first and should talk to the Commission only if you are unhappy with the hospital's response.

Before you leave hospital there should be a care plan for you. This should be drawn up by the doctor who has been responsible for treating you and others who have been involved in caring for you such as a social worker, and community psychiatric nurse. If you have been detained for treatment rather than assessment you have the right to the health and social care services you have been assessed as needing whilst in hospital. Aftercare services can include somewhere to live, social care support, home help and using a day centre.

The doctor responsible for your treatment might put certain conditions on your leaving hospital, for instance you might have to stay at a particular place. They can recall you to hospital at any time. If you have been detained for treatment then your doctor could apply for you to have a supervised discharge which means that when you leave hospital a person (usually a social worker or psychiatric nurse) will be named as your supervisor and keep in touch with you after you leave hospital. You may also have to meet certain conditions such as living at a particular place or going to an outpatient clinic for treatment. Your supervisor cannot make you have treatment if you don't want it. The doctor in charge of your aftercare may end your supervised discharge at any time. You can apply to a mental health review tribunal if you want to end the supervised discharge.

Resources

Adoption and Children Act 2002.
Children (Leaving Care) Act 2000.
Children (Leaving Care) England Regulations 2001 (Statutory Instrument 2001 No. 2874) and Guidance
Children Act 1989.
Children Act 1989 Regulations and Guidance.
Department of Health (2000) *Getting It Right: Good Practice in Leaving Care Resource Pack*, London: DoH
LAC (2004) 4

LASSL (2004) 20: National Protocol: Interauthority arrangements for negotiating support for care leavers resident outside of their responsible authority. Department of Health/Department for Education and Skills.

The Children's Legal Centre (2004) At What Age Can I? Essex: http://clc.live.poptech.coop/Homepage.asp?NodeID=89614

Welsh Guidance, Children Leaving Care: http://www.wales.gov.uk/subisocialcarers/content/CLC%20Act%20guidance.pdf

Welsh Regulations, Children Leaving Care: http://www.wales-legislation.hmso.gov.uk/legislation/wales/wsi2001/20012189e.htm

Supporting Young People Leaving Care in Scotland: Regulations and Guidance on Services for Young People Ceasing to be Looked After by Local Authorities: http://www.scotland.gov.uk/library5/education/syplc.pdf

Northern Ireland Draft Regulations and Guidance: Leaving and After Care: http://www.dhsspsni.gov.uk/publications/2004/Leaving_After_Care_consul.pdf

www.doh.gov.uk
www.drugs.gov.uk
www.informationcommissioner.gov.uk
www.surgerydoor.co.uk
www.yourrights.org.uk
http://www.childsupportagency.gov.uk
http://www.dti.gov.uk/er/individual/matrights-pl958.pdf

Helpful guides for young people to their rights under the Act

- Department of Health and First Key (2001) *Helping You Survive Out There: Your Rights as a Young Person Leaving Care*, London: DoH. www.publications.doh.gov.uk/surviveoutthere
- North West After Care Forum, Fostering Network, and Short, J. *Leaving Care and Foster Care: Financial Arrangements Post 18*, email: ena.fry@fostering.net; www.nwacf.com; www.raineronline.org
- Voice for the Child in Care (no date) *Sorted and Supported*, London: VCC (£1.50), email: info@vcc-uk.org

Citizens Advice Bureau (CAB) your local CAB will be listed in the phone book, and they also have a website: www.citizensadvice.org.uk/cabdir.html

Energywatch – for problems with gas and electricity companies. Phone 0845 9060708
Website: www.energywatch.org.uk

Federation of Independent Advice Centres – Phone 020 7401 4070
Website: www.fiac.org.uk

The National Debtline – for help with dealing with personal debt. Phone 0808 808 4000
Website: www.nationaldebtline.co.uk

Office of Fair Trading – for problems with credit, loans and hire purchase. Phone 0845 7224 499,
Website: www.oft.gov.uk

Useful Organisations

A National Voice is the only national organisation run by and for young people from Care. It exists to make positive changes to the Care System in England. On any one day there are approximately 60,000 children and young people in care in England. www.anationalvoice.org

Centrepoint is the national charity working to improve the lives of young people who are homeless or at risk because they do not have a safe place to stay. It provides direct services to young people, helping them address their personal, social, educational and vocational needs, and it provides accommodation for about 500 young people each night. Centrepoint also works in partnership with local and national Government and with others towards ensuring that all services to homeless and vulnerable young people are appropriate to their needs, and seeks to influence policy and practice to the benefit of young people. Centrepoint Central Office, Neil House, 7 Whitechapel Road, London, E1 1DU www.centrepoint.org

The Care Leavers Association is made up of adult care leavers and supporters of all ages. It exists to challenge public perceptions and negative stereotypes of children in care and care leavers, and to create an environment where care leavers are respected and get the support they need. It runs two websites. www.careleavers.org provides information on various subjects of interest to adult care leavers (such as how to access care files). www.careleaversreunited.com puts adult care leavers in touch with others who they knew whilst in care. It has several hundred registered members. It has an Executive Committee, which meets in Manchester every two months and is made up entirely of volunteer care leavers. It also runs conferences for care leavers, produces a quarterly newsletter for members and tries to organise other forms of support and activity. PO Box 179, Shipley, BD18 3WX info@careleavers.org

Fostering Network (previously NFCA) has, over the past 28 years, taken the lead in raising standards for the 40,000 UK children and young people in foster care. It is committed to seeing that their concerns are given a voice and ensuring services are developed to meet their needs. With a membership of 20,000, including 99 per cent of all local authorities and 18,000 foster families, the organisation is involved in foster care, from the children to the very highest point of policy making. The services it provides include: dedicated workers for young people; advice; mediation; information; and consultancy; as well as an extensive training and publications programmes. www.fostering.net

NCH is one of the largest providers of leaving care services in the UK running more than 60 projects offering a service to young people leaving local authority care. As an organisation this gives it the opportunity to share experiences and learning between projects and thus ensure that it is offering the best possible service to a group of young people who can be incredibly vulnerable and challenging. Through its public policy work NCH lobbies for changes to legislation and practice which will ensure care leavers obtain the services they need and thus facilitate their transition to adult life. www.nch.org.uk

Useful Organisations

The National Leaving Care Advisory Service (NLCAS) exists to improve the life chances of young people leaving care. NLCAS seeks to do this through:
- Providing quality services to those responsible for meeting the needs of care leavers.
- Influencing government policy and society's attitudes towards care leavers and,
- Supporting and facilitating the involvement of care leavers in planning and decision-making that affects their lives.

NLCAS is a part of Rainer, a provider of and gateway to, a comprehensive range of tailored services for under-supported young people. The also offer a free advice service for people concerned about care leavers, and *KeyNotes*, a free quarterly newsletter about leaving care. Email: nlcas@raineronline.org NLCAS, Rainer, Unit 1, Palm Tree Court, 4 Factory Lane, London N17 9FL. See also www.raineronline/nlcas where back issues of *KeyNotes*, briefings, fact sheets, and other information about care leavers can be found.

The Prince's Trust aims to help young people, who would not otherwise have the opportunity, to succeed. It offers a wide variety of awards and provides support, encouragement and financial assistance to enable disadvantaged young people to achieve their goals. www.princes-trust.org

Shelter believes everyone should have a home. It helps 100,000 people a year fight for their rights to get back on their feet and find and keep a home. But it also tackles the root causes of Britain's housing crisis by campaigning for new laws, policies, and solutions. The Young Person's Team at Shelter focuses on improving policy and provision for young people across England. The team also acts as Shelter's centre of expertise on youth issues, aiming to utilise its experience in informing all of the organisations work that relates to 13-24-year-olds. It promotes and maintains educational materials for schools, develops materials and training packages for youth workers, social workers and Connexions advisors and identifies good practice and innovative solutions to youth homelessness. Shelter, 88 Old Street, London EC1V 9HU. www.shelter.org.uk

The Who Cares? Trust is a national charity working to improve the outcomes for children living in and preparing to leave the public care system. It works with central and local government, the voluntary sector and young people themselves to influence practice in the areas of health, education, employability and independent living for this group of children and young people. *Who Cares?* magazine is published quarterly by the Trust for children in care. http://www.thewhocarestrust.org.uk/

VCC (Voice of the Child in Care) is committed to empowering children and young people in public care and campaigning for change to improve their lives. It exists to:
- **Empower** children and young people to speak out for improvement to the quality of their lives by providing information, advice and advocacy.
- **Raise awareness** of children's rights throughout all its work and **promote** the full implementation of the UN Convention on the Rights of the Child.
- **Campaign** for changes in law, policy and practice to improve the lives of children and young people in public care and those in need.
- **Support** the active participation of children and young people in the development of law, policy and practice and in the delivery of services.
- **Deliver** high quality services directly to children and young people and indirectly through its independent services.

The Leaving Care Handbook

- **Ensure** equality of opportunity and anti-discriminatory practice in the delivery of all its services and its employment procedures.
- **Provide** a link for people and agencies who aspire to good childcare practice in their daily work.

www.vcc-uk.org

Other UK-wide leaving care contacts

The Action on Aftercare Consortium serves as the National Forum for the Regional Aftercare Forums. Contact: AOAC Chair, jane.sufian@raineronline.org

The Fostering Network, 87 Blackfriars Road, London SE1 8HA ena.fry@fostering.net Tel: 020 7620 6412 Fax: 020 7620 6401.

QP Regional Development Worker, Wellington House, 1st Floor, 135–155 Waterloo Road, London SE1 8UG Jo.Blake@dfes.gsi.gov.uk Tel: 020 7972 1329.

Dave.Herring@eastriding.gov.uk Tel: 01482 396665.

34–38 Green Batt, Alnwick, Northumberland, NE66 1TU zfrais@northumberland.gov.uk Tel: 01665 603411 Fax: 01665 510236.

QP Regional Development Worker, St James Place House, Castle Quay, Castle Boulevard, Nottingham, NG7 1FW tony.dewhurst@dfes.gsi.gov.uk Tel: 0115 959 7522 Fax: 0115 9597501 Mob: 07747 790763.

NCH Worcestershire Aftercare, Holland House, 12a High Street, Bromsgrove, Worcs. B61 8HQ mdwasn@mail.nch.org.uk Tel: 01527 878196.

QP Regional Development Worker Martin.BANKS@dfes.gsi.gov.uk

Regional Development Worker, Marian Walker House, Frederick Street, Werneth, Oldham OL8 1SW net@nwacf.com Tel: 0161 626 4947 Fax: 0161 652 2821 www.nwacf.com (with discussion forum).

QP Regional Development Worker, 40 Berkeley Square, Bristol BS8 1HP Mcraddock.gosw@go-regions.gsi.gov.uk Tel: 0117 900 1738 Mob: 07968 051871.

Bridgend Aftercare Team, 16–18 Derwen Road, Bridgend CF31 1LH driscsj@bridgend.gov.uk Tel: 01656 655554.

Scottish Throughcare and Aftercare Forum, 2nd Floor, 37 Otago Street, Glasgow, G12 8JJ enquiries@scottishthroughcare.org.uk Tel: 0141 357 4124 Fax: 0141 357 4614 Website: www.scottishthroughcare.org.uk

Aftercare Practitioner Group, c/o VOYPIC (Voice of Young People in Care), 12 Talbot Street, Belfast BT1 2LB vivian@voypic.org Tel: 028 90244888 Website: www.voypic.org

Appendices

Appendix 1
(Chapter 2)

✓ Resilience checklist

Centrepoint, a young people's charity organisation, has carried out some research with young people leaving care. They have identified the following areas where care leavers have told them they need help and advice:

- Self-esteem and identity.
- Communication skills.
- Negotiation skills and problem-solving.
- Interpersonal skills.
- Understanding and identifying with others.
- Exploring and managing feelings.
- Action planning and reviewing.

1. *Do you need help and advice on any of these?*

2. *Are there others?*

3. *Do you know where you can go, or who to ask for assistance?*

Source: *The Leaving Care Handbook*, Russell House Publishing, 2005.

Appendix 2
(Chapter 3)

Personal Support Record Sheet

The **first four** people on this list have a responsibility to provide personal support if you so wish. The remaining group may also be available to help.

Why not keep a list of their contact details for future reference?:

Title	Name	Phone number	Mobile number
Social worker			
Social services emergency contact			
Personal advisor			
Connexions personal advisor			
Advocate			
Mentor			
Complaints officer			
Other people who are important to you			

Ask your social worker for a file to keep all your important documents in. You can include this too.

Source: *The Leaving Care Handbook*, Russell House Publishing, 2005.

Appendix 3
(Chapter 3)

✓ Leaving care checklist

Have you been given:

- Your pathway plan?

- The date of the next pathway plan meeting?

- Written documents on your financial entitlements and when this money will be paid?

- Your health records?

- School certificates, records, and reports?

- Other certificates or achievements?

- Life work books?

- Photographs?

- Any other relevant information?

✓ Pathway plan checklist

Do you have a copy of your pathway plan?

Do you know you can have it amended at any time if you are not happy with it?

Do you feel you were involved in preparing it and that it reflects your aspirations and ambitions?

Did you know . . . ?

- It doesn't matter who you are it must work for **you**.

- You must understand what it means **and** what you can expect.

- It must show

    – How you can make the most of your life now.

    – How it will help you prepare for adult life.

    – How to manage when you are out there on your own.

As well as a suitable case or bag to keep your clothes and personal belongings in, ask for a file to store important documents.

Source: *The Leaving Care Handbook*, Russell House Publishing, 2005.

Appendix 4
(Chapter 4)

✔ Checklist for young disabled people leaving care

Do you know what the Learning Disabilities Partnership Board (LDPB) is?

Do you know what it does?

Do you know who is the Transitions Champion? This person is located within the LDPB.

Do you know what they can do for you?

Do you know who your personal advisor is?

Do you know what they can do for you?

Do you know about?
- Disability equality issues.
- The post-14 review process.
- Transition issues and the role of Connexions in these processes.
- Changes to your benefit entitlements that occur at 16.

Do you know that you are entitled to any, or all, of the following, so your voice can be heard, you can be listened to and notice taken of your views?
- Transport.
- Hearing equipment such as hearing loops.
- Accessible material such as symbol or Braille, parallel text.
- Specialist computer software or other equipment.
- Video or audio equipment to record discussion or decisions that have been made.
- A personal assistant or someone who is skilled in their form of communication: British Sign Language, Makaton etc.

Do you know what financial assistance you should receive? Who can advise you?

Do you know what sort of accommodation you might get? How is the choice made?

Are there any other services or help to which you are entitled? Who can tell you?

Do you need any other information?

Source: *The Leaving Care Handbook*, Russell House Publishing, 2005.

Appendix 5
(Chapter 5)

✓ Working together: care leavers checklist

Do you know?

- Where your Connexions or other similar organisation office is?

- Do you know how to get there if you need to?

- Do you know who your Connexions personal advisor (PA) is? Do you have their contact details?

- Do you also have a leaving care personal advisor? – (in theory you should only have one or the other!)

- If you are not happy with your personal advisor, did you know you can ask to have a different one?

- Do you know how Connexions or other similar organisations can help you?

- Do you need any other information?

Source: *The Leaving Care Handbook*, Russell House Publishing, 2005.

Appendix 6
(Chapter 6)

❂ Accommodation checklist for care leavers

Do you know?

- The local authority's responsibilities to care leavers?

- What the housing department's duties and powers are to help you?

- The different types of accommodation you might get?

- What they offer you and what you need to think about?

- There are different types of tenancy agreement – which suits you?

- When a landlord can evict you and why?

- How to make a homeless application?

Do you know where to go for help on any of these?

Do you need any other information?

Source: *The Leaving Care Handbook*, Russell House Publishing, 2005.

The Leaving Care Handbook

Appendix 7
(Chapter 7)

❷ Do care leavers need help with checklist?

Researchers at the University of Southampton were told by care leavers that they need help with:

- Team working

- Setting educational goals

- Attending school/college/training courses regularly and on time

- Their confidence

- Expressing themselves well and speaking out in discussions

- Boosting their self-image and self-esteem

- Learning to not try using drink/drugs/smoking to cure depression

- Listening to others

Do you need help with any of these?

Do you have a PEP (personal education plan)?

Are you happy with it or does it need changing?

Do you know who your designated teacher is at school or at college?

Do you know what the different types of schools/colleges/universities are?

Do you understand the different types of qualifications and courses?

Do you have support networks in place to help you during your study?

Thinking of going to university? What do you need to know to help you settle in and be successful?

Appendix 8
(Chapter 8)

⬤ Education or employment checklist

1. Education, training and work
- What sort of training or further education are you interested in?
- Do you already attend a course? If yes, which one?
- Do you have any plans to continue in education?
- Are you looking for work? If yes, see next step.
- Do you know what kind of work you are interested in?
- Do you need help with this?
- Do you know:
  - How to complete a job or course application form, or write a CV?
  - How to present yourself well at interviews?
  - Where to go to get further information and help about education and employment?
  - What's available, e.g. college courses?

2. Leisure
- Do you know how to use your leisure time?
- Do you know where local clubs, leisure and recreational facilities are?

3. Culture and identity awareness
- Do you have contact with people from your own cultural background?
- Do you know about cultural activities, clubs etc?
- Do you have knowledge of your religious and linguistic background?

4. Employment (*answer each question*)

(a) What job, if any, would you ideally like?

(b) What sort of experience/qualifications do you think you will need for this job?

(c) What do you think is the biggest obstacle to getting this job?

(d) What do you think are your strong points?

(e) Would you like any further information or training on any of the following? (*Please tick*)
- What type of job you should look for.   ☐
- Where to look for jobs.   ☐
- How to apply, e.g. writing letters, filling in applications etc.   ☐
- How to approach job interviews.   ☐
- Further training.   ☐
- Voluntary work.   ☐

(f) Do you need any further information?

Source: *The Leaving Care Handbook*, Russell House Publishing, 2005.

The Leaving Care Handbook

⊘ Training and employment checklist

1. Which of the following are you doing? Circle the answer and state which school, college or workplace. Also, give dates.
   (a)   Local School/College: Full-time/Part-time

   (b)   Further Education: Full-time/Part-time

   (c)   Work Experience: how much? Where?

   (d)   Youth Training: where?

   (e)   Employed: Full-time/Part-time

   (f)   Unemployed/Other

2. Would you say that you attended the above, a to f – Regularly: More than half the time: Less than half the time?

3. Why do you think your attendance is the way you say it is?

Achievements

1. What school or college qualifications have you got or are expecting to get?

2. What sports or hobby awards and certificates have you got?

3. Have you done any other courses or training (e.g. First Aid)?

4. What personal ambition or resolution have you achieved in the last year?

5. Have you attended any job interviews (including work experience)? Have you been offered a position?

Source: *The Leaving Care Handbook*, Russell House Publishing, 2005.

Appendix 9
(Chapter 9)

✓ Getting a job, keeping a job checklist

The following are skills that an employer identified were important. There may, of course, be other skills you can think of. How do you rate yourself against these skills? Give yourself a mark out of 10 with 10 being the most confident and competent and zero the lowest.

Communication skills	Mark (1–10)
Talking and listening	
Expressing own ideas	
Recording clear messages	
Using telephone, fax, e-mail, IT	
Communicating confidently	
Personal qualities and social skills	
Respecting equal opportunities	
Dealing with the public	
Developing good relationships with colleagues and supervisor	
Being responsible and reliable	
Timekeeping and punctuality	
Dressing appropriately	
Ability to accept praise	
Ability to accept criticism	
Hardworking and willing to learn	
Motivation and enthusiasm	
Ability to understand and follow instructions	
Honesty	

The Leaving Care Handbook

Equipment	
Use of telephone	
Use of fax machine	
Computer packages – Word	
– Excel	
– Other	
– E-mail	
Filing	
Photocopying	
Other work related equipment and skills	
Numeracy and literacy skills	
Using numbers	
Reading, e.g. for research	
Writing	
Problem solving	
Overcoming problems	
Using own initiative	
Being able to ask for help	

If you have given yourself some low marks and they are relevant to a job you would like or you have, think about the reason for the low marks. What can you do to change them or who can help you?

Source: *The Leaving Care Handbook*, Russell House Publishing, 2005.

Appendix 10
(Chapter 10)

✓ Family and friends checklist

1. Which members of your family are you in touch with? For example: parents, brothers and sisters, step-parents, foster family. List their names and telephone numbers:

   ....

   ....

2. Is there anyone you would like to contact or trace? If so, list their names:

   ....

   ....

3. Do you know about your family history? Yes/No (*Circle as appropriate*)

   ....

   ....

4. Would you like to know more? If so, what else would you like to know?

   ....

   ....

5. Do you know where to get more information? Yes/No (*Circle as appropriate*)

Feeling isolated

1. Do you know where to go for help if you really feel bad about something, or someone, or just feel lonely? ☐

2. Have you got an address book with names and telephone numbers in? ☐

3. Have you some ideas on how to overcome loneliness? What are they? ☐

4. If there is a crisis in your life, such as breaking up with your long-stannding boy/girl friend, what would you do?. ☐

5. Do you know how to go about making new friends? Do you need some help?. ☐

6. Do you need any further information? ☐

The Leaving Care Handbook

Worksheet 1: The people in my life.

Leaving care might be a good time to think about who you see and whether there are people you've lost contact with but would really like to meet again. You may already see all the people that matter to you and intend to carry on doing so in the future.

Think about the relationships you have in your life and whether there is anything you'd like to change – perhaps to see more or less of someone, or for them to treat you differently. Enter the names of people that are important to you in the boxes down the left hand side and tick whether you feel satisfied with the relationship, or whether there are things you would like to change.

	Satisfied/feel OK with this relationship	Anything I'd like to change
Parents		
Brothers and sisters		
Most recent carers,		
residential staff		
Previous carers		
Friends		
Work colleagues or students		
Young care leavers		
Ex-boyfriends/girlfriends		
Others		

Appendices

Worksheet 2: The stars in my life!

Another idea to help you think about important relationships, is to give family and friends star ratings!

Think about the person who has really made you feel the most cared for in the whole of your life.

On a scale of 1–10 stars, if 1 is at the bottom (the least cared for that you have felt), and 10 is at the top, (the most cared for, or the most cared for that you could ever imagine feeling) what star rating would you give to different people in your life?

	Name	Star rating (1–10)
Parents		
Brothers and sisters		
Most recent carers,		
Residential staff		
Previous carers		
Friends		
Work colleagues or students		
Other young care leavers		
Ex boyfriends/girlfriends		
Current partner if you have one		
Others		

Source: *The Leaving Care Handbook*, Russell House Publishing, 2005.

Appendix 11
(Chapter 11)

● Checklist of practical things to think about when leaving care

Who can help with these?

- Learning to do things by yourself.

- Cleaning, cooking, looking after yourself.

- Having to pay bills e.g. gas, water, and electricity, and ring the companies to sort out problems.

- Knowing about the nearest hospital, doctors, dentist.

- Smoke detectors and fire alarms; how do they work; how do you switch them off?

- Ensuring your own safety: if someone knocks, ask who they are? If gas or electricity representative calls, ask them for their pass.

- Finding out where the water mains, stop cock and meters are in your house or flat.

- Always keeping a torch that works, easily available.

- Your own company can be great, since it gives you space and time. It can also be very lonely and boring. Discovering what you can do to make friends and enjoy yourself; take up a hobby, join a club, go to the library, visit friends.

Do you need any further information.

Source: *The Leaving Care Handbook*, Russell House Publishing, 2005.

Appendix 12
(Chapter 12)

Checklist of personal things to think about when leaving care

Do I need help with?

- Sharing.

- Knowing when to say 'thank you' or 'sorry'.

- Coping with reality.

- Listening and knowing when to keep quiet.

- Learning social skills.

- How, when and if to tell people I was in care.

- My communication skills.

- My self-confidence and self-esteem.

- Cheering myself up.

- Being lonely.

- Coping skills.

- Making friends and forming relationships.

- Information on my nationality and ethnicity or general information and rights.

- Understanding my own and other people's culture, values, beliefs and religion.

- Knowing more about sex and sexuality.

- Preventing abuse of substances including alcohol.

- Any further information.

Source: *The Leaving Care Handbook*, Russell House Publishing, 2005.

Appendix 13
(Chapter 13)

✓ Participation checklist

Do you know how important it is that **you** are able to participate in decisions that affect your life?

Did you know that your views and experiences are valuable in:

- Recruitment of foster carers and social workers.

- Preparation and training of foster carers.

- Being a member of a fostering panel.

- Recruitment of social work students and involvement in all aspects of their training.

- Recruitment and selection of social services staff.

- Co-leading preparation for adult life courses for other young people.

- Involvement in commissioning services and decision making committees.

- Enlightening government officers.

Want to help or take part? Then contact . . .

Source: *The Leaving Care Handbook*, Russell House Publishing, 2005.

Appendix 14
(Chapter 14)

⊘ Health and health education checklist:

1. Who is your doctor, dentist, optician?

2. How do you arrange to see them?

3. If you move to another area, you may need to register with another doctor, dentist or optician. Do you know how to do this?

4. Do you know where to find your National Health Card?

5. Have you been given enough information on the following? (*Circle*) sex education – contraception – HIV/AIDS – drugs – (legal and illegal).

6. Would you like any more information on any of these subjects?

7. Do you have books or leaflets on any of the above? Which? Where?

8. Do you have any local telephone numbers where you can make contact about any problems you may have?

9. Do you have any health records you may need? See the health record sheets above that you could complete and use for reference purposes.

10. Have you someone you can talk to about these topics?

11. Do you eat a balanced healthy diet – or live on junk food?

12. Do you know what foods are healthy?

13. Do you take exercise – if so, in what form?

14. Do you need any further information?

Source: *The Leaving Care Handbook*, Russell House Publishing, 2005.

Appendix 16
(Chapter 16)

✔ Young person checklist

Some people say they are depressed when they really don't mean it.

Would you say you are?
- sad
- miserable
- mad
- unhappy
- bad
- really upset
- depressed

If you are any of these, who can help:

Name and telephone number: ....

....

List who you would contact if you felt you were no longer able to cope:

....

....

....

Names/telephone numbers: ....

....

....

What further information might help you?

....

....

....

....

Source: *The Leaving Care Handbook*, Russell House Publishing, 2005.

Appendix 17
(Chapter 17)

✓ The Law and Your Rights Checklist

Are you entitled to the new leaving care services?

Do you know the difference between eligible children, relevant children, and former relevant children? And why does it matter?

Do you know which local authority is responsible for providing your leaving care services?

Are you entitled to criminal injuries compensation awards and other money?

What leaving care services are young people entitled to?

Who qualifies for advice and assistance?

Are sleepovers allowed for looked after children?

Can you have access to your files?

Are you a parent and do you know about parental responsibility?

What do you know about maternity rights?

What do you know about child maintenance?

What powers do the police have? Can they stop and search you, search your home, arrest you, send you to prison?

What does the law say about drugs?

Are you in debt? If you were do you know what to do next?

Do you know enough about hire purchase, gas, electricity and phone bills?

What are administration orders, bankruptcy?

What powers do bailiffs and debt collectors have?

Do you have loans and credit problems and are you being harassed to pay?

Do you need any further law or rights information?

Source: *The Leaving Care Handbook*, Russell House Publishing, 2005.